The
Salt
Book

For
The Razal Family
October 1977

The *salt* Book

lobstering, sea moss pudding, stone walls, rum running, maple syrup, snowshoes, and other Yankee doings

edited with an introduction by
Pamela Wood

ANCHOR BOOKS
ANCHOR PRESS/DOUBLEDAY
GARDEN CITY, NEW YORK
1977

Pamela Wood, advisor-trainer for *Salt* magazine, has worked with her students since 1973 to produce the quarterly publication headquartered at Kennebunk High School in southern Maine. A graduate of Radcliffe College and a former working journalist, she has taught English and journalism for seven years, principally at the secondary level. Her publications include *You and Aunt Arie: A Guide to Cultural Journalism Based on* Foxfire *and Its Descendants.*

The Anchor Press edition is the first publication of *The Salt Book* in book form. It is published simultaneously in hard and paper covers.
Portions of this collection first appeared in
Salt Magazine, Copyright © SALT 1974, 1975, and Copyright © SALT, Inc.
1975, 1976, 1977.

The epigraph for the chapter "Stone Walls" is taken from "Mending Wall" from *The Poetry of Robert Frost* edited by Edward Connery Lathem. Copyright 1930, 1939, © 1969 by Holt, Rinehart and Winston. Copyright © 1958 by Robert Frost. Copyright © 1967 by Lesley Frost Ballantine. Reprinted by permission of Holt, Rinehart and Winston, Publishers.

ISBN: 0-385-11423-0

Anchor Books edition: 1977
Copyright © 1977 by *Salt,* Inc.
All Rights Reserved
Printed in the United States of America

Contents

To John

Acknowledgment

How do you acknowledge a debt to a modest man? Simply, and with few words, particularly if that man has an aversion to inflated claims and a highly honed sense of humor. To overdo would be worse than to ignore.

So to Eliot Wigginton I tip my hat. In the ten years since he began teaching English in southern Appalachia, he has changed things in important ways for scores of people in communities all over the United States. As the editor of the *Foxfire* books, working with a young staff of high school students, he has shown us how to harvest rich new fields of material. As a humanist, he has shown us how to bridge the gap between generations. And as an educator, he has shown us how to let students learn by acting upon what is around them, rather than forever being acted upon.

He has done the pioneering that makes this book possible.

Introduction

The signs all point to it. Just as some of the old-time Yankees around here can cast a practiced eye at nature's autumnal signs to predict a long hard winter or a short easy one, so can we look to the signs that foretell the weathering of a book. If I read them right, they offer a hospitable climate for a book that is at once a product of the times and a response to the needs of the times.

Surest of the signs is our national humor. We have been brought down a peg or two in recent years, sobered by the knowledge that we cannot win all things, do all things, be all things. Our intoxication with technology and the power it generates is over. We have a throbbing national hangover.

In the light of day we perceive our limitations. We can win the big wars but not the small festering ones; we can harness nature, but she pulls us to our knees and may drag us to our death if we don't break the traces; we can find our way to the moon, but we cannot find our way in our own country, among our own people.

We see our feet again.

Grounded, recognizing our mortal human state, we look to ourselves and to each other, as we have in earlier times, for comfort, for advice, for knowledge, for laughter, and for whatever answers we can find to living.

And that is what this book does. Its young authors have turned to their own people in their own communities to learn about living. They have documented the skills and crafts and attitudes these people need to survive in northern New England. The answers in this book—sometimes open, sometimes between the lines—are the answers of a sturdy, stubborn folk who have always known life's limitations, always known how to laugh, always known where their feet are.

A second sure sign of the times is that we are again welcoming into our midst whole tribes of forgotten people devoted to nourishing the quality of life. From the dark corners where we have kept them hidden for decades, gaunt from neglect, cobweb-covered but emboldened by our change in humor, out they totter, the humanists, the historians, the religious thinkers, the philosophers, the poets, the musicians.

They hold revival meetings all over the country. And the words they are saying are the same words I heard yesterday from a young Harvard historian exhorting his fellows: We have had hard times, but now are coming upon good ones if we will but reach out to offer our knowledge in meaningful ways.

The Salt Book belongs to a society that is ready to rewelcome its humanists and historians, its poets and philosophers. For it is an intensely human document concerned with the quality of life.

One final sign: the signaling from our young people. They have tried rebellion and they have tried oblivion in drugs, and neither was enough to assuage the ache of wondering why we live and why we die. Quieted now by harder times, they signal us that they continue to search and continue to want more from life than a paycheck.

The authors of this book are themselves young people whose essential wonder is that of other young people: how and why we walk this earth, how and why we live and die. If they sometimes decide (as they clearly do in several sections of the book) that the answers lie in small homely things like a good day's work or a well-made batch of molasses cookies, this in no way diminishes the largeness of their wonder or the dignity of the answer.

Then we can say, perhaps, that it is not by chance that a book like this comes to be published in America in the latter part of the 1970s with the clear expectation that a widespread audience will respond to its underlying message.

When I say, "book like this," I mean a book born from an alliance between young and old, a book that is an act of faith between the generations, a two-way gift rebounding from past to future and future to past. The high school students who are the book's authors and photographers have brought to the alliance their labor, their eager listening presence, their respect, and sometimes their love. The older people who furnish its substance have brought their time, their words, their experience, and their trust.

Chance may have determined the particulars about this book. It is perhaps by chance that the book's authors are these particular kids at this particular high school in Kennebunk, along the southern coast of Maine. It is perhaps by chance that I should serve as the book's particular midwife. It is perhaps by chance that this particular book should be called *The Salt Book* and should have as its subject a seaborn culture on the rugged North Atlantic coast.

But it is entirely without chance that such a book can be written, midwifed, and published at this particular time in our history. It comes as a direct response to our present need for the human answers we have discovered technology cannot give us.

Certainly it is not the first response of its kind. In 1972 the first of the famous *Foxfire* books was published, a remarkable book compiled from the writing of high school students who documented the lives of their southern Appalachian relatives. In the introduction to that book, Eliot Wigginton, who shepherded the *Foxfire* books into existence, made an eloquent plea for reforging the links between students and their culture:

"Daily our grandparents are moving out of our lives, taking with them, irreparably, the kind of information contained in this book. . . . When they're gone, the magnificent hunting tales, the ghost stories that kept a thousand children sleepless, the intricate tricks of self-sufficiency acquired through years of trial and error, the eloquent and haunting stories of suffering and sharing and building and healing and planting and harvesting—all these go with them, and what a loss.

"If this information is to be saved at all, for whatever reason, it must be saved now; and the logical researchers are the grandchildren. . . . In the process, these grandchildren [and we] gain an invaluable, unique knowledge about their own roots, heritage, and culture."

Since that time scores of student projects similar in spirit to *Foxfire* have sprung up across the country. *Salt* was the first New England attempt, beginning its fledgling life in the summer of 1973. Just as *Foxfire* succored a dozen successors, so have those successors nurtured new periodicals and books until today the number grows almost weekly.

And each of them comes in response to our compelling need for the human answers a technological society cannot give us. In this sense, *The Foxfire Book, The Salt Book,* and the host of young periodicals are imminently modern, imminently timely. People who put the stamp of nostalgia upon them mistake their underlying intent. The real subject matter of these publications is how people cope with living, and that subject matter will forever be timely and current.

Lest my generic approach toward *The Salt Book,* with its attempt to place the book in history, fool you, let me now admit my local, biased fervor. I am passionately involved in this particular book, passionately involved with my particular students who wrote the book, passionately involved in the particular culture that nourished the book. You will look in vain for detachment in the pages of *The Salt Book.*

At the base of the effort that produced this book is a strong regional attachment. We all share it, students and advisors alike. Back in 1973 we wrote to explain ourselves in our first magazine: "What is *Salt* about? Very simply, it's about the Yankee seacoast and the people who live here. Our stories are told by the sons and daughters of old-time New Englanders, as well as the children of more recent settlers who have fled the cities to live on these proud unyielding shores.

"Why the name *Salt?* Because salt is a natural symbol for the magazine—the salt of the sea, salt-washed soil, salt marshes, and salty people, the kind that won't use two words if they can get by with one."

If anything, our attachment to the people and the land and the sea has grown in the four years since we began. The better we have come to know our own people, the more we have come to admire them. And as our ties to the area strengthen, so do our loyalties to each other.

You could argue that students everywhere are just about like my *Salt* students, but in vain. Quite impossible to find another Anne Gorham or Herb Baum or Anne Pierter or Mark Emerson. They threw away the mold when they made Chip Zeiner, and as for Kathi and Betsy and Gerry and Ernie and Lyman and Jay . . .

You'd fare just as badly if you tried to convince me that there are better people in the world than those we interviewed for this book. I admire them inordinately because they do not throw things away carelessly, neither string nor old parts nor people nor chicken wire nor pride nor buttons nor ideas that have served them well.

These are people who have minds of their own, who can't be bought, who are tough (life isn't easy up here), courageous, generous, and stubborn. They are not phony; they are not synthetic.

Now my words are the words of a transplant, claiming the area not by birthright but by choice. Imagine how strongly the native writers and photographers of this book identify with its subject matter.

That's good. That's the energy that fires the book. That's what makes the photography strong, and that's what fleshes out the contours of the stories. We are driven by the desire to do justice to our people; we have strained every last gut.

And if the truth be known, it is to our people here along the coast of Maine that we look ultimately for judgment. While we are flattered by words of praise from outside writers, journalists, and educators, while we are awed that a major publishing house is bringing out this book, our real arbiters are at Cape Porpoise Pier, Government Wharf, the Chat and Chew, and the house next door.

Not so long ago, several of the *Salt* kids were down to Government Wharf, where they ran into Stilly Griffin (see "The Stilly Story" in this book). He asked them, "How's *our* magazine doing?"

And last night Stella Wildes called, wanting to know if we would send *Salt* to her grown-up children in California and New York. "They've known the people in those magazines all their lives!" she said.

"You know, I've got every magazine since you started. Won't let them out of the house, not even to my children. I told them to get their own copies. Lester Wildes, he came over and tried to borrow one. I told him he could read it here, but he couldn't take it out!"

So it looks as if we are passing the test here at home, where it counts the most.

The Sea

Willie and Elizabeth Ames

by Anne Pierter

Wilmer Ames and his wife, Elizabeth, are of lobstering stock. In both of their families, fishing as a livelihood stretches back for generations. Elizabeth calls her husband Wilmer, but down around the wharf he is known as Willie. They're island people, too. Willie was raised on Matinicus Island "twenty miles from the mainland out in Penobscot Bay." Elizabeth lived on the neighboring island, Criehaven. "That was a mile across there from Matinicus."

"We could hear the school bells ringing back and forth on the two islands," Elizabeth said.

"Ya, that was a different way of life."

"It certainly was."

As they remembered their island days together, isolated from many of life's luxuries and diversions, it seemed to me that the closeness between them stemmed from those days. Their conversation often meshed as they picked up the thread of thought from each other. Sometimes Elizabeth finished Willie's sentences and sometimes Willie finished Elizabeth's. At the end of one interview, they went off together in Willie's blue Datsun pickup truck to salt down a new supply of bait, working together as they so often did on Matinicus.

Willie described Matinicus for us, "If you landed on the island, you wouldn't know but you wasn't on the mainland 'til you started to walk around and see you couldn't get off. Just the same as being in any other community. It's two miles long and a mile and a half wide. A little harbor in it, a fishing community something similar to Cape Porpoise [where they live now]. I think there was twenty-eight or thirty big lobster boats harbored in there, a store, a grammar school, church,

2. Matinicus Island. (*Photo by Anne Gorham*)

dance hall."

Elizabeth remembered the general store, "You could buy everything from sugar to a mousetrap to a kerosene lamp. They had anything." Then she talked about the island's community church. "I guess originally it started as Congregational, and then of course it was taken over by the Maine Seacoast Missionary Society. But actually it was a community church because everyone on the island went to it. And they were everything from Baptists to Congregationalists to Methodists and Advents, and everything else that lived there. They all went to the one church."

"It was quite a nice little church, too."

"And very well kept."

"They knew how to take care of it. There were little schools on each island. You could hear the school bells ringing, the one over on Criehaven, and the one ringing on Matinicus in the morning." According to Willie, Matinicus' population was, "about one hundred and fifty year-round residents—"

"When we were there," his wife finished. "But then it dwindled until

3. The island's community church.

I don't think they had even a hundred year round. But now they have a terrific summer population. When I lived on Criehaven there were about a hundred, I would guess."

Elizabeth recalled how they met. "Well our families knew each other. My mother and father and his mother and father were always good friends, as long as I can remember. But we didn't know each other really."

"I remember her as a little girl being down at the island," said Willie, "but that is about all I remember of her. She came over to the island to visit after living on the mainland for a number of years, and we met. Married and stayed there thirteen years. Worked real hard, and we come up here [to Cape Porpoise] in 1960. My little girl had to go to high school.

"When I was a kid growing up, everybody had farms. They kept the fields mowed and had cattle, raised gardens. We could get milk of course by the store, and everything else came from the garden. But eventually the gardens growed up.

4. Willie's family homestead.

5. (*Photo by Anne Gorham*)

"I was raised on the south of the island. My father owned the whole south end of the island, eighty acres. A beautiful sandy beach down there. I guess I really loved it. I spent my whole life up there [on Matinicus], until we moved up here in 1960. Well, I take that back. I was in the Merchant Marines a short while, and four years in the Army, but other than that . . ."

Lobstering

Willie began to talk about lobstering. "Well, I'll have to see if I remember something to tell you. Oh, I must've started lobstering when I was twelve, wasn't it, dear?"

"It was 1928."

"O.K. I guess that was about the start of it. I had what they called a peapod, a row boat picketed at both ends. I used to have a hundred traps, and I'd go in the summertime. We'd take that peapod, that double ender, down to the other end of the island and work right out of there. And I used to row over to the neighboring island, Criehaven, 'cause it was nearer of course than our harbor. It was a mile across there to Criehaven, and about a mile and a half to the other harbor on Matinicus."

"So he used to row over there and sell his lobsters in the summertime. This was during his high school days."

"When it come fall, I had to take them up and go to school. We didn't have any high school on the island. I went up to the eighth grade [on the island], and four years of high school [on the mainland]. That's as much as I could take. Shedders used to be later in those days, and about September they started in, and I had to take my traps up and go to school.

"My mother was a school teacher, my mother's people come up from Albion way, and I was born up in there. That's an awful place to send a boy that was brought up on the ocean, to that country. Oh didn't I hate it. I hated it. I wouldn't try and learn anything. Mother said I was going to go 'til I graduated. And I guess if I didn't play basketball, I'd still be going. I had the kids help me do my work so I could play basketball."

Willie began to think of lobstering days gone by, and the members of his family who were part of this life. "Father and Grandfather and Great-Grandfather fished as far as I know. Good old Grandfather was a lobsterman until he was eighty years old, and he fell overboard. He was hale and sound when he was lost."

Elizabeth recalled, "Of course back before the years they had power-boats, the lobstermen had sloops and they went by sail."

"I think they was thirty- to thirty-five-foot long Friendship sloops," Willie said. "A rough guess, I'm gonna say they used them around 1900. Probably along about that time. I couldn't sail a boat out in the harbor if I had a fair wind. But my father could sail, and he used to go in them. He was a good man on the water. It always amazed me how he could make those things go around. That's naught but a sailboat. They wouldn't have anybody with them."

"That was a one-man operation."

"Ya, he'd do everything. They'd sail and haul up [the lobster traps]. He knew just what to do with them."

"But you had to have wind, you know."

This brought to mind a story they had both heard. Willie started it off. "Some old character over to Vinalhaven [an island to the east of Matinicus], I don't know who it was—"

"It was before our time. It was one of the stories handed down that

6. The large boat in the center is a lobster smack, surrounded by lobster sloops.

we always got a kick out of. And that old man said he wished the Almighty would give him a quarter's worth of wind, and he threw a quarter in [the ocean]."

"He'd been becalmed all day," Willie continued, "and he was getting pretty rabid, so he threw a quarter over. It worked all right. Come a squall and it swamped the sloop, rolled her over. He got more than a quarter's worth. Somebody said he ought to have asked for ten cents' worth. Lost the sloop."

"That was years ago. That's a story they told us."

"That's a true story."

"Yes, I'm sure."

"My father went on them sloops all the time. He could do better than in a powerboat. He could never get used to that gasoline engine there." Willie's father lobstered in the sloop both winters and summers, going offshore about eight or nine miles in the winter.

"He'd tell once in a while of the day that he went off there somewhere and he had what they called the tiller, what they used for the steering wheel. He tied it, I think, and went down in the cabin there to put his sweater on. He was cold. And a squall hit her when he was down in the cabin, and she couldn't right herself up. He said she knocked herself right down over, the mast almost level with the water, and the water coming right over the side of her. He didn't have his sweater quite on, but he got out and he cut the tiller rope. And he said that squall come around and knocked her back up again. I don't think he was ever the same on the water after. I think he was a little shy."

"A little cautious."

"Ya, and he said green water was coming right into her."

Willie explained the types of traps used when they went by sloop. "They were made out of spruce, and ballasted very lightly. They had a head [the lobster's entrance to the trap] in each end of 'em. What we call two headers. They could haul easy, but when it come a storm, they went adrift and stove up, and they lost most of them. They'd be cleaned right out. With seventy-five traps as it was, they couldn't tend many more than that. And they'd haul them by hand, those sloop boats.

"In later years, after we made the oak traps and ballasts heavier, we didn't have, oh, pretty near a tenth of the loss of them others. We fished afterwards in the same place, and you wouldn't lose hardly any traps. Boy, the old-timers used to haul them by hand. They'd haul their worth then."

Elizabeth tells how in later years the lobstermen were assisted somewhat in hauling their traps. "The hauling wheel I remember was the one that had a flat belt that ran from the fly wheel of the engine to this pulley, you know, the winch. The big winch head would go around and those little flat belts were forever—"

"Coming off."

"And breaking, and having to be repaired. Or they'd slip and fall off, and you had to stop and put them on all over again. My father and grandfather had them, too."

Willie talked about the engines they first used. "The only kind of engine they had on the boat that would start one of those things was six cylinders. But before that, they didn't have anything. They had to haul 'em by hand, when they went completely by sail. I don't know if my father went completely by sail or not. I don't believe he ever did. I think he always had some kind of engine on it."

"They didn't run as well as they do now either," Elizabeth added.

"They didn't run at all."

"There were a lot of imperfections. A lot of the old folks couldn't get used to them, the engines."

"Ya, they all hated them. One old fella got mad. I don't know who it was, I heard them tell about it. His engine wouldn't run and he uncovered it and threw it overboard. Fired it."

"He was better off without one."

"Ya. My cousin, Ivan, once tried to throw his overboard, but he couldn't get it over. This was a Model T or a Model A, I can't remember what year it was. He got it all out on board, got it partly up on the side, but he couldn't get the whole of it over. He was through with that."

"That's a true story."

When Willie first started lobstering in his peapod, he fished a few of

7. Four-header trap lobstering on Matinicus.

the double-headed traps used on the sloops. But he mainly had square traps. "Course, I just started in and had the first square traps. We used square traps out there. And then we got away from them. I asked a fella once, 'How come we quit making square traps out there?'

" 'That's easy,' he said. 'There's so many sea urchins out there, and there'd be a bushel in the trap. You couldn't take them out of a square trap without pickin' 'em all out. And a round trap, you could just roll 'em out. So that's why we made round traps. Ya,' he said, 'that's easy why we quit making square traps.' I couldn't remember why, couldn't remember what reason we had for quittin' usin' 'em.

"Course, it made sense. There'd actually be a bushel of those things in one trap. You'd be very careful touchin' 'em. They were just like a porcupine with the quills. They'd get you in your hand or somewhere and it'd work its way right straight through you. Just like a porcupine quill would."

The round traps that he fished with on the island had four heads in them. Willie started using them, "Oh in 1934 I guess [a year after he graduated from high school]. My uncle bought some from a man on Criehaven, the neighboring island. They started using them down there first. An old French fella from Shag Harbour made them. Nova Scotia. They use them altogether down there. I told Mother [his wife], I said, 'There's the home of the four-headed trap.' And he [the Frenchman] brought the pattern back.

"The Criehaven people used them first, quite a number of years. My father used them some, too. And my uncle bought a whole string of John Anderson's, and he liked them so well, I built ten. Fished so well, I never used anything else. I always used them. I used them up here [Cape Porpoise] for a good many year. But they got too big for me. They were four feet long. They weighed a lot."

"They were heavy, let's say. He's got a few left now."

"Ya, this will be the last year that I use them. Too heavy for me."

"But we've seen them fish, haven't we, in our time?"

"Oh gracious, yes."

After Willie bought his first lobster boat, he used the four-headed traps. He didn't haul them by hand. "No, no. I had a winch. Didn't have a hydraulic hauler like we got now, though. We had niggerheads or winch heads, or whatever you call 'em."

"Ran from the belt in the engine. Called a V belt."

"The first of my lobstering offshore, I had a place that I'd go. I wasn't too sure of myself about running down there about ten or twelve miles to make my gear. I got down there one day, and just got started hauling when the belt broke on the thing. I stayed down there all day and hauled those double traps [two traps attached to the same line] up by hand, sixty fathom of rope on 'em. And you know, the next day I couldn't even open up my hands, they were so tired. I didn't want to come in after I was lucky enough to get down there and make 'em. So I stayed through and hauled 'em.

"I have three hundred traps out now. It's the first time in my life I've ever had that many out. I usually fish two hundred and seventy. But inflation is kind of catching up with me, so I'm spreading out a few more. Getting more out and working harder.

"There were more lobsters out there [on Matinicus]. But the weather was worse, too. Lots of times you could haul up here every day, but there would be northwest winds that would get you out there. And I've seen a week at a time we couldn't get out, and these inshore boats'd be hauling every day."

"So it all evened out."

"Yes, they get bigger hauls [on the island], and here much less."

"Costs more money out there, too."

"I've fished forty years, and it's about the way it was then. I didn't think so when I first come up here from the island. I was never so discouraged in my life. About ready to head back again. If my girl didn't have to go to school, I know I'd have gone back. I hadn't sold anything. I came up here in an icy winter, 1960–61. That was the worst winter that ever got to be. The harbor was froze over. We never saw it [a frozen harbor] until we come here. That's something all new to me when I got here the first year and got my boat frozen in the ice. It's a nice place here, and I like it. I wouldn't go back to where I came from now, it's changed so much."

"Not that much I guess."

"Well it's changed a lot. They're hauling five or six hundred traps. I wouldn't know how to keep up with them. The island changed a lot after World War II. An altogether different place. I don't know what changed it, but it seemed to be different. All the fishermen seemed to be more graspin' and greedy than they was before. When I was young and growin' up, if anybody had anything to do, everybody would turn to and help them. Then after the war, everybody would sit down and look at you as if to say, 'Do that yourself.' That's the way it was. It seemed to be different. We had an awful good time working together."

8. (*Photo by Anne Pierter*)

I wondered if the island people did any other kind of fishing besides lobstering. "We used to do a little herrin' fishin'," Willie said. "We didn't do any other kind of fishin' for the simple reason that there was no market out there. You had to go to the mainland with your fish. It was a lovely place to catch fish, like codfish and all those things. It was right around Rockland and Vinalhaven that you'd sell your fish. And that took all the profit out of it.

"When I was a young fella growing up, there was what they called the salt-fish business. You used to catch this fish and salt them all summer long in great big hogsheads, barrels. And in the fall we had a vessel that would come and pick them up. And I think they took 'em to the West Indies or somewhere. When refrigeration come, that ended the salt-fish business. Oh they were salty. They'd pile the salt right on them all summer long. That was the only way that they could keep 'em. And they'd take them out and kind of dry them out and throw them in the hold in the vessel.

"Sometimes, well I guess it was Cape Porpoise and Portland vessel fishermen would come there in the wintertime and go trawling. And we used to follow them around. I can remember being with my father,

9.   On the left in the foreground are the fish flakes, wire racks used in drying fish for the salt-fish business.

hauling, and board a vessel and help him dress the fish for the fish heads. I think it was the *Richard Nunan* that come out here."

The kind of bait they used for lobstering was "herrin' altogether. All we could get. You'd go in the fall of the year, just like you'd be gettin' your potatoes in your farm or anything. You used to torch it. You'd go with your torch and dipnet. It had a big bow on it, maybe three, four feet across the net. Oh, that could hold four or five bushels of herrin'. You see that frightened them, the light, and they'd follow it. It'd thicken up and thicken up and get thicker and thicker, then you'd dip the net."

"You don't dip the net until the fish look just right," added Elizabeth. (One man would hold the net, while the others rowed.)

"There would be about four men in a crew. And each man felt he had to have a hundred bushels of herrin', salted. And you'd go and get them and work all night and the next day, and another night."

"Salt 'em."

"Salt 'em. That's all we had for bait. If you didn't have any bait, you were out of luck. You had to have it. Sometimes you'd have to take your boat and go the whole length of the coast, hunting for someone who had herrin' in weirs and buy 'em. That's all we used for bait. Ya, we torched those herrin' and lug 'em up. And in the spring of the year, what we didn't use, we'd have to lug 'em back down to the beach and dump them out again."

"And they really smell, them herrin'."

"There's no way, except hauling your traps after you've baited them up, where you could get the smell off of your hands. You had to wear it off, hauling your traps. I used to keep them herrin' sometimes for shedders. There wouldn't be any bait, and I had to have some for shedder fishing. [This was after they started using red fish (ocean perch) for lobster bait, also.] Real good bait, but oh wouldn't they stink! I was hardly allowed in the house. I'd stink it up."

"Well, not really you know, but . . ."

"There's no way you can get that smell off of your hands. We tried everything. Washing, soap, be damned. You'd go haul your traps, and it'd be gone."

"And that's after he had his hands in salt water all day. It would eventually wear off. But then when you got home, when you got in that night, you baited the bags up again for the next day. So you see, you had it on all over. That was part of his living."

"I can remember when there was this redfish, brim, and they used to give it away. There was a plant over in Vinalhaven. We used to go over and get a whole boat load. They give them to us. Then they started chargin' fifty cents a bushel for them, the first ones we bought."

"Now they're five dollars a bushel," said Elizabeth.

"Close to five dollars a bushel. And that's some difference. There's hardly a day now I don't spend thirty dollars or better for bait. And I can remember one winter, we hadn't torched for herrin'. Hadn't many there. And there was a seiner out there. It was coming on a storm and we had to have a bushel of herrin'. The seiner wanted to get in so he wanted to sell his load. My father had been talking to him, and he said he'd sell them for thirty cents a bushel. He said, 'Do you think we can afford to buy them?' I said, 'We've got to have bait anyways.' He said,

10.   A boy on Matinicus Island throws his dad's salt to attract the pollock. (*Photo by Anne Pierter*)

'Ya, we'd better buy 'em.' And he paid the man, I guess it was some thirty dollars for a winter's bait. And he thought that was an awful price to have to pay."

"And it probably took more than one haul to pay for that, too."

"I guess it did take more than one haul to pay for it."

"Yes it took several. Probably lobsters were ten cents a pound then."

"Oh, it might have been a little bit more," Willie said. "Right after they closed the banks in '33, they were ten cents a pound. They worked them up to maybe twelve, fourteen cents the next year. I had just one season that they went for ten cents. We lugged them over to Rockland for three cents a pound. You'd get the freight, three or four cents extra. That's when they was ten, twelve cents a pound. And we'd get fifteen, sixteen cents [by bringing them to Rockland]. And we thought we was really doing something when we had three or four hundred pounds to take over. You thought you were doing something if you were getting three or four cents a pound then. It was a trip to Rockland, anyhow. But those days went out. If you got ten dollars worth of lobsters, you thought you'd earned a good day's pay. Twenty dollars, and that's cookin', if you got twenty dollars worth of lobsters in a day."

"You were rich."

"Ya, you thought you were pretty prosperous."

"Everything Wasn't Handy"

Willie described Matinicus as, "A real nice place to live. But you're so far away from everything in order to go somewhere. We had a grocery store on the island, but it was real high out there. So anything we wanted, why shopping or anything, we used to go to the mainland. The prices was so high out there, and I could get a pretty good price on the lobsters if I'd take them into the mainland. When we were first married, we'd get up early in the morning before it got hot, and take our lobsters in and sell them. She'd buy her groceries and we'd get something to eat, and go back home again. We'd very rarely go one way or the other when we didn't get spray all the way across us going or coming. If it was good going over, it'd be bad going home."

"Or else it'd shut in thick-a-fog."

"Course the main problem out there was fog. We'd get more fog. There'd be lots of days we'd go over to Rockland, that's the nearest [on the mainland]. Just before we got there, coming out of this fog bank, there'd be sunshine. Nice and clear in there. Just the same as before we got to the island, hit that fog bank.

"We was going home one night. I had bought all my supplies out there, and on the way back it shut in thick-a-fog. I was steering by compass. She was sitting right along me. All of a sudden this whistling buoy come up right in front of us. It loomed out of the fog, and she said, 'What's that?' And I said, 'I have no idea what that is.' So I went back and got the number of the buoy, and run down and looked at my chart. I don't know how far off course we was. So that gave me something for me to check the compass. That's how lucky we made it to be. I don't know where we'd ended up that night if we kept on running. We were going right to sea."

"So then you have to study the chart and find out where you are right now, and where you should be, and how much time you've run, and how you have to correct it."

"That was barnyard navigation, I called it."

"Well, we made some wild trips sometimes," Elizabeth said. "If it blew too hard to go haul the lobster traps, that probably would be a good day to go to Rockland and do all your business and your shopping and stuff."

"Of course, we didn't want to go," said Willie.

"Well, we had things to do, we had to go of course."

Willie remembered the waters of Penobscot Bay between Matinicus as being quite rough at times. "She's made some wild passages, too, across the bay. Just as bad as I ever had, probably. Remember the time we were going back to Matinicus there and it was blowing a gale?"

"Yes," answered Elizabeth. "We'd been in Rockland several days and the weather was really bad. We were anxious to get home. We had done all our business and our shopping and so forth. We waited for a chance. We saw it was moderating a little. And Max Young asked me if I was going, too. I said, 'Course I'm going if the boat's going.'"

"Ya, and he said, 'You're not treatin' the little woman very good today, I guess.'"

"Of course it was kind of breezy before we got there," Elizabeth continued. "Sitting there on the edge of the engine box by the muffler on the back end of the engine, it was nice and warm. I'd sit there with my back not on it, you'd get burned, but right close to it to keep warm. And hang on to the engine box, otherwise you'd be on the floor. So that made it an interesting trip. It wasn't a very good day."

"Course the big power boats we had would go in gale winds," said Willie.

"With a good man at the wheel. Very important."

Willie used to go lobstering in his 36-foot boat off Cashe's. "That's a ledge, three and a half fathom water on it. You see, it was sixty miles from Matinicus out there, and Matinicus was, oh, twenty miles from the mainland. You'd get about half way off there and the Camden Mountains, you'd see 'em going down, down, down, and sink right out of sight. You wouldn't see anything more until you got half way back. Oh, we used to go off there in the summertime. We'd go and lay four days off there. When we got our crates full, we'd come in, in four days probably."

"He's been there several times. More times than he should have."

"But I come back anyhow."

"And he's here to tell the story."

"I had a couple quite close ones out there. The last time we was out there, my brother and I was coming in. It was fall. And that's no place to be out there in an open boat in the fall. We had a few traps that we was bringing in, and got caught in what we call a 'smoky sou'wester.' He was having a new boat built at that time. Gonna be a size smaller than mine. He says, 'Well, Willie,' he says, 'if we live to get in and they haven't laid the keel on the boat, I'm gonna have one made just as near like this one as I can.' And they hadn't laid the keel, so he had one just like it.

"Ya, that was the time I walked through the door and she looked kind of surprised to see me when I come in."

"I didn't know where I'd see him again. And at the time it was very important that he came back because I was pregnant. No doctors on the island. There were three registered nurses out there. When you had a baby, you couldn't have it on Matinicus, you know. No hospital. So you had to plan for this in advance. And you usually go over to Rockland about a month ahead of time to wait. Of course, you can't tell, if you're out there in the middle of the winter, what kind of day or night you might have to make a wild crossing. It'd be a ways through the storm, and you might not make it. So your doctor makes you come in about a month ahead of time and wait. That's what I had to do. That was a long month.

"On the island I grew up on, there was a lady who went into labor in the middle of the night. So they started for Rockland—her husband and another fella. They didn't make it in time, so the baby was born on the way. The stork made it first. So, jokingly, someone asked the fella who was operating the boat, what did he tie the cord with. And he said, 'With a bait bag string.' Which was all just a joke you know, but it was something."

"There was an old, old man up there," remembered Willie, "when I was a young fella, and he said, 'No one ever died up there for lack of a doctor.' Didn't matter naught what kind of night it was or what kind of day it was, if anybody ever thought they ought to have a doctor, they'd go. There was an old doctor at Vinalhaven, he's the only one they could get to go. They'd give him about a pint of whiskey so to get him primed up before he'd go, to get his courage up. He'd go with them. And then they'd fill him up with black coffee when they got him out there."

"He'd sober up and then he was good."

"He was a real good doctor."

"Real good."

"He'd always go," Willie continued. "Of course, in later years we got a telephone on the island. For most years, there was no telephone. The only telephone was on the Matinicus Rock Light, which was five miles outside of us, and they'd bring the messages up from there. But, oh I guess probably in the '30s sometime, they run a cable up from the Matinicus Rock Light to Criehaven to Matinicus, so all the stores had a telephone to call up. Well, the registered nurses would practically be the doctors. And they'd call up the doctors to see what to do, and they'd tell 'em. That's a lot better than the old days.

"There was no way of gettin' any communication. They had to call 'em in, go get a doctor in a howlin' gale. And there's some awful bad chances some of those fellas used to take 'cause they didn't want you to die for lack of a doctor. It wasn't a very nice place to bring up an infant child, either. You'd worry all the time in the wintertime if they was sick. But we had three real nice nurses; they were good. They never got away when they come out there, a nurse, 'cause somebody latched on to them.

"Oh, everything wasn't handy out there. If you got hurt or anything, you had to call up the Coast Guard or somebody to come and get you."

"For instance, he broke his leg one morning about, oh, six o'clock. And he got it set that afternoon around five. Cause if there's an injury on the island, you have to get him home and decide if the leg is broken. And then call the Coast Guard boat because it's miserable weather and you couldn't make the trip in a small boat. And by the time they got out there from Rockland and get him loaded aboard, and back to Rockland and so forth and you get an ambulance, and get to the hospital and get your leg fixed, it's around five in the afternoon. A long painful day. And the funny part of it was that the postmaster—"

"It wasn't funny, but . . ."

"No. The postmaster had broken his pelvis the night before. In his dooryard, he had slipped and fallen the night before around seven o'clock. They thought at first he had broken his hip. They weren't sure. And of course they couldn't do anything until morning. So the Coast Guard boat was already coming in the morning. But he [Willie] went down early in the morning to put his boat on the beach. He had a leak and he thought he was going to get his boat on the beach to check this out early. And there was only one patch of ice. And he had to step on that. He wasn't looking where he was going. He was looking off to see how fast the tide had gone. To see whether it was time to put the boat on the beach now or not. This is all tide work, you know. He stepped on that patch of ice and down he went."

"I sat on it. Ya, and when I walked home, it was with my boots on."

"His boot, of course, supported his leg and served as a loose cast."

"Colder than all cold."

"Well you couldn't just stay there, you'd freeze."

"When I got to the house, she said, 'What do you want?' I said, 'Get my boot off, I think I broke my leg.' And I was standing on the porch. 'You broke your leg?' "

"Well, he was standing on it."

"I said, 'I think so.' We got the boot off and she agreed with me then."

"I had to pull the boot off. I knew if we probably didn't get it off in a hurry, that I might not be able to. So I took hold of it and I gave it a yank. Off it come. I hated to do it. And then it turned black and it was all sort of swelling by then. So I got him bedded down on the sofa and got my little jeep out, and went down to the other end of the island and got one of the nurses. She come back with me and she—"

"She decided it was broke."

"Oh yes. She knew and she said, 'Well, don't worry, there's another broken bone on the island. And the Coast Guard boat will be here on the tide when it's right, so we can get you off. So we'll have two going instead of one.' Course it wasn't funny then, but we laugh about it now."

"I don't believe there had been a broken bone on there for ten years, but there was two in the same day.

"It was a pretty good life. But you missed an awful lot. We take for granted what people thought was a luxury out there. Like electricity and telephones and going for a ride in the car, and all those things. Going somewhere to a restaurant, that was all a luxury."

"And a bathroom in your house," Elizabeth continued. "We had electricity, we had our own generating plant, and then we had a well drilled. And then we had a bathroom installed because then, see, we could generate the power, and pump the water and make it work."

"And when the power plant would go out of order, we was out of luck."

"Ya. My water, my bathroom, my electricity. So when you would lose your power, you'd lose everything."

"Now, they have electricity and they have telephones. Microwave telephones, and a generating plant up there. We didn't have any of those things. We had to have our own."

"Ya. I told you about our artesian well we had drilled out there. You just didn't contact a man that drilled wells and say, 'I'd like to have a well drilled.' You'd have a meeting on the island, and then about six or eight people got together and said they would have a well drilled if they could get a well-drilling outfit out there. So then one interested man said yes, he would come for so many wells. I think there were eight who had to be promised before he would bring his equipment out there. He

11. "Going somewhere to a restaurant [as Willie and Elizabeth are about to do in photo above], that was a luxury on Matinicus," says Willie. (*Photo by Anne Pierter*)

had to bring it out on a scow; it had to be towed out. The tide had to be right so he could unload it on the beach."

"The weather had to be good."

"Everything had to be perfect. It took some timing, this whole operation, to get this done. And these eight people who had already signed up had paid part of the money also, to make sure they didn't back out on your deal. That's how we got the well drilled. Of course after he got there, he'd drill several more than the original eight who said they would. We were one of the original ones because we wanted water so we could have a bathroom and—"

"We got rusty water," said Willie. "They drilled through and hit an iron ledge."

"We got rusty water, but we got water. At least we could run the bathroom and so forth."

"There's a lot of iron in it. When we had it tested, they said it was pure, wouldn't hurt you, good for you."

"About nine times as much as permissible. It was orange really, when I heated it."

"That was a heartbreaker. We went down thirty feet and got seven gallons a minute in an artesian well. And got rusty water. Some people got beautiful water."

"Then I told you something about the power plant. We generated our own power and so forth," Elizabeth said. "Well, I got to be a pretty good engineer. And you always made sure that if you ran the washing machine and you knew that the water pump would probably run if you were running water and so forth, not to have too many lights on. You could only generate fifteen hundred watts at a time. So don't overload anything because you're going to blow a fuse. And I did once before I came to, to what I was doing.

"I mean, I knew I wasn't supposed to do it, but I couldn't quite figure out how many things I was using at one time. Well, pretty soon I knew how many watts the washing machine took, and how much the pump took, and how much the lights took. And don't take on anything else running, or else you might be out of business. And I learned how to change fuses very soon. And another thing, this was expensive to run this power plant by gas. In the wintertime when the days were short and you had to have a light on early, it used to cost us about thirty dollars a month for gasoline to run the plant. And that of course, wouldn't mean electric everything. That was only the bare necessities. The water pump and some lights, and I had a toaster and a mixer and an iron. Of course, we had a gas stove.

"I remember doing my ironing at night when the lights would be already on, so that you wouldn't be burning up all that extra gasoline that cost so much. You had to plan everything. You didn't just go ahead and do it the way we would do it here, and not even think about it. In order to have a refrigerator, it'd run on this bottled gas. I had a combination gas and oil stove unit, and that's how we heated the home. We didn't have a furnace. And we kept warm."

"We had those little radiators the heat run off from gas."

"That was a very poor heating method."

"It was kind of a damp heat. It would go *whhhsk!* and blow off steam just as you'd go by there."

Of Ships and Shipwrecks

"Of all the years and all the people went back and forth—some boats went all the time—just one boat that I ever know of was lost [among the islanders], the mail boat. That was before they had a telephone on Matinicus. I couldn't have been over four years old."

"It was 1920, and you were four."

Willie recalled, "The mail boat was going back into Rockland and the bay was full of ice. And I remember one of them picked me out of my dory and lugged me up, and asked my father what conditions were. And he said, 'A lot of ice in there.' It was one of those calm, cold days. So they went in, they had a good trip in. They couldn't get into Rockland, so they left Owl's Head that night to come back [to Matinicus], which they had no business doing. The night when they left, the bay was full of ice, and it come off a squall.

"There were three of them. And one of them wanted to get home, the captain. I think it was his twenty-first birthday or something. They were giving him a birthday party, and he wanted to get home. His mother burned the lights on the north end of the island, course she knew he was bringing mail. It was one of those kerosene lamps with a reflector in it. She burned the light for him for years. So she always burned the lights there in that window after the mail boat sank. Your uncle was one of them."

"Ya, he was just a boy. I never knew him."

"Course nobody ever give it any thought that the boat hadn't come, no telephones. Come a good day, the lighthouse people come up from the Rock to get their mail. They said, 'Where is the mail boat?' And old Tom Hall used to run the store, sitting there with his feet up on the barrel. And he said, 'It was over three days ago that they left.' And he says, 'They're in hell,' he says. 'That explains that.'

"They never knew what happened. They never found a trace of them. They found the mail sacks all along the coast. They hunted all over the

12. The *Gladys M. Taylor* after she wrecked on Malcolm's Ledge.

islands all that next spring, hoping to find something. They found the boat."

"Remnants."

"Remnants of it over by Vinalhaven."

Then Willie began to talk about Criehaven's original name, and why it was so aptly named. "The original name of it was Ragged Island. Ya, and it *was* a ragged island. It was rough."

"Rough and ragged."

"There was more wrecks picked up on the back of that island. More old sailing ships got stoved up there than anywhere else on the coast, I believe. You run into Matinicus Rock Light, and you'd get caught in there [on Criehaven]. Even the people who lived there didn't know, I don't think, all the ledges there was off of there."

"No."

"I lived on the neighboring island, and there were places I didn't dare to go down there, there were so many sunken ledges. They used to lose a good many ships. There weren't so many that went on Matinicus, cause they'd get to Ragged Island or Criehaven first. There was just that one wreck across Whaleback Ledge. I remember a dragger went ashore there on it. She was lost, a small boat, about a hundred feet long I think."

I asked Willie if he remembered any other wrecks. "Yes I do, I know of just one. Well there were an awful lot of wrecks out there. The last one was when I was probably a dozen or thirteen years old. A four-masted schooner went ashore on Malcolm's Ledge in the fog down there, the *Gladys M. Taylor*. That was one of the highlights of my life. We went down there. Of course, when anything went ashore, they went down to the wreck to get off it what they could, after they had abandoned it."

"Piracy, I believe," Elizabeth added.

"The next morning we went down. I wanted to go awful bad and my father said I could go. So then my grandfather, father, and I went down. He wouldn't let me go aboard until the tide got down. My father was the first one up aboard there. He crawled up over the chain, hand over hand.

"My father was real busy trying to get the bathroom out of it [the schooner]. We didn't have any bathroom and he was going to get all the things. So he lowered the tub down to Grandfather and me in the dory. Grandfather didn't take to a bathroom anyhow. So we tied a rope to it and shoved it overboard because we couldn't get it in. [They had to tow it.] And when we got back it chafed off. My father said Grandfather did it on purpose. He didn't want it. The tub was gone."

"It was too big, too heavy to get into the dory."

"Too big for us to get her over, an old man and a kid. My father worked his heart out getting all the plumbing out, and lost out. The crew all got off of her and got into a yawl boat [lifeboat] when she wrecked, and moored in the bay until somebody came. She laid there

13. The store on Matinicus Island. (*Photo by Anne Pierter*)

all that summer and way into the fall until the fall gales broke her up. That was the last major wreck out there.

"I could tell you another little story about that same ledge. It's a half-tide ledge. A half-tide ledge means the tide covers it. There was always rocks there. We used to go down there and shoot ducks in the fall. And my father was down there one time. He had two men on the ledge there, and he'd stay off [in a dory] and pick up the birds when they'd shoot 'em. He was in the dory, and a little duck there [drifted by after it was winged], and he made a swing at him with his oar and hit him. And when he did, he slipped and went overboard. Those two men was on the ledge, no way of getting off, and he was overboard. He worked a long time, and he finally got himself over the side of the dory. He was long enough doing it though, so they were contemplatin' what they were going to do. Wonderin' if they should shoot themselves before they drowned.

"And he was always very careful when he went down there again. He said, 'One man alone should never put anybody else ashore. There should be two men [in the dory].' He said, 'You could have a heart attack, anything could happen and they couldn't get off.' So he was always very careful.

"What about that trip we made there, dear, the Thanksgiving gale we had in 1950? Now that's an interesting story for you. One of the worst gales we ever had in the history of the coast, I guess. We'd been on a hunting trip up in the country there. We'd been hunting and we'd come back to Rockland. We used to haul our boats up over there [on the mainland], and have them painted and all worked up the winter, and go hunting for a week. We come back and got the boats launched. And my cousin had a deer. He was taking it out of the freezer and he wanted to get it home. But I didn't think there was a chance to go and nobody else did. The storm had knocked the telephone out over on the island. It broke the cable or something. And I was a little bit anxious to get home 'cause my daughter was staying with somebody out there."

"She wasn't quite two years old."

"And we didn't know what had happened out to the island and everything. So we started out. Thought we'd go out and look at it. We got out a ways and it was awful rough. Two boats going in company. And my cousin said, 'Let's go a little farther.' And the missus says she knew that was the end of the run right there. She says, 'If you go any farther, you're gonna go all the way.' So we got out there. And I've never seen it as rough on the ocean as it was. No wind. I mean there was a ground sea, and I've never seen it as rough as it was that day. But we think we was making it pretty good. It was hazy, and I was goin' by compass of course. We got within five miles of the island, and it shut down thick-a-fog, just like that. And I says to myself, 'I guess that's the end of the run.' I knew we'd probably make it in the breakers there, but that'd be it, when we got there. But we hit her on the money didn't we?"

"Ya."

"Everything was breaking toward the bottom. And we hit the mouth of the harbor. It was real rough trying to get into that harbor. We knew we was there, and we knew we had to go. And there's always three big seas that'll come, three big ones, and then you'd get a little lull in it. We waited three big ones, and let her go. We pretty near hit the steam boat wharf before we stopped."

"We zoomed right up the way, almost on the beach. You see, it wasn't so bad because the wind wasn't blowing so hard. It had calmed down."

"No wind, just unrestful around there," Willie added. "It was the roughest I've ever seen the ocean, to be on it. I mean no wind but ground seas."

"But there was times that the wind blew and it was rough. That's really bad. That time there was no wind, it was just rough. But I remember looking at Ivan's boat, that's his cousin's. His boat was little, compared to us. And one minute you'd see it and the next minute you wouldn't. It'd be in the trough of the sea. And I'd keep watching it and every once in a while I'd think, 'Why, I can't see Ivan.' I didn't know

14. Willie's boat on Matinicus named for his mother. The steamboat wharf is on the left.

where he was. Down [in the trough] while we were up, you know. Oh, it was wild."

"I'd told her if we had been there a half hour earlier, we wouldn't have got in the harbor. The tide was coming, so we never would've gotten in there if we got there a little earlier. Oh, I had a hard time. I had a whole boat load of people on it."

"Everybody wanted to go home with us so they went. And we spent a cold day out on the bay one day. Five above zero with a thirty-mile-an-hour wind."

Willie remembered it as "Just a fair breeze. We started out from Spruce Head. We left about eight or nine o'clock in the morning. My brother lived over there. We figured fair wind would be a good chance to get home. We got out there four miles and broke the water pump. Of course, he'd called up that we'd left, and we'd normally been about an hour and a half making the trip. He'd come out to the dock to see us off. Then he went right up and called them [on Matinicus] that we had left. Course, they were looking for us to get out there in an hour and a half, and we didn't show up. And when we didn't come, it got blowing harder and harder. It got blowing so hard they said they couldn't leave Matinicus. They didn't have any boat that was able. So they had the Coast Guard out there hunting for us. The Coast Guard hunted all day. They thought we'd blowed offshore somewhere, and they were way outside looking for us. I had her and my nephew with me. Sick, wasn't he sick."

"Ya, he was seasick. We had a little gas stove with two little burners down in the cabin to keep warm. And then as the day wore on, I wondered how long that gas tank might last before it'd go dry. We might be spending all night, I didn't know. So after a while we thought it over, and we shut one of the burners off—"

"Shut it right off."

"To conserve you know, 'cause I thought it might be better to be warm a little longer. Course, then it wasn't as warm, but we managed that day. Along about four o'clock in the afternoon or later, we heard this plane."

"We'd been hearing them all day."

"Ya, we heard several planes. It flew over, and then it came back and flew over again. And then it took off again. So I rushed down in the cabin. There was an old red shirt he had, and I grabbed it and I ran out. And I waved that shirt. And I waved it and I waved it, and they saw us. And they came back and they hovered right over us, that time."

"He stayed over us like an old mother duck. Went right around and around and around us."

"And then, of course, on their radio they contacted the Coast Guard boat, and radioed them right to our position. And I guess it was nine o'clock that night when we got to shore. That was a long day."

"The weather didn't do what I thought it was going to do. It kept breezing up as I say. It was blowing about forty miles an hour. And I thought it was going to blow harder and blow about a week. And I had a pretty poor anchor on her. I knew before the night was over she'd break it. And I knew that was the end of us if she did. We'd go right to sea. And she wouldn't go very far, but then she'd ice up and roll over. The only thing I had in mind was I'd run the engine a little while, and pile her ashore. 'Cause there were cottages, there were camps. I figured that was the only chance we'd have, 'cause if we went to sea, we were out of luck. But it died right up pretty. When the Coast Guard boat picked us up, it was just as nice as could be."

"The boat had a lot of ice on it," Elizabeth said. "The wind would blow and that spray would go across the bow, and then it would freeze. It was cold, awful cold. We had to go up and run out another line. The one we had wasn't very good, it'd been sitting there for a long time. We had to pull the anchor up and put on another line, we had double."

"Getting ready for night."

"That's when we made our preparations for night. That's when I shut off the other burner in the stove, and put an old coffee can over it to conserve the heat. To get all I could get out of it, you know. And it was one that he had used to put his paint brushes and stuff in. And when that paint mixture got going with that gas in there, oh the air was fragrant. If you had a tendency for seasickness, that made it worse. But when he went up there in the bow to get that anchor up and get that line on it, I really held my breath, because there was so much ice up there. And I was just scared to death that he would slip, and there wasn't much I could do."

"Had to be done."

"That had to be done. We were out all day and strangely enough, I wasn't even hungry. I didn't even think about it."

"I think that was the best cup of coffee I ever had when we got aboard the Coast Guard boat."

"I guess it was."

"They pulled us up, they towed us astern. When we started out it was so rough, they couldn't take us along side. Course it was moderate after, died right out, and they pulled us right along towed right along side of them. They come pretty near pulling her [Elizabeth] overboard, the Coast Guard boys. I was tying the boat up [to the Coast Guard boat]. And he was going to help her aboard, and the boats started to yaw [pull] apart. And he was still hanging on to her. She was stretched right out there. That'd been something if you had fell overboard and got put in that cold water, wouldn't it?"

"Ya, it would."

"I had hold of one hand and he had hold of the other. Finally, one of the officers cussed him out. He said, 'Let go of her.' And she hollered, 'Let go.' Boy, it was an awful cold day. It was cold when we left. This fall wind and everything. You didn't have far to go, and you didn't think anything about making a run out there. There'd been nothin' to it if the wind hadn't come. It's one of those things."

Island Living

"Let's see, what did we do for recreation? I don't know. Worked, I guess."

"Well, in those days people played cards and made ice cream in the wintertime. That was real fun," Elizabeth said.

"That was all before World War II, we had a real good time then. It used to be nobody ever left the islands—"

"They didn't have money enough."

"They wouldn't have gone anywhere else. Some of them spent most

15.   (*Photo by Anne Gorham*)

of their life on the island, never went on the mainland. There was people there that haven't been on the mainland I bet you, for ten or fifteen years. I don't believe Marion Young never went for a good many years did she, on the mainland?"

"When we was first married she used to go every winter for a while. But the last few years we were there she didn't go. She didn't leave the island. Why should she? She had everything she needed right there."

"Now they was real nice people, them people there before World War II. Very, very nice people. You couldn't find any better I believe, anywhere else than on that island. In fact, they perhaps made a little better living out there than they did on the mainland, No one out there owned

16.   The mail boat, the *Mary A*.

an automobile on the mainland. That was a dream if you ever owned an automobile. We started out having a few old cars along the islands. We had a jeep. Fall of the year, we used to take it off on the mail boat and go hunting."

Elizabeth remembered that on the island, "You knew everybody and everybody knew you. The mail boat came three times a week in the summer and twice a week in the winter. And that was the highlight of your week."

"I used to tell her to be careful when the mail boat come that she didn't break an arm or something, 'cause she was small. They all made a run for it."

"They'd unload crates of fruit and bread and milk, and everything was brought up from the wharf. Everybody'd have to hurry to get their groceries and stuff."

"They wouldn't order any more than they were sure they could sell," explained Willie. "They didn't want it spoiling on them, so you had to be around to get it."

"Ya, you had to be around to get what you needed. Course, it was always a joke on the island if the mail boat couldn't make the trip, or for some reason they couldn't deliver all the things that were ordered. All the men were very happy because then the wives would make them homemade breads and all those things. And they hoped the boat would never come in, some of them did. So then they had homemade biscuits and homemade bread, and homemade everything."

"That mail boat missed very few trips. I think she was sixty-five feet. There'd be days they couldn't come, but they tried to get in. Then they'd come two days together to make it up. And old Stuart Ames [Willie's second or third cousin] in a lifetime of running it, I believe he missed only two or three trips."

"He made some wild trips, but was an awful good man."

"Oh, he was an awful good man on the water," Willie agreed. "His

17.   Some of the supplies brought over on the mail boat the day we went to Matinicus. (*Photo by Anne Gorham*)

father, of course, lived on the island, too. It was breezing up one afternoon, a screechin' nor'west. His father was chafing. He said, 'Stuart,
you better get goin',' he says, 'it's goin' to blow real hard.' And he
looked and he says, 'Pa,' he says, 'I don't believe it's goin' to blow all
the water out of the bay.' Didn't jar him a bit."

"I remember when I was a girl, he broke his ankle. I guess he slipped
on the ice or something like that. And I think he missed one trip. The
next time he came on crutches—"

"With the mail."

"Ya. He had something tied around his foot here, and I guess he
hobbled on [the mail boat], and he managed to get up the ladder and
get to the post office and so forth. I don't know how he did it. Everybody liked him, he was an awful nice man."

"Very accommodatin'."

"And I've made a good many seasick trips with him on that mail
boat."

"Seasick, everybody would be seasick."

"Terrible. And I was a pretty good sailor, too," Elizabeth said. "So I
could hold the bucket for the other people."

"It didn't take me long to get seasick down in that cabin if there was
two or three of them sick around me. Didn't like that. A lot of tourists
have discovered the island, and have bought up all the land out there.
When we left, we had a hard time to sell our place. Several years selling
it. And I think now it's just about the same as buying a piece of land in
Cape Porpoise on the ocean front, the way it is out there now. No one
ever dreamed of that ever happening."

Years ago on the islands the tourists were called boarders, and they
were taken into the homes of the island families. "Oh yes, Mother used
to take them," Willie recalled.

"Ya, his mother used to take them. And on Criehaven they did, too.
And that was possibly the best vacation they could have. They'd stay
with the people for a week or two."

"Well fed."

"Well fed is right. Welcomed right into the family. And they did everything you did. Went with you every day."

"Course I've seen them come out for two weeks and never see the
sun all the time I was out there. That's the chance they took. That was
the only trouble on that island out there in the summer. If you had a
good summer, that was just heaven. I've seen summers they'd be up
there, it was nice clear weather all summer. But when you got one of
those drippy summers all summer long . . . You'd get so sick of the
fog. I went lobstering one summer, and I think it was two weeks that we
never saw the sun at all. We'd be up every morning and go by compass

and haul traps. It just got to be routine. You didn't notice when the fog come down your ways."

Willie described Criehaven, and told how the fog would put a damper on his fun. "Nice little community over there, about as big as Matinicus. They had a school, church, and a dance hall. There's recreation in the summer. You'd have dances from one place to the other. Oh, I'd get burned up, always what a fog out there. My father wouldn't let me go across there at nighttime if it was foggy. And we always watched that fog bank all day long so we could know if we could go across to dance. No go, if it come in foggy.

"Sometimes we went over there and got caught in the fog. And the people on Criehaven would put us up. Or the other way around if they was up at our place to dance. If it shut in real thick and it wasn't safe for them to go back, they'd stay over on this island. We had a lot of fun. It was our own boys that would play. They played real good. Played accordion and violin and guitar—"

"And drums."

"They'd play all the dances. The dances were different then. There was a square dance and waltz and a two step. You'd figure they'd play three dances. Now this dance hall, the one on Matinicus, has been made into a dwelling, and the one on Criehaven has fallen down.

"During the war was the end of Criehaven 'cause they couldn't get kids enough to go to school, and they lost the school. There weren't enough families there to maintain it. When they lost the school they lost everything."

Elizabeth added, "And they couldn't get a teacher. 'Cause during the war you couldn't get teachers, and certainly they weren't going to go to an island."

Willie agreed that there was quite a bit of intermarriage between the island families. "Yes there was, more or less. Just three or four different, about that many names there. You'd get new stock in there once in a while. They married someone else from away. Most of the girls left anyhow. There's nothing for a girl out there. They go to high school and meet somebody and go away. And a good part of the boys did. Just didn't want to go fishing. A lot of them didn't care about fishing, so they never came back.

"It seemed rather odd on this island, when I went to school I think there were twenty pupils in school and three girls out of twenty. There always seemed to be that ratio up there. We had more boys than there were girls. That's why when the girls come over, they usually didn't get away."

As for the ratio on Criehaven, "Well, I think it was about half and half," claimed Elizabeth.

18. "Oh, every old buoy or something I hang up, there's a story that goes with it. I saved this one [the buoy in the center] 'cause my sister-in-law fired at it once with a rifle and hit the side of it. She said, 'That's too bad I hit your buoy.' I said, 'I don't care.' Out three hundred yards and she fired at it. You know, she was a crack shot."

"Most everybody liked it that came off the island. I loved it. I really liked it. It was beautiful. I guess that's why she married me, to get back on an island."

"I guess so."

"She'd been on the mainland how many years, dear?"

"Eleven."

"Eleven years before she came back. We had a nice life out there."

At twenty miles out to sea, it would seem Matinicus winters were unusually harsh. But according to Willie the winters were, "Much milder out there. I've seen winter after winter when there wouldn't be a patch of snow out there."

"But a lot more wind," Elizabeth added.

"You get a tough snow storm, and it'd usually turn to rain out there. But other winters, I remember when I was a child, there'd be great big drifts of snow. There'd be this much wind and there'd be bare ground. And it'd snow and drift as high as this room, somewheres. But very few winters that we had very much snow out there. As I say, it always turned, when you got out on the ocean, it'd turn to rain."

"The salt air also eats it up, and if it lands, it doesn't last very long. And then, too, the wind blows it. It just sweeps it off. It doesn't have a

19.   Willie's "own wharf and fishhouse and pier."

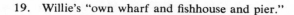

chance to accumulate."

"It used to be a beautiful spot out there for a garden," Willie said. "We had a lovely garden out there. It was another hobby I had, tending my garden. We could raise a vegetable garden way into November out there if we didn't get any frost."

"We used to can everything out of the garden. All our vegetables, all our berries we canned, and make jam and make pickles. I canned mackerel and halibut. Everything that we caught. And we had a well-stocked cellar of everything."

"Oh, we had a lot of good times. What we used to do for recreation after we was married—you asked me what I did—we used to go pick berries a lot. That was great fun. The island was abundant with strawberries and cranberries and raspberries, and anything. That was our fun."

Elizabeth remembered, "One of the things that I really loved out there was going cranberrying. The cranberry bogs were just beautiful way out there in that salt marsh."

"They grow pretty good up here, but I think there was more out there on that island."

"Always berries."

"Ya, all kinds."

"Strawberries, wild strawberries."

"I don't think of anything that can beat a wild strawberry."

"We used to pick them a lot."

"We used to go down to Mother's place on the southern end of the island," said Willie, "and we'd pick two or three quarts every afternoon, wouldn't we?"

"Yes."

"And great big ones, almost as big as cultivated ones."

"They were lovely."

"Great big things there. There'd been cattle for a good many years that grazed there in the fields. And then after they got through, it come up with strawberries. We had a special little place that we'd go after I'd get done hauling traps. And bustle down in there and go strawberrying."

"And we got the raspberries also," said Elizabeth.

"Not every year though, we didn't get them every year. Strawberries were almost a sure thing every year. Strawberries and cranberries."

"Of course, there were blueberries. The sea gulls like to chew them. We used to have a running battle to see who could get there first."

"And my brother stocked the island with pheasants, and they used to like the island berries. Those great big island strawberries. And them buggers would get the raspberries, too. They'd whack their wings and knock the berries off'n the bushes—"

"And they'd pick them up underneath. We saw 'em doing it, we knew what was going on."

"They're quite the bird. We had one there that used to come in the back yard in the morning. And he flopped his wings and crowed just like a rooster. Oh he'd do a terrific wing beatin', and then you'd hear that funny crow right under our window. We had a bird feeder out there, and about three pheasant hens that would come up. The blue jays, they'd scatter the bird seed, and the pheasant hens would come up and get it off the ground. Puttin' the garden in there, I've seen the old fella around there, and he wouldn't come up. And then he finally did come up to get some of the seed. He was tamer than the hens was. Standin' right around the house. A beautiful thing.

"We used to go watch the birds a lot, too. There was more birds stopped there than any place along the coast, I believe. In fact, I used to belong to the Audubon Society there and count birds, one from another. I told them I wasn't a very good Audubon man 'cause look at all the guns I had hanging on the wall. I used to just go check for them, tell them what I had seen. Take them around the islands.

"I guess the thing I enjoyed most of all was hunting when I was a kid growing up. There was a lot of ducks out there, no deer or anything like that. I used to row out into the harbor and chase ducks. Probably more than I should have sometimes. There weren't no game wardens out there."

"Kind of a little poaching."

"We don't eat them [ducks] anymore, since we got up here. She seems to have lost the taste for them. Well, I'm getting so I don't care so much for them myself."

"No, I'd rather watch 'em. We had all kinds of birds, everything."

"When I was a boy growing up, they never nested out there. The sea ducks, eider ducks, would come. Probably it was around the last of September and October. They'd been to Labrador or somewhere and nested. But during the war years I think, or previous to that, a few started nesting there, and it grew right up. Oh, they nested there by the thousands. They decided to make their change. I don't know why or anybody knows. They had the whole length of the Maine coast. But they lay right here. Had some young ones right out here."

"We used to watch them in the spring," said Elizabeth, "the eiders, when they had their babies. And they nested right out to the island. And those little ones looked just like little bumble bees. And they'd get on their mother's back when they were frightened. When they were afraid. We spent hours watching them. They'd crawl right onto their mother's back and she'd swim off with them. Oh, they were the dearest little things. Now how could you bag one of them?

"The mother ducks would baby-sit for each other. A lot of the times, we'd see one mother with two flocks, while the other mother was probably off feeding or something. And they'd baby-sit for each other's flocks. We watched them do that. It's almost unbelievable but they did."

"Black-back gulls were the worst enemy they had. They'd swallow the whole flock of them if they'd get a chance, the little ones. We'd go down there, they'd have a convoy. Four or five mother ducks gathered up there to keep them all together, so they could fight off the gulls. Course, those black-back gulls are protected, but I used to make short work of them when they got after those little ducks. They knew what a shotgun range was all right, those black-back gulls. Herring gulls don't bother them. But the black-back gulls, they're bigger. They're miserable birds. They'd goffle [eat] up a whole flock of them little ducks all a kickin'. Make me some angry to see them do that.

"Lots of times in the fall and the spring, little birds were migrating, and get strayed off at night. And they'd [the black-back gulls] knock them down and swallow them if they'd get the chance. A lot of little birds come aboard the boat with me, and I'd take care of them. They say it's good luck if a little bird comes aboard your boat. Bad luck if he dies, after he comes aboard. I'd take good care of them when they'd come aboard."

"Didn't you put one in your compass box one day?" asked Elizabeth.

"Yes, she was tired. Sometimes they got so tired they'd die, them little birds. Oh, their little heart was just—"

"Just all tired out."

"I'd drive them down the cabin so they couldn't get out. So they'd stay there and rest up. I used to feed them crumbs right out of my sandwich, too. They're hungry and sometimes they pick up something that's salted like redfish. And that fixes them right up good.

"I'll tell ya a funny one. We used to dump our garbage offen some steep rocks down at the cove there [below their house]. That was a good garbage disposal, that flat rock."

"We'd take our garbage pail out there and dump it, and then it'd wash it all down there. High tide would wash it out to sea."

"There's a lot of ocean out there. I was hauling up the cove one day, and I hauled up an old vest. Draped right around my trap. And I said, 'Mother, you've thrown my leather vest overboard, didn't ya?' Went out there and draped right around one of my traps."

"I had cleaned house. And he had this old, well it was a sheep-skin type vest, that he used to wear in the winter under his oil clothes. But it was worn out, and I knew it couldn't be repaired anymore. It had had it. It was spring. I cleaned up the sheds and everything. That old vest was hanging there, and it was time for it to go. Now's my chance. And

20.   (*Sketch by Holly Berry*)

so when I got through cleaning, I marched everything down to the cove and dumped it overboard, before he got home to see what I was throwing away. And I made sure that vest dropped in the cove. And then it wasn't for some time later, it must've been in the fall, and I did this in the spring. But in the fall one day—so help me—up comes this vest."

"She said to me, 'How did you know?' I said, 'I hauled the vest up on my trap out there.' But I recognized it all right, though."

"It was only remnants you know, by then. It wasn't in very good shape when it went in. So it's always been a family joke ever since.

"We had a darling little house on the island, a kind of bungalow, with two bedrooms upstairs. And we could look right onto the cove. Old Cove was the name of it. The first thing in the morning, you'd open your eyes and look out there to see what kind of day it was. Of course you'd know when the sun came up, on account of those windows faced east. And also in the wintertime, he could always tell in the morning whether we should get up early or not. If there was a few puffs of wind on the roof, that meant it was blowing real hard. So stay where you are. You're not going out today."

"I used to keep five traps in that cove [Old Cove] in the summer and I'd finish up hauling there so she could see me. And she could walk down to the dock. Oh I guess it wasn't a quarter of a mile down to where the wharf was. She used to walk down and wait for me and then walk home with me. I didn't catch any lobsters in those traps."

"Oh, sometimes you used to get a lobster."

"Oh, just a few, there wasn't very many in that place."

"That was his last place to haul on his way in, in the afternoon. He'd wave to me, so then I'd walk around and visit with him while he was baggin' up his bait and doing his chores and things. Of course you had your own wharf and fish house and pier."

"My own wharf and fish house and pier at the mouth of the harbor."

"It was nice."

Fishing

Fishing has always been a way of life for people along the coast of Maine. It is not unusual for a family to have three generations of working fishermen. A boy will begin to work as a helper for his father when he is eight or nine years old, and his grandfather may still be fishing at eighty.

From the quiet inlets that offer shelter along Maine's rugged, weaving, 2,000-mile coastline, the boats leave their mooring by dawn to go "outside"—the fishermen's term for the sea beyond the harbor. When the sun is strong, the only evidence of the fishermen at the wharves is their empty trucks. Midafternoon the boats begin to return with the day's catch, and by dusk the wharves are busy, as the men unload their haul into the waiting trucks.

Once the day's catch has been sold to nearby dealers, the fishermen return to the wharves to hose down their boats and prepare for the next day's fishing. At this time they usually swap yarns and drink a few beers. By the time they get home, carrying empty lunch buckets, they've had a twelve-hour day.

There's an old saying in Maine that the fishermen have to be as rugged as the coast they fish. On their feet in choppy water, hauling heavy nets or lobster traps, rolling bait barrels on the wharf, the fishermen do not lead a soft life.

And it's a risky business. "You can set your traps and you don't know if you're goin' to get them in the mornin' or not. Maybe a storm'll come up and clean them out," says one lobsterman, Arnold Stinson. A boat builder, Herb Baum, adds, "You have to be a different person to work on the water. You might get one dollar one day and one hundred dollars the next day and nothing the day after that."

So what draws a man to fishing? "Nobody tells you what to do or when to do it. You're your own boss," says lobsterman Herb Baum, Jr. "I guess it runs in my blood. My father, my grandfather, and my uncles were all in the business. Everyone was." And Arnold Stinson agrees,

21. The Kennebunk River. (*Photo by Herbert Baum III*)

22. Two lobstermen talking it over after a long day (*Photo by Herbert Baum III*)

"Yes, you can go and come when you want to, knock off when you want to."

The principal kinds of fishing done along the Maine coast are lobstering, dragging, shrimping, gill netting, and trawling. By far the most fishermen are lobstermen. Fishing a stock of lobster traps that might range in number from 150 to 1,200, the lobstermen work alone or in pairs on boats that vary in size from a 15-foot open dory to a 36-foot boat with a canopy.

While lobstering is done with traps, dragging and shrimping are done with large, funnel-shaped nets towed along the bottom of the sea. Draggers bring in codfish, flounder, hake, and haddock year round, while shrimping can be done only in the winter months.

"The difference between lobstering and dragging is that in lobstering you usually own your own boat," explains Herb Baum, Jr. "A lot of the businessmen or dealers own the draggers, and they hire someone to run them. The lobsterman is usually an individual. He owns his own boat and his own gear."

Gill netting is different from dragging or shrimping in that the fishermen leave a curtain of netting in the water overnight. The fish swim into the net and are caught by their gills. With the exception of flounder, which are a bottom-feeding fish, gill netters catch the same kind of fish that draggers get: codfish, hake, and haddock.

Trawling involves a long line of baited hooks furled inside a wooden tub and unwound into the water. The trawler sets his lines in the morning and hauls them in the afternoon, bringing home mainly hake and cod, with some haddock.

Over the years, changes have come in the fishing industry. Very few fishermen haul their traps by hand now, using hydraulic haulers in-

23. Doane's wharf. (*Photo by Herbert Baum III*)

stead. Some of the wooden boats have been replaced by Fiberglas boats. But basically, the operation of fishing remains what it has always been: a small independent enterprise of men who work alone to harvest the sea.

"Fishermen are funny," says Lester Orcutt. "They hate change. It is like the lobster trap. Try to get these guys to use plastic traps or something and no way."

by P.W.
with Herbert Baum III,
Anne Gorham,
and Anne Pierter

Lobstering

THE STILLY STORY

by Herbert Baum III
  and Kristy Bunnell

Photography by Anne Gorham

"There was this guy lobstering in a 15-foot dory. First thing he hauled up a lobster trap, and this great big lobster was hanging on it. Right when he hauled it up, the lobster come up and bit the dory right in two. He [the man] jumped in the stern and sculled her ashore."

This old sea tale was told to us by Stilly Griffin, a lobsterman in Kennebunkport, Maine. "Well, that's good enough for ya," Stilly laughed (a good-enough story) as he unloaded the lobsters from his boat.

Stilly has been lobstering for forty years. Hauling fifty traps with the help of his father, he first worked out of a small power dory, a rowboat with a motor. Now he owns his second boat, the *Lorraine E.,* and has increased his stock to 230 traps.

Stilly has had this boat since 1954. He named it after his only daughter. His boat is thirty feet long and pretty near ten feet wide. He just had his boat hauled up to have a new engine, new ribs, and a new floor put in.

During the winter months, he gets ready for spring by building up his stock of traps. He builds approximately 150 traps each winter. It takes him an hour and a half to build one trap including the trap head. His traps are the box type and are made out of oak and hard wood. He uses only square traps because he says they pile up better and handle better

24. Stilly Griffin. (*Photo by Anne Gorham*)

on his boat.

Stilly's buoys are black, white, and red. These buoys are used to mark the trap in the water. They float and are tied to a rope which is also attached to the trap.

In June or July lobsters shed their shells. Stilly explained, "Its back will open up and the top shell will go off. Then he'll squirt his tail out of the back and he'll wiggle his claws right out through."

It takes a lobster six to seven years to reach the legal size. It has to be $3\frac{3}{16}$ inches long before the lobsterman can sell it to the market. A lobster is measured from the eyes to the back of the body. In Maine, a lobster cannot be kept if it is over five inches long. This is because they claim it's a breeder. If a lobsterman is found with a short lobster or a lobster that is too long, he is fined $5 apiece for the first five lobsters and $25 for each one after that. The lobsterman may possibly be sent to jail for it.

Stilly says that when a lobsterman catches a lobster with eggs on it he puts a V in the tail. He does this so that the lobster can have her eggs and also have other eggs in the future. If this lobster is kept by the lobsterman, he may be fined $50 if he is caught.

Right now in Kennebunkport and in other fishing villages, lobstermen are faced with a bait shortage. Bait has become very scarce and expensive. Bait now sells for $12.50 a barrel. Stilly uses redfish (ocean perch) and herring to lure the lobster into the trap. The herring are so small that they cannot be put on the bait line. So they are first put in a bait bag made of nylon and then put on the bait line.

We asked Stilly what he thought of part-time lobstermen. His reply was "no good. Matter of fact I don't think they should be allowed in the business." A part-time lobsterman puts down ten or fifteen traps in his spare time, but doesn't depend on lobstering for his livelihood.

It will cost a lobsterman an initial expenditure of $25,000 to get started in the business. This cost covers boat, traps, buoys, rope, and a

25.

26.   Edgar Campbell unloading his catch. (*Photo by Herbert Baum III*)

license, which is bought from the state at a cost of ten dollars, and is
good for one year.

After Stilly catches his lobsters (and checks that they are of legal
size), he puts a peg in one of the lobster's claws, which prevents the
lobster from attacking and crushing the others in the tank. This tank is
filled with circulating water to keep the delicate crustaceans alive.

When Stilly has finished hauling his traps, he goes in to the wharf
where he unloads his lobsters, then takes them to market to sell to the
dealer. Stilly is selling his lobsters to the dealer now for $1.30 a pound,
though the price varies with the season. Market price is $.60 to $.70
higher than Stilly gets.

This has been a long day for Stilly. He got up at 4 A.M. and now, 12
hours later, is ready to jump in his old truck and go home to his wife
and family.

Before he leaves, Stilly sheds the bait apron and rubber boots he
wears over his work clothes. Still, the fragrant fish odors remain. We
wondered what his wife thinks of his smelly clothes. "Not a thing,"
Stilly replied. "She doesn't mind them because she says the dollar bills
are clean!"

BAIT GIRL

by Anne Pierter

For the past two summers I have been getting up at five o'clock every morning. I am a bait girl on a lobster boat.

When I get down to the wharf, the sun has just come up and in the distance the sea sparkles like diamonds. It's very peaceful. Usually the only sounds are the occasional cries of sea gulls and the hum of lobster boat engines.

I wait outside the bait shed for Dan Wentworth, the man I work for. Dan is rowing his dory from the bait shed to the mooring to get his lobster boat, the *Charlene,* named after his wife.

When he gets back with her, I climb aboard while he goes into the bait shed for the bait we'll use that day. In the bait shed are barrels of ripe redfish that Dan says "smell so bad they'd gag a maggot." They've been watered down, and their own heat within the barrels has had them cooking for days, even though salt was added to slow down the cooking.

Drums of herring are also in the bait shed. Herring are a favorite with lobsters because they're an oily fish. But they're popular with people, too, so we have to settle for the heads and tails, called "cuttings," to use as bait.

Dan and the other lobstermen take big drums down east to Yarmouth to be filled with the cuttings, which have to be put in bait bags before

27.

going into the traps. Herring don't smell as strong as redfish.

Dan's barrels of bait are painted yellow with his initials scrawled in orange. Each lobsterman has his section of barrels in the shed.

Dan wheels three barrels of redfish and a barrel of herring onto the wharf, enough bait to last us for the day. Using the hoist, he lowers the barrels down to me. I guide them into the boat and try to line them up.

We cast off and head down the Kennebunk River toward our first string of about twenty traps. Dan has 270 traps and he fishes half of them a day, spending six to seven hours on the water.

We're both wearing heavy hip boots, rough work clothes and bait aprons made from the same material as rain slickers.

The first thing Dan does when he comes to his string is to gaff the buoy. After the gaff has hooked onto the buoy, he pulls the buoy out of the water and with his automatic hauler starts to pull up the trap.

This is done by putting the rope attached to the trap in the turning wheel of the hauler. Once the trap is pulled up, he places it on the wash rail of the boat.

He opens the door of the trap and begins to measure the lobsters. The measure is marked for $3\frac{3}{16}$ inches on one side, five inches on the other. Any lobsters shorter or longer than those lengths have to be thrown back into the water.

28. Dan gaffing a buoy. (*Photo by Anne Pierter*)

29. Hauling the trap. (*Photo by Carl Young*)

Sometimes you'll have as many as twenty lobsters in the trap that have to be thrown back over. No lobsterman likes to get a trapful of snappers (small lobsters) that he's just going to have to throw over.

A good haul for a trap would be twelve "keepers," that are within legal size. You don't get too many like that. Most traps have on the average of about three lobsters.

After he's measured the lobsters, Dan puts the keepers in the peg box. The peg box is a small wooden box about three inches high and about fifteen inches square. One of the corners is sectioned off and that's where the pegs are kept.

It's my job to peg the lobsters. I grab the claws separately with each hand, then transfer one claw so that I'm holding both claws in one hand, with the crusher claw on top and the pincher claw beneath it.

With my free left hand, I put the peg in the crusher claw so that he can't open his claw. This is to keep the lobsters from attacking each other in the tank. Then I throw the lobster into the tank, which is a big drum fed by a hose that keeps the salt water inside circulating.

While Dan is hauling traps, I have already baited the spudge iron (pronounced "spudgin"). The spudge iron looks like an ice pick that has a hole near the end of the point. First I put the bait bag on the spudge iron, then poke the point of the spudge iron through the eyes of the redfish.

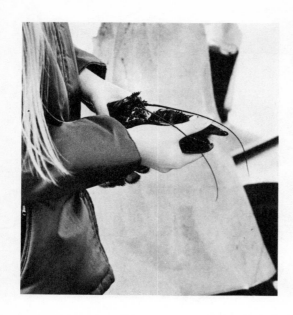

30. Plugging the lobster.

31. Dan baiting the spudge with redfish and a bait bag. (*Photo by Anne Pierter*)

After Dan finishes measuring the lobster, I hand him the spudge iron. He threads the bait line attached to the trap through the hole in the spudge iron, transferring the fish to the line. The bait line keeps the fish from floating outside the trap.

He closes the door of the trap and pushes the trap over, trying to place it in the same spot he hauled it from.

Setting the traps the first time, Dan uses a fathometer which tells the depth of the water and what kind of bottom is below.

We fish close to shore in the summer months because the lobsters come in then to shed their shells so that they can grow. Toward the end of the summer they start to move back into deeper water, and we move our traps along with them.

The fishermen have their own special names for the kinds of days we run into on the water. If it's a nice warm day with no waves and the sea is smooth as glass, Harley Jackson will call it a "grandmother's day."

If it's raining and there's strong wind with the sea going, Milt Maling will say "it's some buggerish out there." If it's foggy you don't say it's foggy. You say "it's thick-a-fog."

About 12:30 or 1:00 each day we head in. As we pull into the wharf, Albert Hutchins is usually there. Albert is the lobsterman with the most seniority at the wharf we fish from. What he says goes. In Albert's absence, Stilly Griffin takes over. Of the seventeen or eighteen lobstermen that fish from this wharf, Dan is one of the younger men.

After docking, Dan pours out the "pickle" from the empty bait barrels and puts the barrels on the wharf. He loads the lobsters into baskets and takes them to the lobster pound across the street, where they are weighed and he is paid. While Dan does this, I wash down the boat and empty out the bilge.

A lot of people have asked me why I'm a bait girl. Two years ago when I was fourteen, Dan lost his bait boy and was looking for a new one. One night when he was visiting my father, he jokingly asked me if I wanted to bait for him.

The more I thought about it the more I liked the idea. I wanted a job outdoors, and it was something new and interesting.

About a month later I called to ask if I could have the job. He was surprised that I had taken him seriously. That spring I went out for a few trial runs to see if I would like it. Would I get seasick, would I mind using the bait, or would I bug Dan?

I didn't get seasick, could stand the raunchy redfish, and I didn't seem to bug Dan. We decided what my daily wages would be, which included ten of my own traps. Any lobsters I got in my own traps were mine to sell or keep. The next year I got a raise of ten more traps, so that now I have twenty.

At first my mother had strong reservations about my being a bait girl. She had heard the language around the wharf could become quite colorful and was worried about the kind of influence it might have on me. I might become a "wharf rat."

But it didn't turn out that way. The lobstermen laugh and joke with me. There's a mutual liking. I have their respect and they have mine.

Lobstering is hard work, but it doesn't seem like work to me because I enjoy it so much. My summers as a bait girl have been good ones and I'm already looking forward to working again next summer.

GETTIN' WHERE SOMEBODY HASN'T BEEN

Story and photos by Herbert Baum III
Interviewing by Herbert Baum III,
Anne Pierter, Karen Eames, and Jay York

"It isn't where the lobsters are now—it's where they're gonna be next. That's what makes the difference between a good fisherman and an average one," Herbert Baum, Jr., told us. "The secret of bein' a good lobsterman is gettin' where somebody hasn't been and knowin' where they're gonna be next.

"It depends on the time of the year what kind of bottom you're lookin' for. Spring of the year you fish the hard bottom. Summertime you fish the sand and you try to fit it [the trap] in just off the black edge, which is kelp or similar to that." (During the summers, lobsters go in under the rocks to shed, and the lobstermen try to put their traps right next to the spot where the lobsters will come out to feed.)

"You turn your fathometer on when you first leave the river, and you never turn it off. You watch it and every day you learn something else about the bottom you're fishin'. A fathometer tells you the depth of the water from the keel of your boat to the bottom. It gives you an echo. It bounces up to the boat and back down to the bottom again. If it's a bright flash on your machine, it's hard bottom. Soft flash, you know you're in the mud."

Herb went on to explain about the depth at which he sets his traps. "Well, that varies, too," he said. "In the summer you're gonna fish from —I dare say ten feet, eleven feet up to twenty feet. Then as the season goes on, the temperature of the water decreases. You go off deeper and

32. Herb Baum, Jr., at the wharf.

deeper and deeper [because the lobsters move to deeper water].

"If you fish all year, you're off in a lot of tall water. Anywhere from a hundred to two hundred feet of water. Varies on what type of fisherman you are. Off shore some fishermen fish the gullies, some fishermen fish the hard bottom.

"That's what makes fishermen different than anybody else. They can fish where they want to. Some can catch lobsters on a hard bottom and some can't. I don't know why, but that's the way it is.

"To figure how much line to use [for the traps] well, you want about —it's six feet to a fathom, and you just figure it from there. And you have to allow for your tide, and the size of your buoys and how many bobbers you have. The spring of the year you have more line and more bobbers. If it's the back end of the moon, new moon, the tide doesn't run as hard. You don't need as many bobbers or as much line.

"The bobbers hold the slack off the bottom so the line doesn't tangle up around other objects, like rocks, on the bottom as the tide turns."

We've discovered during our interviews that lobstermen keep a pretty sharp eye on each other. When a lobsterman sees traps on the stern of another lobsterman's boat, he can be sure that the other fellow has found a place where the lobsters are crawling better and that he's moving his traps to that place. He, in turn, is likely to load up his traps and follow the other lobsterman, unloading his traps in the same area.

33. Herbert Baum, Jr.

34. Herb smiles at his good day's catch, 430 pounds.

Occasionally you'll hear a lobsterman complaining that somebody has hauled up his traps and taken his lobsters. Some lobstermen go to great lengths to find out whether this is happening. One local lobsterman staples his bait line to one of the top laths of his trap. A missing staple and an empty trap confirm his suspicions.

Arnold Stinson, who lobsters out of Cape Porpoise, tells a story that illustrates the point. Arnold claims lobstermen are "pretty honest people. They're pretty good," but he laughs and remembers that not everyone who fishes the sea would agree.

"I knew an old fella here years and years ago. He'd always get through [lobstering] early durin' the week, but Saturday he was a long time doin' it. So I says, 'I'm goin' to find out what he's doin'.'

"So I hauled slow and waited 'til he went home. Then I went down around the point where nobody'd see me, and I hauled one of his traps. And he had a spool of black thread, he'd take that thread and put it round two laths so when you opened the door you'd have to break that thread. That's why he was so long on Saturdays in tyin' up them things! Poor old fella. He's long dead now."

We asked Herb Baum, Jr., if lobstering has changed much over the years. "Yes, I'd say it's changed quite a lot. The traps are getting better, the bait's gettin' harder to get, the price is better, but overall, things don't look up like they should."

If things don't look up quite the way they should, maybe one reason is the increase in the number of traps being set each season. "There's so

35.   Lobsters loaded in the truck going to the lobster ground.

36.   Weighing the lobsters at the pound.

many traps here that you really can't put traps where you want to. There's so many there, you know," Herb explained.

"So you try to put them where somebody isn't and hope your guess is better than theirs."

WINTER LOBSTERING

by Herbert Baum III, Margo Brackley, and Kristy Bunnell

If you go down to the wharf at Biddeford Pool, Maine, in the winter, it's almost empty. One of the few boats you might see tied up there is the *De-Dee-Mae,* a 42-foot Fiberglas boat owned by lobsterman Marshall Alexander.

37.   (*Photo by Seth Hanson*)

Winter lobstering is so much rougher than summer lobstering that the *De-Dee-Mae* has to be well equipped to handle choppy water and heavy gales.

Marshall has outfitted the *De-Dee-Mae* with radar, Loran, fish-finding sonar, CB radio, and ship-to-shore radio in addition to the fathometer most lobster boats carry.

The *De-Dee-Mae* is named after Marshall's sister and is powered by a Nissen diesel engine. She's the fourth boat Marshall has owned in his years of lobstering. We asked him if he liked this one better than the others.

38.   Loading the bait into barrels. (*Photo by Herbert Baum III*)

"Yup," he replied. "But you always hope that you'll like the next one better."

Marshall started lobstering when he was eleven years old as a helper on a boat in Biddeford Pool. He now fishes five hundred traps both in the winter and summer.

We asked Marshall how important his equipment was in winter lobstering and got a strong answer.

"If my fathometer quits, I would go home. Course I got two of them now, but before I did, I would go home. I found you could be fishing right along a piece of bottom and lose more money dumping gear where

39.   Marshall Alexander. (*Photo by Seth Hanson*)

you didn't know where it was.

"The difference in being up on top of a hill trying to plant potatoes and being down on good soil trying to plant potatoes—that's the difference, and the bottom of the ocean is the same way."

What's the best bottom for lobstering, we asked Marshall.

"Well, different times of the year it changes as to what's best," he told us. "The spring of the year you want hard bottom.

"In the fall of the year while your lobsters are headed into the mud to kinda crawlin' and hibernate for a while, right on the edge of that bottom is usually the best, or right in the mud itself.

"You know, that's why you like a machine to show you both. But also it comes in handy because you know the bottom the draggers can fish on and it's advisable to stay away from it."

Draggers are boats that drag the bottom of the ocean with a big net that scoops up the fish. Lobstermen lose gear and catch fewer lobsters in an area which is being dragged if they set their traps there.

During the winter months fishermen have to put ice stripping on their wooden boats to brace them along the water line where the ice hits the boats. Usually for ice stripping, they use wood, Fiberglas, or copper sheeting. Marshall doesn't have to use ice stripping on his boat because Fiberglas boats have done away with it.

Marshall starts his day a couple of hours before daylight in the winter. He has to start early because his traps are so far off shore that it takes a couple of hours to get there.

During the winter season, Marshall wears different clothes than in the summer because it is so much colder. He wears clothes that would keep him warm on shore, such as wool pants, wool shirt, and heavy socks. Then over all this he must wear something to break the wind.

He takes a man with him all the time because he hauls so many traps that it would be very hard to do it alone. In the summer he also takes his dog, Mate, with him.

"She goes lobstering with me all the time in the summertime. They're a lot of company, you know. She likes to chase toggles [bobbers to hold the slack on rope]. A couple of times this summer she grabbed right hold of them and a couple of times she held on too long. Pulled her over the stern twice."

The price of lobsters in the winter is a lot different than in the summer. You can get a better price for lobsters in the winter time because you get a better-quality lobster and the demand is greater. There's more demand because there are not as many lobstermen in the winter, so the dealers want all the lobsters that the lobstermen can give them.

We asked Marshall how he kept his lobsters alive in the winter and he told us that he keeps a stove up forward in the boat. This stove

40.

keeps the lobsters alive, or if it is real bitter cold he throws them in a barrel with water in it.

Offshore the lobstermen get wind that they don't get on shore. So on-shore there might not be any wind but when Marshall gets offshore it might be blowing hard. Then he has to turn around and come in.

"You have to use a little common sense" in the winter about how hard to run a lobster boat, Marshall says. If it is choppy, the spray from the water will freeze to the boat and "weight it right down with ice."

We asked him if he communicated a lot back and forth with other boats. "Yea, a lot. I mean when you're out there I think you regularly use it for navigation, to know where your other boats are, so you can keep track of them.

"For it's lonely out there. I mean, you know, you and your helper. A

41.   Government Wharf. (*Photo by Herbert Baum III*)

lot of the guys are alone. They like to talk to someone once in a while. But," he added, "you can't be talking on the thing all the time or else you wouldn't get any work done."

For many years Marshall built his traps, but now he buys them because he doesn't have enough time to build them. We asked Marshall if he loses many traps in the winter, and he said that as long as he fishes in water over twenty-five fathoms he won't lose any. When the traps are that deep they won't move in rough weather.

Marshall has tried many different types of traps. He tried wire traps, but they didn't fish good, he said. He has also tried the round ones. These round ones fish good, but Marshall said, "They're a lot heavier and everything. But the difference is in the fishing. If you fish round ones, you have to have a big boat because it doesn't take many to fill it up."

We asked Marshall if he preferred a Fiberglas boat to a wooden boat, and he replied, "Well, I like this one if that's what you mean. But I don't think anybody really can say what Fiberglas can do if you give it twenty years. But as far as maintenance goes, it's terrific!"

In Biddeford Pool, where Marshall fishes, there are many part-time fishermen. We asked Marshall if he thought that they hurt the business, and he said, "I am death against part-time fishermen. It all goes back to whether the lobster business is going to be an industry or whether it's going to be a sport. We'll find out in a year or so," he predicted.

Marshall puts in long days lobstering—from before light in the morning until almost dark at night. We asked him if he enjoyed lobstering.

"You got to enjoy it, really," he said. "If you don't enjoy fishing, you'll never make it. It's the same with any job. When you like what you are doing, you can usually make a go of it."

Dragging

Story by Herbert Baum III

*Photography and interviewing
by Herbert Baum III
and Anne Gorham*

We headed out at four o'clock one summer morning to go dragging with Lester Orcutt on his boat *Minkette* at a fishing spot called Wood Island. Lester had agreed to let us go with him so that we could learn the daily routine on a dragger.

It was a very cold morning when we started out, but when we arrived at the fishing spot, the sun had broken through the clouds and the haze was lifting. On the way to the fishing "grounds," Lester had made a check of all his equipment to be sure that everything was in perfect working order for the day's chores.

"The basic operation of dragging is the method of setting the net, the type of net," Lester explained. In dragging, "there is very little difference from any kind of fishing, ground fishing, shrimping, or what have you.

"The difference is the size of the mesh [loops in the net] and mainly the season." Shrimp nets have a smaller mesh than ground-fish nets, he told us. "In the wintertime it is supposedly mainly shrimp and there are very few ground fish mixed up with the shrimp." For this reason, dragging is done mostly in the summer and shrimping is legally limited to the winter.

"The first thing that you set is the twine [net] overboard. The cod end goes first. That's the back end of the net. That's the business end of the net where everything winds up eventually, in the bag [the bag is an-

42. The *Minkette* at the wharf. (*Photo by Anne Gorham*)

other word for the cod end of the net]. There is chafing gear on the bottom of the bag." (For the names of the parts of a net, see diagram 44.)

The chafing gear consists of hundreds of strands of frayed rope tied to the bottom of the bag. It looks somewhat like a mop. The purpose of the chafing gear is to keep the bag from chafing along the bottom of the ocean, creating a hole in the net.

"When you get fish in the net, flounders are heavy and they won't float up like some other fish will. This puts weight in the cod end and makes it drag harder over what you are towing, whether it be mud or what have you," Lester explained. "It will chafe the knots out and even though it doesn't actually chafe through the twine in the mesh, once it chafes the knots out, the thing lets go and then you have a hole. When you have a hole, you start losing fish."

43. Heading out to Wood Island. (*Photo by Herbert Baum III*)

The net used in dragging is a wide mesh net of four and one half inches. "That lets the little stuff [fish] out so you don't destroy them," we were told in an interview with another local fisherman, Dave Burnham. The small fish can swim out of the net while the bigger ones are trapped.

"When you are dragging for codfish, you use rollers on the bottom of your net," Dave said, "and when you are dragging for flounder you use chain on the bottom of the net. Course, if you got chain on the bottom of the net you have to stay on perfectly smooth bottom."

Nets themselves have become very expensive. "They have tripled in price in the last five years," shrugged Dave. "You used to get a net for two hundred and fifty to three hundred dollars. Now they cost well over a thousand."

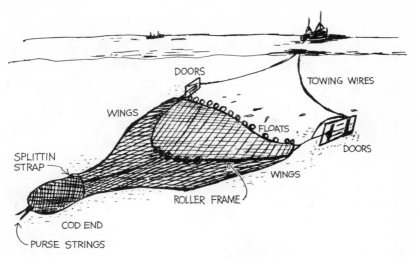

44.   Parts of the net.

45.   Chafing gear on the cod end.
(*Photo by Anne Gorham*)

46. Lester Orcutt tells *Salt* Interviewer Herb Baum III how he got into fishing. (*Photo by Mark Emerson*)

47. The main body of the net. (*Photo by Herbert Baum III*)

We asked Lester where he gets his nets. "Often you'll buy the webbing and build it yourself," Lester replied. By that he means knitting all the sections of the net from twine and joining them together. Lester usually knits his own nets. Building a net takes a long time, however, and "if you're in a jam and you have to have a net right away, you'll have it built for you. There are two places—either in Gloucester, Massachusetts, or in Warren, Maine," that build dragging nets.

Lester continued his explanation of how to set the nets. "Once the cod end drifts away from the boat, then the main body of the net goes next." Dave Burnham had described to us the design of the main body of the net. "In the outer extremities of the net are the wings. You have a lower wing and an upper wing on either side. Then you have the top belly and the bottom belly of the net." The belly of the net is the middle section of the net and this is made into two sections. Dave then went on to explain the next section of the net.

"You then have what they call a square, which is an extension of the top belly that lets the net ride over the top of the fish before the bottom of the net [cod end] gets the fish. That way if the fish get scared and jump up, they already have a roof over their head. If they go to the sides, they have the wings around them. If they turn around and go back, they're in the net.

"That's basically how the net works," explained Dave. "And then, you have the lower end of the net—the back end of the net—which is the cod end or bag. Usually there is an extension in between the net and the cod end which, just as it says, extends the length of the net to the cod end. You don't really need it unless you get a lot of fish. It makes it easier to work the fish into the net when you're handling the gear [net] at the side of the boat.

"Anyway, that is the net and the two doors that open the net. It's got rollers on the bottom of the net to protect it from the rocks. Got floats on the top of the net to lift it open, so what you get is a large funnel. The net is seventy feet across the bottom, fifty feet across on the top and probably sixty or seventy feet long.

"The doors that open the net are six feet long and forty-six inches in depth, and they are made of a combination of iron and wood. They are approximately two inches thick and the total weight of our doors is five-fifty to six hundred pounds apiece. They have to be able to go to the bottom and hold the net down.

"They have to be rugged enough to take a tremendous beating on the rocks and ledges. The doors are a very critical part of the net. If they are off balance one half of an inch, the net won't fish at all and it will put you out of business."

With Dave Burnham's explanation of the parts of the net in mind, we

48. The roller frames. (*Photo by Herbert Baum III*)

49. The door.
(*Photo by Herbert Baum III*)

could now follow what Lester was telling us about operating it. "When your cod end and the main body of the net have drifted away from the boat, you put the roller frames overboard. Then you go ahead on the boat and run the legs and ground cables out.

"The legs go from a figure eight, which is a link that you can run two cables through from one point. One of these cables goes back to the bottom part of the net and the other cable goes to the other side of the net to allow the net to open. They [the two wires] are cut so that they are the same length. That's so your wing end as it comes through the water is straight up and down.

"The ground cables, well, fish are funny in that most fish will be tempted to go away from anything that is making a disturbance in the water. Ground cables are put ahead, between the legs and the doors, and as they go through the water they sort of vibrate. This vibration sets up a . . . almost a curtain of air bubbles in the water. The fish will have a tendency to go towards the middle or to go away from it, hopefully staying low enough so we can catch them.

"It is sort of a herding, actually.

"The ground cables are cables that connect the door to the legs. The ground cables hook onto the towing chains, which are on your doors. We run out ten fathom, sixty feet, of legs and then we have sometimes five fathom, thirty feet, or ten fathom, sixty feet, of ground cables.

"When you have run your ground cables out, that brings you to the stopper link which stops in the Kelly's eye. The Kelly's eye is a ring made up quite heavy that the two chains that come from your doors are hooked to. Everything runs through the Kelly's eye. Then there is a stopper link that comes along that your legs and ground cables are hooked to. This stopper link, the main body of it, will run right through the Kelly's eye, and then the stopper link has ears on it and those ears can't go through the Kelly's eye.

"So this transmits the strain from the ground cables running out through the Kelly's eye to the Kelly's eye and from that to the chains on your doors.

"After you have come to the stopper link, you have a chain between there and your main wire which is called an idler chain. And you hook that up to your main wire to your door. This makes it all one line from your drum on your winch through to your door, through to the stopper link in your Kelly's eye, back through your legs to your net.

"Then your doors, which are chained up to your galisframes, have to be lifted and unchained from the galisframes and then set. The galisframes hang from the side of your boat and your doors are hung on these when they are not in use.

"The doors are set by steaming full-speed ahead in a very slight arc

50.   The Kelly's eye. (*Photo by Herbert Baum III*)

to keep the doors away from the side of the boat. Then you run out the amount of cable that you want. Usually three to one—if you are in fifty fathom of water, then you run out one hundred and fifty fathom of cable.

"The doors are heavy, and if you let the wire out too fast, the doors will have a tendency to slide like a sled sliding down hill. They'll slide one across the other. And that will turn everything upside down and your doors are on the wrong side and you just won't catch anything.

"So once your doors are set and you have a spread on your wires and everything looks all right, you have a towing speed that you tow by. You tow for whatever length of time you feel is going to be efficient, and then you haul back.

"Hauling back you just about reverse the procedure. You start the winch and you haul the two main wires in. You haul the doors into the galisframes, hook them up and unhook your main wire from your door. That puts the main strain back through the idler chain back through to your legs or ground cables. Then you haul the net up alongside the boat, and then you bring it aboard as you need it.

"If you have a lot of fish, you have what you call a splitting strap on the body of the cod end. A splitting strap is put around the cod end, and it is loose so it doesn't hinder the cod end from opening. It is put through beckets that will keep it in place.

"If you are fortunate enough to get more fish than you want to heist aboard the boat at once, then you take your fish tagel—which is a long

51. Dropping the doors into the water. (*Photo by Anne Gorham*)

stick with a hook at the end of it—and you put it in your splitting strap. This cuts off your cod end and keeps the fish that are below the splitting strap in the cod end and runs the other fish up into the net.

"That's the basic operation of dragging," Lester told us. "That is all I have been doing all these years. Setting out and hauling back and wondering where all the fish are."

The day we went out with Lester we noticed that he often consulted electronic equipment in the pilothouse. When we asked what equipment he used, the answer was "More and more every day." Then he went on to tell us how fishermen had managed before they had electronic equipment.

"The old-timers years ago used to drag . . . I used to talk with some fellers down to Small Point off Sebasco. They told me how they went out, threw a lead line over to find bottom and then threw their net over the side and started dragging. On the end of the lead line was a cup that would hold some grease. And then the line was knotted at various intervals.

"The lead man—the man who threw the lead line—would throw it overboard ahead of the boat, and if he was good, the line would hit bot-

tom directly below the bow of the boat. He could tell by countin' the knots how deep it was.

"When he hauled it back, he looked at the cup and if it filled with mud, gravel or nothing [meaning rocks], he knew what kind of bottom he was on. They would then tow . . . either until they had towed enough or they had fetched up and couldn't tow any longer. Then they would haul back and usually spend the next day mending their nets.

"But now," Lester continued, "you have to have sounding machines, radar, and Loran. The radar, of course, is because of the increased traffic. You don't have to have radar to fish, but you do have to have it because of the excess traffic around. I've seen times down off Half Way Rock, which is near Sequin [Maine], where there would be twenty boats setting out in an area no more than a mile square, and you know you have to know where the other guy is or you'll set into him.

"Radar is an electronic machine that transmits a signal from a revolving antenna, and constantly the signal is being beamed on a very high frequency. The signal travels out until it hits an object, and when it hits an object, it bounces off. A lot of it bounces off in different directions, but some of it bounces back and is picked up by the antenna. Then it is sent down to the display unit and is converted to light that displays on a screen.

"Loran," Lester explained, "is a machine that is used to fix your position so you know where you are when you can't see landmarks. A scanner is nothing more than another sounding machine, but it has a

53. The bag.
(*Photo by Anne Gorham*)

52. Getting a strain on the net. (*Photo by Anne Gorham*)

54. Radar. (*Photo by Herbert Baum III*)

transducer on it and it looks ahead and to the sides. It will tell you if there are rocks ahead of you or on the side of you. A sounding machine is just like radar except it sends a signal to the bottom [of the ocean], and it [the signal] bounces back up and tells you what the bottom is like.

"It's one of those things where you get a couple of guys who buy one and put it in their boat and they do a little better at fishing and then everybody has to have one. Now, of course, we had to go from the old AM set to the VHF, and most everybody works with a Citizens' Band radio now. So if you look around the pilothouse, you find anywhere from fifteen to twenty-five thousand dollars' worth of electrical equipment, and it makes you sick.

"You're running an old boat that you can't afford to do any more than paint her up every year, and you have all this sophisticated equipment in the pilothouse. And you still don't have it all. There is still more that you can put in, but for the inshore fleet you don't need it. For the offshore fleet they do need it in order to be able to compete with the other guy, and that is what it is, competition. It's me against you and everybody else."

We were curious about how Lester became involved in fishing. "I used to think years ago," Lester remembered, "that anybody that set a lobster trap in the water and expected a lobster to crawl into it so he could make his living was a damn fool, and I don't know, maybe I'm back to thinking the same way.

"I've always lived here on the coast, and my family, they ran the grocery store here. That's what I was brought up in. I got married to Emmy in 1935, and in 1936 [Lester and his wife] spent the winter down in Pennsylvania. I worked in a steel mill. Needless to say, I didn't like that worth a darn.

"Finally I got a skiff and an outboard and a few traps. I've gone from bad to worse ever since," he grinned. "I started dragging seventeen or eighteen years ago.

"My first experience with dragging was in a boat that was primarily a lobster boat. The net was one that we had bought from a feller that had had it quite a while, and when we came to haul back, we got the wings of the net up to the side of the boat, but we couldn't get the rest of it up. It was full of rocks.

"We left it over the side of the boat and headed for shore, and when we got to where we knew there was a rocky bottom, we lowered the net till the net touched bottom and it put a hole in the cod end and let the rocks out and anything else we had go out. So we brought it in shore and attempted to mend it, but I don't think we ever did get it right after that.

"From that, I bought a boat down in Stonington and I worked with her for about eight years, and then we got this thing here, the *Minkette*. She is twenty-six years old now."

While we were out fishing with Lester, we watched other boats around us, and we began to wonder how his boat compared with them. "This is one of the smallest boats in the fleet," Lester replied. "It's a little small. Most of the boats are fifty feet or over, and this boat is forty-six feet overall. But she is a good sea boat. For a while, I was fishing any day that anyone else fished. Since then I've quit that. I go out when I feel like it.

"I think there's a tendency now toward western rigs, which are mainly a southern boat. Most of the northern boats for years and years have been eastern rigs, and most of the southern shrimpers that are built down south are all western rigs. So a lot of fellers are now going down south and gettin' those boats and they will get anything from a 64- to 83-foot boat. That is what they are coming back with. One feller down in Boothbay just bought a 72-footer and brought her back. They are goin' to steel boats a lot down there now, due to upkeep and maintenance and a few other things. They are a hard-time boat and not as comfortable as this style of boat [the *Minkette*].

"This is a round-bottom boat and she'll roll, but she'll roll easy. She won't yank your head off like the hard-time boat will. She is a good little boat. She isn't all you'd want, but she's decent. I've caught quite a few fish off her. Not lately though."

We asked Lester what the difference is between an eastern-rig boat and a western-rig boat. "An eastern rig," Lester explained, "is a rig where the pilothouse is aft and the fo'c'sle is forward. The fish hole is in between on the deck.

"A western rig has the fo'c'sle forward, but it also has the pilothouse up over the fo'c'sle, so it's also forward. This gives it much more deck space. It also has its fish hole in approximately the same place, although usually in an eastern rig the engine is aft of the fish hole. They load it differently, too. On an eastern rig, they will load down by the head [front] so that if an eastern rig draws—this one draws six feet of water—it doesn't make any difference if she is loaded or light. She'll draw six feet of water simply because she goes down by the head, and the head only draws three and one-half feet when she is light.

"A western rig will draw more water when she is loaded because the stern is always the deepest part, and as you load in a western rig, you load the stern down so she'll draw more water when she has a load in her.

"There are a lot of stern trawlers being used now. They are a lot more practical I think because you are towing right straight ahead and with one of these boats you have to tow with a side pull. You have both your doors and your whole net hanging from one side.

"There is an inshore fleet and an offshore fleet. The difference is mainly the size of the boat. The Gloucester fleet, the New Bedford fleet, and the Boston fleet average from seventy-five to eighty feet in length. They run the same gear that we do, but they're an offshore fleet.

"The inshore fleet runs off maybe twenty-two miles and maybe even farther. I guess Tommy Jordan [a local fisherman] has been out to Doggers, that's a new fishing ledge. That is probably twenty-eight to thirty miles, and that's as far as they go.

"Some lobstermen are going to Cashe's Ledge, which is about fifty miles off shore, and they are fishing out there with a 32- to 35-foot boat. They take a gang of traps with them and some bait, and they go out and set the traps, haul them the next day, and bait them up and haul them again. They will stay out there three to four days. Then they will leave the traps there and come in and sell their lobsters and get some more bait. But that is an awful small boat to go out that far. They are asking for trouble, I think.

"I remember once there were line trawlers on Cashe's and they were some enormous time getting in and they had windows stove out and everything else. They came back and they were miles from where they wanted to be. You have to watch the weather and listen to the weather reports and then make up your own mind. If you are going out that far off course, it can be a long time getting home. Some of these nor'westers come up, and to come back in you have to head northwest. When you are running right dead into chop, you have to take it slow and it takes a long while. You think you're never going to get home.

"The main fleet of boats has deteriorated quite a bit in the past two years," Lester told us. "Since the shrimp let go [became scarce] in the wintertime, there have been six to eight boats sold out of Portland, and they have nowhere near the number of boats that they used to have.

"Fishing is for an optimist, I think. If lobstering would pick up so that there were a lot of them around, there would be a big influx in the lobster industry. Everybody would be buying boats and traps and going fishing. I think there is a hard core of people who will remain in the fishery and keep it going, so that it won't be completely depleted.

"Some of the boats in this area fish anywhere from Eastport [Maine] to Gloucester [Massachusetts]. The small fleet will fish the area from Sequin to Boon Island. There are no big areas up here that you can just go to and put a whole fleet of boats in without having to be careful not to get fouled up with somebody else. If you go down south off the Carolinas, you can set out and drag for miles in one direction. Here you might be able to tow one hour, which is usually three miles, in one direction.

"There is no great big area. I think probably Jeffrey's Basin is the largest and that is mostly mud. You can go over some rough bottom out there and you have to look out for wrecks. There are a lot of wrecks out there."

After Lester had completed his first tow, we could see that he had dragged up many types of fish. "It is in seasons," he said. "In the wintertime we have had shrimp in the past ten years. And mixed in with the shrimp will be codfish, hake, flounder, all in limited quantities. In the summertime, up until about four years ago, we had whiting, which are called silver hake and they are a food fish. When they come, they usually come plentiful, but they are also a cheap fish. When I started dragging, they were a cent and a quarter a pound. Now they are around a dime.

"You can do all right if there are enough whiting around. Gloucester now has a good whiting fishery going. They'll go out and catch a hundred thousand pounds in one day, and when whiting are here they will come pretty clean, with not much other fish mixed in with them. The

55. Cleaning the fish. (*Photo by Herbert Baum III*)

same way with shrimp. If shrimp are real heavy—if there are a lot around—why then usually they come pretty clean.

"Now in the summertime, if you don't get whiting, there isn't much else you can get. Ground fish, but they tend to go up on hard bottom—rocks—and we stay on the soft bottom or mud. We mainly get hake and a few flounders. Hake, as I said, is a cheap fish. I think it costs you four cents a pound to truck them, and probably one cent for commission, so you don't wind up with much. It is a lot of work and they have to be dressed [cleaned] and have their heads cut off."

We asked Lester how many fish he gets in an average tow. "Lately," he shrugged, "if you could get a hundred to a hundred fifty pounds an hour, you are doing average. It's pretty hard to keep one of these boats going without being able to gross in the neighborhood of four hundred dollars a day. Maintenance, fuel, and having enough so you can buy

56. Loading the fish into the fish hole. (*Photo by Herbert Baum III*)

57. Unloading the fish at the wharf. (*Photo by Anne Gorham*)

58. Fifty thousand pounds of redfish (ocean perch) caught by a Rockland fisherman outside of Matinicus Island.

twine if you lose a net, and so you can take home a day's pay and not have to worry about fishing every day.

"You have weather days when you can't fish. You have to look ahead and try to plan for those days as well as the days you do fish."

For the past three years in Maine the fishermen have been fighting to pass a bill that would increase the 12-mile limit to 200 miles, and they have won that bill. "I think the 200-mile limit is ten years too late," Lester smiled. "But it is here, and as long as they don't sell us down the river on it, it will work. It will be a very good thing as far as the fishery is concerned, especially for the East Coast. I don't know much about the West Coast.

"It's going to take time, a lot of time, probably eight to ten years before the fishery is back to where it is a good viable fishery like it used to be thirty years ago. But it stands to reason that if it is managed correctly, so that there is enough stock left to reproduce and build it back up, it almost stands to reason that it has gotta help, gotta improve. I can't see any other way it is going to be done. We have to take the pressure off the fishery." Lester has just been nominated to serve as one of Maine's two representatives to the management council that will control the rules and regulations for the 200-mile limit.

We asked Lester to tell us whether he would advise a young person to enter the fishing business. "Well, I would advise a young person just starting out to be a lawyer or a doctor. But I think there is a good future in dragging. There is a good dollar in dragging if this is the type of work that you want to do. You have to realize you're going to be gone long, long hours and you probably will be away from home quite a bit and the conditions are not always the best.

"It depends on the individual. I think there are some individuals that it would be a good livelihood, if they went into it. But I wouldn't advise them to go right out and buy a boat and just go dragging. I would advise them to go on a boat first, and there are two or three schools around that will teach you about dragging. Teach you how to mend, how to build nets, and they can take you out on a boat and show you the procedures and everything else.

"If there is anybody that is going into the business, they should learn all they can about it first, either from talking to other people, going to

59. "It has been a long haul and I have made mistakes, a lot of mistakes, but I was lucky."

school, reading books. Not the way I did it.

"I went out into it cold, and I didn't know how to mend a simple three-legger net. So it has been a long haul and I have made mistakes, a lot of mistakes, but I was lucky. I had a pretty good man with me for a while. He knew how to mend, he was a good rugged individual. He wasn't afraid of working. He'd been fishing all his life. I learned a lot, an awful lot, from him.

"It is a simple business, but it is not a simple business. It's rewarding at times, but it is also frustrating. It's something that I think will improve in the next ten years because of the 200-mile limit."

Shrimping

Story and photos
   by Herbert Baum III

I got up at three o'clock one cold March morning and went down to the wharf to go shrimping on the *Capt. Jim* with Dave Burnham and my father, Herbert Baum, Jr. We arrived at the wharf around four o'clock and started out towards Wood Island, off Biddeford Pool.

Shrimping is basically the same operation as dragging, or you could say that shrimping is one form of dragging. The main difference is that the mesh of the shrimp net is smaller than the mesh of the ground-fish net used in dragging. "Our shrimp net," Dave explained, "is one-and-three-quarter-inch twine. This is small enough to hold most of our shrimp, but the openings are still large enough to let the tiny ones escape without getting destroyed."

Shrimping can only be done in the winter, due to a law that prohibits shrimping during the summer breeding season. Dave and his crewman, my father, start shrimping around the first of October and they finish around March.

Dave told me that setting the net and hauling it back are done the same way as when dragging for ground fish. We set the net overboard and about three hours later we hauled it back, hoping for a net full of shrimp. As Dave and my father worked to bring the net up to the side of the boat, they shouted directions to each other.

"Start the winch," one of them said.

"Hook that door up tight."

"Pull on the forward wire."

"Get ready, the net is almost here."

The net was lifted aboard the boat about fifteen minutes after we

60. "The man on deck pulls the purse strings and lowers the bag and dumps the catch on deck."

61. Shrimp falling out of the bag.

started hauling it back. Once the net has been unloaded onto the deck it is immediately thrown back overboard.

"You don't waste time," Dave laughed. "Before you sort out the fish, you tie the purse strings back up [the strings that tie up the bottom of the bag] and throw the net back overboard.

"Then you reverse the whole procedure. Hook your net to the doors, disconnect the doors from the galisframes, and then start the boat in a gradual circle until you get a good strain on the net and everything looks all right.

"Then I signal the man on the winch and he drops the doors and, as they spread open, the net spreads open and down she goes.

"The man on deck then goes to work and cleans the catch and dresses the fish. [Cleaning means taking all the trash fish out and throwing them overboard. Dressing simply means cleaning out the insides of the fish and cutting off their heads.] Then he also packages the shrimp. This is all done while we are making our second tow.

"Normally our tows will run from one hour and a half to four hours, depending on what kind of fishing we are doing. Shrimp, you usually tow longer, because you don't catch as many at one time. If you are

62.   Sorting out the fish.

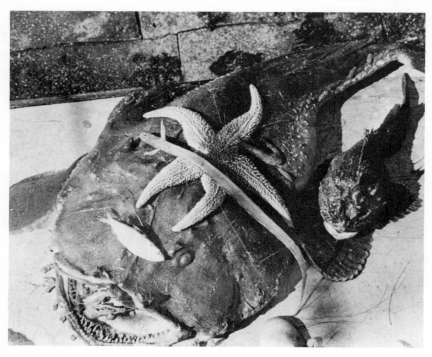

63. Not everything in the net is shrimp.

ground fishing, you can go over a piece of bottom with a lot of fish on it
and you can tow for five minutes over something like that and get seven,
eight, nine thousand pounds, with no time involved—if you are lucky.

"You have a fish finder that tells you whether you are fishing on bottom where there is any fish or not. You can see it on the machine. Some
of the time you get fooled, but most of the time the machines are right.
All they are, actually, is a fathometer with extra powers, and the frequency is such that it registers on the bladders of the fish. So if there is
a concentration of fish down there, it will give you an echo on the machine.

"Shrimp don't have a bladder so they don't show up very good, so
you turn the sensitivity of the machine way up high, and if the shrimp
are concentrated enough or in big bunches, you can see the little clouds
or what looks like grassy fields on the screen."

Dave told me that the first year he went shrimping he had two men
working for him. "We used to cook the shrimp then," he explained.
"We had one man and all he did was cook. We'd haul back the net and
dump the shrimp on deck and Smokey Coil [one of the men] used to

pick the trash out of the shrimp. He'd give the clean shrimp to Sherm Thompson [the other crew man] and he'd put them in the cooker, and he'd cook them for four or five minutes. Then he would take them and put them in the trays to cool and then store them down in the fish hole.

"Then the shrimp went to Norway. That is where the market was in those days. Then they got away from the foreign market and got more of a domestic market for the shrimp, so we stopped cooking. It wasn't necessary to carry the extra man, and looking at it from an economic standpoint, it was cheaper to go two-handed and not cook than it was to go three-handed and hire the cook and pay the extra insurance and everything else. That's the way we've been doing it ever since."

Shrimp have become very scarce in the last few years. Both the foreign and domestic fishing boats have been pounding on the shrimp so hard that they don't get a chance to breed. My father told me how the shrimp breed. "As the temperature of the water drops, the shrimp come into shoal water and shed their seeds. They change their sex life and transform from one to another and then go off shore."

Every fisherman has a particular fishing day he likes to brag about, and Dave was no exception (after a little prodding.) "The most fish that we have ever caught in any one day was when we were down to Sebasco fishing. [He was dragging, not shrimping.] We had close to twenty thousand pounds of whiting. That same day we caught a five-hundred-pound tuna fish. I think we had thirteen thousand whiting in one tow. That doesn't happen very often, though. Usually we feel good

64. The *Capt. Jim.*

65. (*Photo by Herbert Baum III*)

66. Dave Burnham.

if we get a thousand to fifteen hundred in one tow."

I was curious about how Dave became involved in the fishing business. "My father and my grandfather were both fishermen and I wanted to go fishing. But my father wouldn't let me go, so I went to college. Instead of going to a conventional college, I went to the Maritime Academy. I came out of that and I couldn't afford to go fishing. It cost too much.

"So I went to sea for sixteen years, and I saved my money so I could buy a boat, and I bought my lobster boat. Then I went lobstering in the summer and went to sea in the wintertime.

"I sold that lobster boat and I bought this boat that I own now. I sold the lobster boat to use for a down payment on this boat, and I bought it seven years ago. It has worked out good. This boat is seventeen years old now and she was originally built in Gloucester, Virginia. She was built for oyster fishing, so when I bought her I had to completely rerig her for this type of work."

I asked Dave why the *Capt. Jim* always gets into the wharf so late. "We try to arrange it so that we arrive at the fishing grounds at daylight, and we usually stop before sundown," he replied. "It makes a long day if you steam off two hours, and then you fish till five o'clock, and then you have a two hours' run to come back in and unload the fish. It makes a sixteen hour day anyway. But you don't do that every day because of the weather.

"We use our radio basically to call and make plans with the trucking company that handles our shrimp. We call them and tell them how many fish we have and what time we will arrive at the wharf, and when we get in, they are there."

I asked Dave if he had ever been caught in a storm. "Oh ya, three years ago we had an engine failure and we were being towed in and we missed the entrance to the harbor. While we were trying to find our way into the harbor, the boat rolled so bad that she rolled a wire off the deck and the wire got hung up in the rocks. It anchored us in the breakers, in a blinding snow storm. I think we got hung up around nine o'clock and before we got cleared, it was close to midnight.

"We were out there two and a half to three hours anchored right on the rocks. I'll give Lester Orcutt credit. He was towing us in and he never let go to the tow line. He was in the rocks, too."

Now this cold March morning has turned into a cold March night. We got into the wharf around seven o'clock. By the time we got the shrimp into the trucks, it was close to ten.

Gill Netting

*Story and photos
by Keith Euler*

Early one foggy April morning I put to sea from Biddeford Pool with
Herbert Hutchins. As we rowed out to the boat, the first light of new
day broke through the fog. Soon after, through the aid of radar, we set
a course for the Cape Porpoise Peaks, about ten miles off Wood Island,
to haul Herb's two strings of nets.

After an hour's run we came into sight of the first net's marker buoy.
Herb ran the length of the nets to see which way would be the best to
haul the nets with the weather conditions.

"The nets are made up of fifty to one hundred fathom [one fathom
equals six feet] segments connected together to form strings of nets
from five hundred to a thousand fathoms," said Herb. "The gill nets are
set right on the bottom. A sixty-pound lead line on the foot of the net
holds the net down, while a polyethylene float line with plastic bobbers
holds the top of the net up, keeping it open."

The gill nets are anchored at both ends, and each end is marked by a
buoy. "Right now," Herb said, "I am using a monofilament twine with
a mesh of five and a half to six and a half inches." Herb uses other
meshes when he is fishing for other kinds of fish.

"The principle of a gill net," said Herb, "is to have the fish swim into
the net and get its gills caught in the meshing. In trying to escape, the
fish further entangles itself, and is therefore caught."

Herb fishes out of a two-year-old Bruno and Stillman 44. Herb's
boat, the *Helen W.*, is powered by a 250-horse-power caterpillar diesel
which has many functions. It runs the net lifter, which hauls the nets,
and it also runs the salt-water pumps which are used for washing both

67.   Herb picking fish from the nets.

fish and the crew's work gear.

Herb fishes with either a two- or three-man crew. When fishing with a three-man crew, one man, usually Herb, runs the net lifter and keeps the boat broadside to the way that the net is running. The other two men pick the fish and fold the net after it comes around the net lifter. When Herb is fishing with a two-man crew, there is only one man to pick and fold. The other man runs the net lifter.

Once Herb has determined which end he will start to haul, the buoy on that end is picked up, and the line to the anchor is hauled by the net lifter. The net lifter is like a rotating barrel with jaws to clamp onto the line.

The net comes up over the side of the boat into a very large roller and around the net lifter. It then comes onto a table where the fish are picked out and put into boxes that are built into the side of the boat.

68. The net is hauled over the side on a roller.

69. The net lifter hauling nets.

70. Crew of the *Helen W.* folding nets.

71.   Resetting the net.

72.   Tommy Brennan gilling the fish on the way back to the pier.

73. Boxes of fish ready to be loaded into the truck.

Next the nets are folded and put into another compartment, where they will be prepared for resetting. When the last buoy of the net is hauled, the anchor on that end is hauled aboard the boat with the buoy.

The net is reset through a stand shaped like a goal post that is on the stern of the boat. The buoy on the end that was last hauled is put over that side of the boat, and the line is let out. Then the anchor is dropped. Once all the line between the anchor and the net is out, the net follows through the stand. The lead line goes out one side of the hump in the middle of the stand, and the float line goes out on the other side. This keeps the net from twisting. When the net is completely out the anchor for that end is set and then the buoy.

For resetting, you have to find a good spot where there are fish, and this takes practice and experience. Not too deep, fairly flat bottom, not too rocky—these are some of the things you look for.

Herb told me that he has been fishing three main areas: Jeffrey's Ledge, Tanner's Ledge, and the Cape Porpoise Peaks.

"We have been averaging two to three thousand pounds a trip. But as you know, there are your good times and your bad times. Sometimes you get next-to-nothing, and other times you can get thousands of pounds."

Herb, unlike a lot of other fishermen, nets all year. He does not convert to lobstering or to any other business during the summer months.

In the early afternoon, after resetting the nets, we started for home. On the way in we had to clean the fish for the market. This process is called gilling the fish. The gills are cut loose in the front and back and then they are pulled out. The belly is then cut open and the insides are removed.

Once at the pier, the fish are washed and loaded into boxes which are then put onto a truck. The truck will take the fish to be weighed and sold. In another one to three days, weather permitting, the crew of the *Helen W.* will head back out to sea to haul their nets once again.

Trawling

Compiled from interviews
by Maureen Campbell,
Laurie Smith,
Fran Ober,
Kelly Emery,
and Sandy Frederick

Back in the days when men fished off sailing vessels, they caught their fish individually on long lines of baited hooks that were unwound into the water. This was called trawling for fish.

Trawling is rarely done full time for a living as it was in the old days. It is now a form of fishing practiced only part time. Some lobstermen go trawling in the winter months and lobster in the summer, spring, and fall.

Even though trawling is no longer practiced full time, when it comes to eating, people in fishing communities place a higher value on fish caught by this method than other methods. This is especially true of old-timers who grew up on fish taken off trawl lines.

"A trawl fish is a better fish than a gill-net fish," claims Sam Wildes of Cape Porpoise, "because they let gill-net fish stay in the net for a couple of days. They drown and the taste goes out of 'em. They ain't so good as a trawl fish.

"But there's hardly a few that goes trawlin'. One reason is that there's more dragging business going into it. They go into draggin', but they don't go into trawlin'. It's hard to get the bait stuff nowadays." In dragging or gill netting, no bait is needed.

One man who used to trawl was Kenneth Hutchins. Ken is one of the last natives of Kennebunkport, Maine, who fished off a sailing vessel in the early 1900s.

"In 1917 I went fishing on the *Richard J. Nunan*," Ken told us. "It carried fourteen dories and twenty-five men all together, including the engineer. I went eight years, winter and summer. I went swordfishin' in the summer and trawlin' in the winter.

"We trawled all day long and had four tubs. They had four tubs to trawl to a dory. They were like a flour barrel sawed in two. You had ten lines to a tub and about fifty-two hooks on each line. It made up a trawl."

We asked Ken what was used for bait on the trawls. He replied, "Well, they used mackerel, herrin', squid, and a lot of times you'd run out of bait. Sometimes we'd go out and get bait to make another set before we came home.

"When the trawls were all strung out, they would reach about maybe four or five miles. Of course, we had fourteen dories.

"We fished just about every bank there is. You name it and we fished there. There's Grand Banks, Georges Bank, Jeffrey's Bank, Middle Bank, Brown's Bank, and Lahays."

Ben Wakefield is another person who used to go trawling. He was telling us about a big storm that he lived through while he was trawling out at sea. "It happened the day after Christmas 1933," he said. "I was

74.   Trawl tub.

75.   Kenneth Hutchins on the
Richard J. Nunan in 1917.

76. Baiting the trawls.

77. Ken Hutchins.

twenty-six years old at the time. I was married. I'd just been married about four months at the time.

"That was a scary episode. We were trawlin'. Do you know what trawlin' is? We had these trawl tubs and they have a hook on 'em and you have to bait the hooks. We have five tubs and each tub was about a half-mile long, and it's got about five hundred hooks on each trawl. We had five trawls, you know what I mean, five tubs.

"We left here about four in the mornin' and went up off Boon Island, outside Boon Island about five miles and set these trawls all baited, see.

"We're after codfish, haddock—haddock mostly—and then after they sit awhile [the trawls], after about an hour, you start pulling 'em back and take off the fish and coil it in the barrel. And that was what we was trying to do that day until that big gale of wind come up on us and blinding snow storm. We lost part of the gear cause we didn't have time to get it all back.

"The storm got so bad we had to leave part of it. We never did get it. And then instead of going back to Cape Porpoise, because the wind would be directly straight and we'd have to go right straight into the wind, we tried to go into York Harbor which was nearer, and quarter into the wind like.

"But we never made it. We come back awful early that afternoon and couldn't find the entrance to the harbor, so we turned around and went back out to sea again, cause it was the only chance we had. Stayed around those rocks and we'd be lost.

"My father was with me. Course he was the one that knew everything. I didn't know much. I didn't see too much, see. He was way ahead of me by experience.

"We went back off shore about two or three miles, and we started to get ready to try to spend the night and live the night out.

"We put out what you call a sea anchor. You took three of these trawl tubs, wrapped them all together and put them on the end of your anchor line way out ahead of the boat but it stays on top of the water. You know how hard a bucket draws through the water. Well, these big trawl tubs pull hard so they keep the bow of the boat up into the wind headin' into the wind as best you can.

"And by putting the sea anchor out and by tying the small sail we had—we tied it down low so we had about half a sail, between the sail and sea anchor, it saved our lives.

"We kept the motor just idling all night long like you would in a car, just let it idle cause we didn't want it to stop. In case anything happened, we thought we might possibly have a chance to get off a rock or something.

"Many times that night I thought it was the end of us cause those

78.   Ben Wakefield shows us a forty-year-old newspaper with artist's sketch of his battle with the raging winter seas.

Wrestling With That "Wolf of the Winds" a No. Atlantic Winter Gale, Two New England Fishermen Had Adventure of Their Lives

Capt. and Bob Wakefield of Cape Porpoise Beat the Raging Sea at Her Own Game---But It Took a Bitter Night of Beating Off Ice and Maneuvring Through Mountains of Black Water to Do It---They Finally Won Through to Safety in Rockport Harbor

great seas would come over the boat and you figure if one more comes it's going to fill your boat and you're gonna sink.

"But each time we just had time to pump her out again. Just as we were pumpin' her out she'd fill up again, and you kept that up all night long.

"The only thing it done was scare me about to death. I guess probably my father was the same. He was pretty scared. I thought it was the end of me. Nobody wants to die at twenty-six years old.

"And we pumped all night long. Cause, see the sea would come in and we'd pump and pump by hand. We got so tired. If ya do somethin' for as long as you can do it, like pumpin' and still have to do it twenty minutes more, ya know, that's what we were runnin' into.

"And I'd pump and he'd pump because there was nothin' else we could do. You couldn't get in and we just had to stay there and hope that you could live the night out, you know, and hope the snow storm would get over by mornin'.

"The boat was icing up all the time and getting colder and colder in the blinding snow. We really went from York Harbor to Rockport, Massachusetts, backwards with the anchor out, drifting slowly up the coast. We spent a horrible, horrible night.

"Until close to mornin' it got just a little better when the wind shifted and cleared the air up and we could see the land. It saved our lives [having the wind shift].

"We looked in at the land and as far as I was concerned it [could have been] the coast of England. But he [his father] looked it all over and he sees that high land in there and he'd been there many times taking lobsters up there, by boat. He recognized that land. We was about twelve miles off the shore then, and he said that's the land right above Rockport.

"I was tickled to death. The storm had stopped, the only thing that saved our lives cause we couldn't take much more of it. The wind shifted, come off the northwest about fifty miles an hour and it made us head right into Rockport. After about five or six hours we come into Rockport Harbor.

"They see us coming. Sixteen below zero, they knew we was in trouble cause the boat was loaded . . . loaded with ice. Oh, you couldn't see the boat. On the bow there was at least eight inches froze right down over it, hanging down over the sides and on the windows. In what we call the shallow here on the front windows, like the windshield of a car, here was eight inches froze right over that.

"The inside of the boat was full of ice. The stern was covered, even up under the roof of the canopy, we called it, there was two or three inches of ice under that, where the spray would go up and hit.

79. The dragger, *Seahorse.* (*Photo by Keith Euler*)

"We were driftin' and we finally did make it to Rockport Harbor. They come down and helped us tie up the boat. The fishermen, they rushed out and helped us tie the boat up. They knew what we had been through. They thought we might be freezing but we had plenty of clothes on. We were cold but not freezing.

"They took us up to the police station, got us warm coffee and then we went to the Coast Guard station. They called down to Cape Porpoise and let my wife and mother know that we were in safe because they'd already given us up for lost.

"That afternoon there was five men lost out of Portland, that same afternoon. All the fishermen and everybody had given us up for goners. There was just no hope for us to live through that.

"In fact, we were the only ones who did. The rest was lost. There was two men on the trawl out of Portland a hawlin'. They never heard from them again. And there was three more men on a small fishing vessel, that was in dories hauling trawley, lashed dories over 'em ya know. Each man hauls so many trawleys, then they come along and pick 'em up again. Heist the dories back on the deck of the ship. And they was lost. He lost his son and his brother and another man, the captain lost them.

"I've been in a few more episodes . . . We come in once southeast of Jeffrey's Banks, that's a famous fishing banks. It wasn't snowing. It was raining. We just about made it that night, too.

"We had great seas running behind us, comin' before the wind. The great seas get big. They come right over the back of ya, keep crawlin' up on ya."

Ben Wakefield's story had come to an end. We asked him if that storm after Christmas was the worst storm he'd ever been in. He sat silent, then with a nod of his head said, "That topped 'em all."

How to Build a Lobster Trap

by Elizabeth Tanner

Building a lobster trap is no simple task, as I found out from Stilly Griffin. Stilly is a Kennebunkport lobsterman, but during the winter he builds and repairs lobster traps (or pots as they are sometimes called) in preparation for the upcoming season.

"Got two hundred of 'em outside in the yard. These are the new ones I built for another fella, an' I got some new over here." He pointed to the huge stacks of traps which cover his yard. "Then I got another hundred twenty or twenty-five more over there to repair."

I asked Stilly just how long he had been building traps. "Oh boy!" he replied with a hearty laugh, "since I was in school. I'd have to do it every day."

Stilly builds the square traps rather than the round type. "I like the square traps better," he explained, "they handle better. An' when it's choppy they're [the round traps] rockin' an' rollin'."

His traps are made out of red oak which costs about forty dollars for two hundred feet of wood. Stilly told us, "Should be more this year since lumber's gone up."

There are many different pieces needed to build a lobster trap. Stilly has these parts cut ahead of time making it a little easier for him.

"Ya get started here with the bottom bed piece. You need three of these. These are twenty-six inches long," Stilly explained. "Then you take three of these. These are bed pieces, too, only these are twenty-two inches long.

80.   "It's kinda too bad to put that trap in the water, isn't it? Takes all day to make it an' two minutes to stave it up." (*Photo by Jay York*)

"Now you take two of these standards for each side." A standard is a piece approximately twelve inches long which fits into two holes about the size of a nickel, approximately one to one and a half inches from the end of the bed piece.

"First ya pound the standard into the [bottom] bed piece. Now the other side. Now you put the top bed piece on 'em an' pound that. Then nail it." Stilly uses six-penny nails to make it stronger. This is done two more times so that you have three shaped pieces.

"Now I gotta have two runners. They are thirty-four inches long and two and one-quarter inches wide." One of the three pieces is placed at each end of the runners, and the third is placed approximately twelve inches from one end. Holes are then drilled and the pieces are nailed into place with eight-penny nails.

Stilly picked up the partially built trap and set it, bottom side up, on his work bench. "Now we gotta nail the laths on. Some people call 'em slats, but they're laths to me." The laths are thirty-four inches long and one inch wide. The ten laths are placed along the bottom of the trap.

"Ya nail 'em just the nose of that hammer apart [about half an inch]. Ya put two nails [eight-penny] on each end of the lath. I gotta put special nails in there, three and a half inches long. [You put the nails] right down the middle.

"That way she can't get adrift," Stilly explained, "David Jones y'know is a rugged bugga.

81. The top and bottom bed pieces are nailed to the standards.

82. Drilling the runners to connect them to the bottom bed pieces.

83. Bottom bed pieces connected to runners.

84. Lathing up the bottom.

85. After lathing the bottom, the trap is turned, and the ballast is put in.

86. Lathing up the side.

"Now I gotta get three bricks for the ballast so to sink it an' to keep it on the bottom [of the ocean]." Stilly placed the bricks (actually there are about two and a half bricks used) against the center. "Now you take two of these. Ballast strips they call it. They're twenty-five inches long. I got 'em all cut up perfect," Stilly said, "an' you put 'em right on top to hold those bricks. Now we gotta drill right through. Now hammer it." He pounded in the nail with authority. "See, there's nothin' to it." He lifted the trap off the bench and set it on the floor.

"Now ya gotta get some copper nails." Stilly took a handful of the copper nails and leaned over his half-built trap. "You start in the corner of the trap, inside by the bricks. Next, [drill] eleven holes across [the bottom bed piece] an' I got four up each side. Then you got seven along the bed [bottom bed piece]." Then the copper nails are hammered into each of the drilled holes. These nails are for putting each of the meshes of the parlor head into the trap.

Then it is necessary to drill four holes along the top and four along each side standard. After that, you need six along the runner. This is then repeated on the opposite runner. The copper nails are hammered into the holes. The two side (fishing) head meshes are put on the nails. The hoops of the heads are then tied together.

"I sometimes knit my own heads, but my brother knits most of them. Then Kenneth [Hutchins] knit mine this year. I ain't knit a one."

Stilly began to tie the parlor head in. He took a piece of twine and tied each corner of the head to the standard with a piece of nylon twine. He then went outside the trap and back around the standard and tied it

87. Pounding in nails to attach the heads.

to the mesh. This is done to all three corners. He burned off the excess
string with an electric gun so it wouldn't unravel. "We used ta use
matches," he told us with a smile. "Burnt a lot of fingers!"

88.   After the corners of the heads
are tied, excess string is burned off
with an electric gun.

Next he put the bait string in. The bait string is tied to the bait
caulder which is a loop nailed to the back of the trap near the center.
The bait string is a long piece of black nylon. You take double what
you need and, holding on to each end, twist the string. Then you tie it
to the loop (bait caulder).

Stilly leaned on his almost completed trap and began to tell about one
of his sea adventures. "One time I was goin' out at another fella's on
the river, an' he wanted me to go out mackerel draggin' with him. We
was up about midnight, an' it started to rain hard an' we wanted to haul
the net an' come in, but the rain was too hard. I steered awhile an' then
he took over there. About half an hour afterwards, I says, 'I'll go out
an' get me a sandwich.' I opened up my dinner box an' I had a lobster
sandwich in it.

"I took just one bite of it an' we run right up on the fishin' rocks. The
sea laid her [the boat] down and I rowed her down forward an' I
grabbed six life preservers—three for him and three for me. An' we tied
them together and then we put them on us.

"The sea hit us. I felt it all over. It was right on my feet an' I could
feel a crunch.

"I says, 'We put a hole in her.'

" 'Oh, no, she didn't,' he says.

"I says, 'She sure did.'

"So the next wave come and take the boat and set her right off. She
floated—we thought she was gonna sink. An' I went up around the canopy. I cut my wrist on the window an' the wave washed her out. The
engine set on top o' the canopy. It was about two o'clock in the mornin'.

"We had the hatch way down on the cover an' I pried that cover up an' then I reached down in there an' pawed aroun'. I got ahold of the . . . middle of the rope an' we dragged her way over to Watson's Cove before she rest off Kennebunk Beach.

"I couldn't get the flashlight to work all night an' the cars would go 'round the beach. We didn't know who it was. I see this car come down the road over the hill an' I took that thing [flashlight] an' gave it a wallop an' when I did, that thing came on. An' I kept flashin' it, y' know?

"He peeped out of his car an' looked an' the fella with me said, 'I'm gonna get in the engine box,' an' I says, 'Oh no you're not! You're stayin' with me, by Christ! The boat floated all this time an' this far an' we're gonna stay with her!'

"Y'see she had copper tanks in 'er—kept her up. An' then the fella in the car went around the beach an' he says, 'He didn't see us.' I says, 'Oh yes he did. I can tell.' "

The man in the car, Dan Wentworth, took his boat out to rescue them.

"When he hit those terrible waves he just flew. There was a wicked thunder storm that mornin' about one o'clock. He went an' got us.

"He says, 'What yer gonna do? Tow 'er in?' I says, 'No, the heck with her. I want to get in a tight boat for a change.'

"So we jumped up there an' got a new change of clothes, an' I was wet just about every part on me. The only dry spot on me was my sou'wester.

"We went back an' got her the next day an' put 'er on the sand beach, nailed canvas over the hole, painted it good an' took her up to Clemmy Clark to have him fix her, an' that was the end of my mackerelin' life," he finished with a big laugh.

"Now we'll build the door. There are three door buttons. Them are nine inches long." You take two of the thirty-four-inch laths and nail them to the top of the trap. These are spaced about an inch apart. "Now you take four laths an' nail them to the door cleats. Put 'em side by side." You nail them in place with two small nails and two larger nails.

"Then ya take three rawhide strips an' nail them to the second lath [on the top of the trap]." This is done with two large nails in each of the three strips. Then you take the partial door and set it on the trap approximately one inch from the second lath. Next, nail the pieces of rawhide to the door to form a hinge. Now you have a door.

"Gotta lath up the front. These are all supposed to be cut the right size. The short one's nineteen and a half [inches] and these long ones are twenty-six [inches]." You take two of the long laths and place one

89. Attaching the door to the top of the trap. The ends are then lathed up and the heads attached.

just below where the bed piece comes out. This is nailed in three places (to each of the three standards) with two eight-penny nails.

The second lath (twenty-six inches) is then placed on the projection of the bottom bed piece and is nailed to each standard as before with two eight-penny nails in each place. You then take the three shorter pieces and, beginning from the top lath, nail each of the three shorter laths approximately an inch apart on to the end and middle standard with two eight-penny nails.

"Now we need the green wire. I use the wire. It costs more, but I won't have to repair this trap till it's worn out. It's stronger. If it were laths you'd need four an' one up the middle," Stilly continued as he stapled the green wire to the standards.

I asked him how many staples he used and he told me, "Oh, it varies . . . use your own judgment. Now cut off the edges even with the sides and pound 'em down. It'll take a lot of bangin' when it's rough." This is repeated for the other end.

The back of the trap must be lathed up. "You need six of these [twenty-six-inch] laths." These are placed between a half inch and an inch apart and nailed with two eight-penny nails at each end to the sides of the trap.

For all practical purposes the trap is completed. However, Stilly brands his trap to tell it from any other. The branding is done on the top (under the door). Each lobsterman has his own number and Stilly brands his on the first top bed piece.

"My number's 6334," he said as he plugged his special branding iron in a nearby outlet. The same is done with his initials. "S-M-G. I put it right here in the middle."

Then Stilly stepped back and admired his work. "It's kinda too bad to put that in the water, isn't it? You might lose it the first time out.

Takes all day to make it, an' two minutes to stave it up." Actually Stilly can build a trap in an hour to an hour and a half.

Finally, Stilly picked up the trap and set his work of art on his workbench. Of course, every fisherman's trap has its own distinct quality and differences, and this is a "Stilly Special." "Now you see there's nothin' to it," he finished with a hearty laugh. "Nothin' to it."

90.

Knitting Lobster Trap Heads and Bait Bags

TRAP HEADS

by Fran Ober

Photography by Carl Young

Let me introduce you to Albert Hutchins, the man who showed me how to knit a lobster trap head. He's never told me his exact age, but when I asked him how long he had been knitting the heads, he told me, "About sixty-five years. Yes, since I was a kid."

Albert is a Maine lobsterman who has lived in Kennebunkport most of his life. We asked Albert who taught him how to knit the lobster trap heads. His answer was, "Oh, my father taught me years ago. He always went lobstering . . . that's all he ever did."

Albert then went on and told us a childhood story:

"I have a brother. Well, I have two brothers. The oldest brother was about seven years older than I was. Of course, we was kids and he didn't like to knit heads, my older brother. So he'd say to my younger brother, 'I bet Albert can knit heads faster than you!' Kenneth, my younger brother, and I would get racing, knitting those heads. Yes, that's the way my older brother got his heads knit. Of course, we didn't realize he was pulling a stunt like that."

Albert told us quite a few people around here know how to knit heads. But "the young fellas don't like to knit them so they hire some-

91.

body. They just plain don't like to do it."

What is a lobster trap head? It's a funnel-shaped net tied inside the trap that guides the lobster to the bait. There are two different kinds of heads, the fishing heads and the parlor head. The two fishing heads are located on either side of the trap. The lobster first crawls through one of the fishing heads, goes to the bait, and then continues on to the parlor head. The parlor head is located in the second half of the trap. It is the last head that the lobster must crawl through to be finally trapped.

Quite a few materials are used in knitting the head. The smooth wooden needle is made out of maple. Albert carves his own needles. He makes them in sizes ranging from six to twelve inches in length, and a quarter to one and a half inches in width. The smaller the needle, the less twine will fit on that needle. For this reason Albert prefers a larger needle so that he can make a large head with one needle full of twine.

The twine he uses is nylon. This also comes in different sizes. The size Albert uses has 550 feet in a pound. This size costs about six dol-

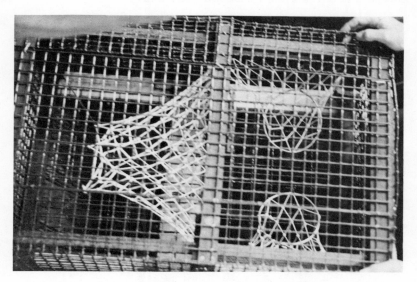

92. The lobsters crawl through the fishing heads at right and then through the parlor head at left.

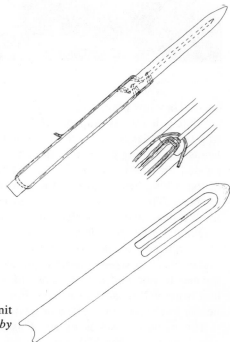

93. Wooden needle used to knit lobster trap head. (*Sketches by Regan McPhetres*)

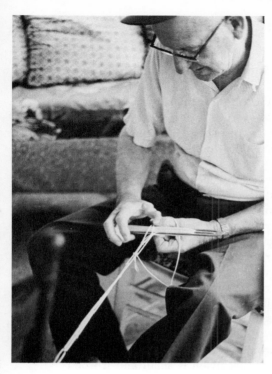

94. Going down twenty-two meshes.

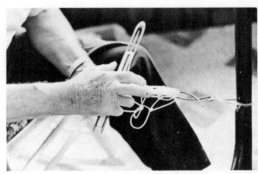

95. "I'll hook it up."

96. Knit across six times, adding a mesh at the end each time.

lars a spool. Albert said the amount it takes to make a head is "maybe eighteen fathoms."

He told us how they used to make the lobster trap heads.

"Before we had nylon, we used sisal, sort of a jute. It's splintery and won't last at all. If you set traps in the springtime, maybe in just two months the heads would be worn out. You wouldn't have any head in your trap at all.

"After I knit the head itself, we would dip the sisal head in hot coal tar. That coal tar is great stuff—putting your hands in it! The coal tar would stiffen the head, see. There wasn't much body to that sisal. Oh, that's terrible stuff, and we had it for rope, too!"

Albert went on to tell us about dipping the sisal head in hot coal tar.

"You had to take some lard and rub your hands all over with it. It was awful messy, oh yes, you bet it was! Then we'd cut the feet out of long knee socks and pull them up to our elbows. You'd dive your hands into the hot coal tar. It burnt all the time because your hands were covered with tar. It was black—it was just terrible stuff!"

The first time Albert used nylon was during the second World War. He used to use parachute cord. It wouldn't rot, so he started knitting heads with parachute cord. Albert said that nylon is small and it won't rot. "It's wonderful. It won't deteriorate in the water at all."

To thread the needle, Albert explained, you place the end of the thread on one side, bring it up around the spindle in the center of the needle, and down around the bottom again. You continue with this until you have a full needle.

After you have threaded your needle you set up some sort of a hook to put your thread through. Albert had a large brass hook.

"That's a hook, see. I made it yesterday. You can use most anything for a hook, a piece of twine, but it's easier to snap it on this brass hook."

To start knitting the head, you must bring the end of the thread through the hook and down about two or three inches. You then bring your thread up around your "mash" board to form a loop.

During the three afternoons and one evening Albert took to show me how to knit heads, he always called the small completed loop a "mash." The dictionary spells it "mesh." But for me—and for Albert—it's pronounced "mash," and that's the way I'm going to spell it.

A mash board is a small piece of maple used to determine the size of the mash. The larger the mash board the larger the mash. The smaller the mash board the smaller the mash. Albert used a 1″ by 2″ by $\frac{3}{16}$″ mash board. A mash is four sided and looks like a diamond. These small diamonds knitted together form a head.

After you make a loop around the mash board, you bring the needle

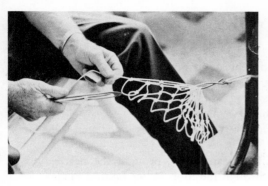

97. Albert knits down four times.

98. He doubles the twine.

99. Albert now has ten down, thirteen across.

100. Albert has now decreased, and is knitting eight down, five across.

back up over the top of the thread. Then you pull the needle through the loop and it forms a small knot. Remove the mash board and you'll see that you have one mash.

Then Albert knit a series of mashes.

"I'll go down first. I'll go down twenty-two mashes and then I'll hook it up."

He made a second loop around his mash board, brought the needle up over the top of the thread and through the loop. After he had made twenty-two mashes he placed each mash in the hook. The first time across, he added one mash on each end.

Now there were seven down, thirteen across. Before he came out on the end of the seventh row, he doubled the twine. Albert explained why. "I start here and put it in double for the simple reason that when I start right here it will be double up in the corners of the trap."

He continued using double thread, going down till there were a total of ten down, thirteen across. After having reached this point, he decreased, knitting five across eight times down. Now he knit it together. Albert explained:

"I knit it together now. You'd have a mile if I kept on, so I have to knit it together. It's the same stitch [only you don't use the mash board to measure it]. To end the thread you just burn it in two. You now have your finished head.

"It's ready to go in the trap now. A lot of people wouldn't know how to put the head in after they got it, see. I can show you how I tie the strings on, but I ain't got no trap to put it in, see."

He tied each corner to the standard with a piece of twine. He went outside the trap around the standard and back in again, tying the string to the mash. This he did in all three corners.

"This head here should last three years . . . a couple of years anyway," Albert said. "Nylon doesn't deteriorate a bit. The only thing that deteriorates is the lobster walking over it, see, trying to get out.

"Some of the little ones [lobsters] get in the mash. Of course they're small and they wiggle through and sometimes they'll cut a mash."

Albert told us that the head he knit was his own. "I mean there's nobody else that knits them like this. This is my own head." Albert's brother Kenneth also has his own way of knitting the heads.

Albert took us down to the cellar of his house where he makes his lobster traps. He told us that he didn't make wooden traps much any more. "The last couple of years I've been kind of experimenting with wire traps. I don't know just what grade of wire this is. They call it perm-a-guard. It's got a plastic covering on it. I use oak to make the frame, then I just wrap the wire around it.

"They work pretty good. It's not much bigger than a wooden trap.

101. Albert now knits it together to form a funnel.

102. The funnel head takes shape.

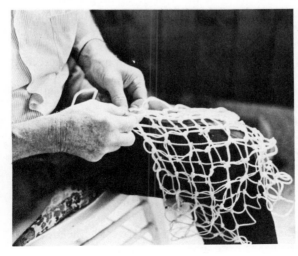

103. "It's ready to go in the now."

104.

The only thing is it's square. They're not heavy, hauling them in the boat, not as much as the wooden ones, the reason being, there isn't so much to soak. They don't soak up much water. The only ones that do that are the wooden traps.

"Dry, the wooden traps weigh about sixty-five pounds. After they soak up the water they weigh about one hundred and ten pounds. They're not too hard to haul, see. We haul them up hydraulic. All you have to do is to work a lever with your hand.

"You know we don't use those old wooden buoys anymore. Oh, no. We buy the buoys already made. They're sponge rubber. The wooden buoys soaked up water, of course, and that's not so good, not so good as these.

"We used to make our own buoys. Oh yes, we used to turn them on the lathe. Sometimes all we had was a piece of four by four and hew the end out."

Albert paused. I watched his hand move quickly over the head, as he showed us how to knit the heads once more.

"If anybody brings me a head, I can knit it the same size. Any size anybody wants. I knit quite a few for different fellas in the wintertime.

"If I'm knitting something I don't know, sometimes I keep going, and it's according to what you knit. You can knit bags and heads, everything. But, you kind of have to figure things before you start . . ."

BAIT BAGS

by Anne Pierter and Stephanie Wood

Photography by Anne Pierter

"When I was about ten years old, I learned to knit bait bags. My aunt taught me and I've been knitting ever since. Quite a number of years. She had girls, and we [Ada and her cousins] thought if she could knit them, we'd like to. So she told us she would teach us. And, of course, everyone was so anxious to do it better than the other one—so we all accomplished what we were doing. She was very happy to think she was teaching us to knit them. So it was real interesting. I guess that was about the beginning of me knitting."

Ada Foss of Cape Porpoise showed us how to knit bait bags. Working from the house's plant-filled entry, she patiently guided us through each step. But during our interviews, we learned more than how they're made. Ada's pride and skill in her craft is as much a part of her bait bags as the twine she knits them with.

"Why, of course I didn't do too much of anything 'til after I was married. Then I used to knit for my husband and my father. We used to keep them supplied. I had two sisters, and we all three learned.

"But we didn't used to knit any to sell until after my husband and I went into the lighthouse service. My children went to school there for a while. We had a traveling teacher, but then I had to go ashore with them, so I had a chance to knit for a man by the name of Clarence Wallace. He lived in Cutler, he was a dealer, and I knit for him steady then. I didn't get very much out of knitting, but it was fascinating to do it and I always loved to work.

"I knit for a number of the fishermen. And then I don't knit any unless I have them on order. If someone wants me to knit, why I do it for

105. Ada Foss.

them, and I like to."

Now Ada took us step by step through the process of knitting a bait bag. She used nylon twine which comes in spools, each weighing two pounds. "I use the Yarmouth [brand] 10/20 because I think it's the best. I like that to knit. It makes a firmer bag—well that's my idea. My son-in-law has got bait bags that he's had, oh, it must be fifteen years. And he still uses them."

Ada walked out to the entryway, sat down in her rocking chair, and picked up one of the needles she uses in knitting bait bags. All of her needles were handmade, most of them by her husband over thirty-five years ago.

"My husband made this needle for me years ago. I'm very choiced of it. And when I'm knitting, I'm very careful. I have several needles. I don't know what kind of wood it is, but it has to be something that's quite strong. They do have plastic, but they're not so good as the wooden ones. I like the wooden ones much better."

It takes Ada approximately one full needle's worth of twine to knit a bait bag. "I'll knit one bag, and I'll have a little left over to start another one."

Ada first pulls the twine through the prong of the needle, leaving about one half inch of the end hanging free on one side. (See photo 106.) She has burned the end to keep the twine from unraveling. Now with her right hand, she wraps the twine underneath the fork in the needle, and then turns the needle around to the other side. She then brings the nylon twine straight up and around the prong of the needle from the left side to the right. (See photo 107.) Bringing the twine under the fork and then turning the needle over, Ada continues doing this, working from the spool. She doesn't cut a certain length of twine off first. "And you go around like that. It's easy once you see how it's done. When I fill my needle I fill it full."

The next step after filling the needle is to make the beginning loop that the bag is knit onto. (Later this will form the drawstring of the finished bait bag.) Ada cuts a piece of twine about thirteen inches long and secures the ends with a square knot. She loops this over a hook in the window frame of the entry where she knits all her bait bags. (See photo 109.)

Ada then pulls her needle through this beginning loop, leaving about an inch of the twine on which she ties a knot. (See photos 110 and

106 and 107.   Filling the needle.

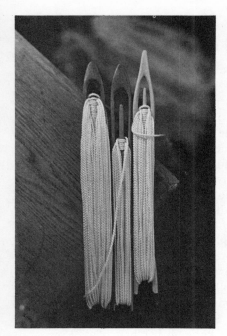

108.

109.   The drawstring which the bait bag is knit onto.

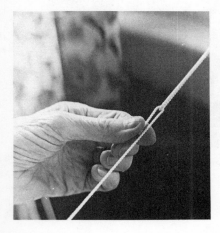

110.   Ada brings the twine from her needle through the drawstring about an inch.

111. She makes the knot for the first loop of the bait bag.

112. Completing the second loop of the bag.

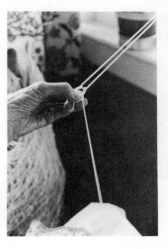

113. "That's the basic knot. See, you have to hold your fingers just right."

114. Ada begins to knit loop sixteen, the first loop of row two.

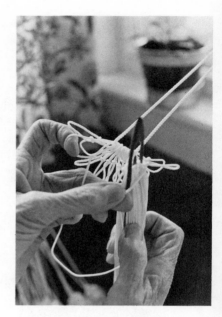

115. Joining the bag together.

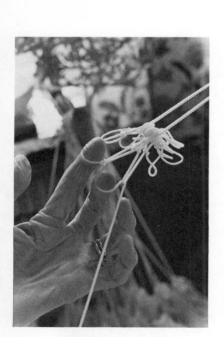

116. Ada makes loop seventeen.

117. The first loop of row three.

111.) "You have to hold your fingers just right in order to tie that knot. If you don't it will slip, and if it slips it doesn't work out that way." This is the basic knot for knitting a bait bag. Now she makes another loop and again ties a knot around it. She continues looping and knotting until she has fifteen across.

Now the bag begins to take shape. Holding the last loop (number 15) in the index finger of her left hand, Ada grasps the first loop she knit between her left thumb and middle finger. (See photo 114). Taking her needle, Ada knits a loop under loop 1. The twine, still attached to the knot in loop 15, is brought through loop 1 the same way it was brought over the beginning thirteen-inch loop on the hook. (See photo 115.) Now with this new loop (number 16) on Ada's middle left finger, she ties the basic knot used to tie the other 15 loops. (See photo 116.) Then she pulls the needle through loop 2 and knots another loop below that, completing the second of the 15 knots in row two.

"It's the same thing as the first, only now you're starting to make your bag. Then you keep going around like that until you have the length of the bag you want, which is 10, 10 times down. See you count these [knots]." You continue knitting until you have 10 rows of knots down. That's the length of your bag.

"There now, when you start narrowing this off, you pick up these loops way down there [with the needle] but you hold this one." With her

118. "Well when I was knitting regularly, you know steady at it, I could do one in ten minutes. I used to knot twenty-five or thirty of these a day. But I don't do it anymore. I just do this more to pass away the time."

119. Ada draws the needle through the final row.

left hand, Ada holds the last loop she knit and threads her needle through the rest of the loops of the final row. Ada draws the needle through the final loop which secures the bottom of the bait bag. (See photo 119.)

For an even firmer bait bag, Ada divides it near the bottom, pulls the needle up through the opening, and makes a knot. She separates the bag once again so it is now divided into quarters. Drawing the needle through, she makes a second knot. (See photo 120.) About a quarter of an inch below these two knots, Ada ties a third knot and burns off the remainder of the twine. (See photo 121.)

"I burn all of my twine. Then it doesn't have a chance to ravel. And then I always turn my bags [inside out] there, see? And that is your bait bag. All done."

120. She divides the bag for the second time.

121. "I burn all my twine. And then it doesn't have a chance to ravel."

122. "You see, it's one hundred per cent nylon, and it really makes a beautiful bag."

Save the Tail for Last

Photo story by Jay York

Eating a lobster may not require as much skill as catching it, but there's more to it than crushing every shell in sight. If you end up with a plateful of tiny red fragments, you've worked too hard for your meal.

This particular chapter, demonstrating how to eat a lobster the way old-time Mainers do, was enjoyable work for eight *Salt* students. Gathering around a picnic table one warm sunny day in Maine (outdoors is the best place to eat a lobster), they exhibited the expertise gained from years of lobster eating.

An important thing to remember is to avoid overcracking, the immediate sign of an amateur. With deft use of hands and fingers, other instruments are necessary only occasionally. Use butter—real butter—liberally. And, of course, save the tail for last.

123. Ken Hutchins shows off one of his larger lobsters.

124. The first step in eating a lobster is to remove the legs. Twist them off.

125. The best way to get the meat out of the legs is just to suck them.

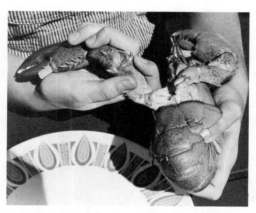

126. Now break off the claw where it joins the body.

127. Break the claw from the knuckle. To get the meat from the knuckle, push it through with your finger. Douse the meat in butter.

128. Open the claw and break it. Now break off the end of the claw.

129. Push the meat out. This is the biggest piece of meat you've had so far.

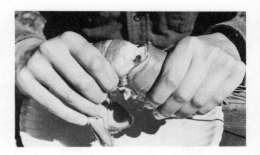

130. Grasping firmly the tail in one hand and the body in the other, break the tail and body apart. Set the tail aside for last.

131. Pull the back off the body. (If you like the tamale, this is where it's found.)

132. Split the body down the center and pick out the pockets of meat in the body.

133. Now attack the tail. Pull the end of the tail off.

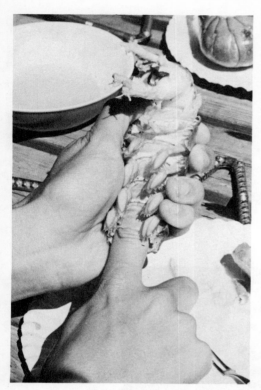

134. Use your forefinger to shove the meat forward and out.

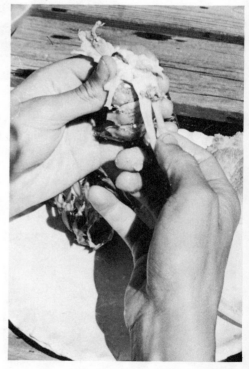

135. To remove the vein from the back of the tail, grasp the two protruding prongs of flesh and pull toward you, all the way to the end of the tail.

136.

Rum Running

"Rum row" . . . *"dark of the moon"* . . . *"drop"* . . . *"picket boats"* . . . *"code book"* . . words that summon up an era in Maine when liquid cargos of liquor lay wallowing on the high seas three miles offshore, highly visible on a clear day. Cargos that were slipped stealthily ashore by night into the isolated inlets of Maine's 2,000-mile coastline.

We have wanted to tell the story of those cargos, of rum running, of prohibition days, ever since we started *Salt* four years ago. Most of us had heard just enough about those days from our grandparents or parents to whet our curiosity. Often what we heard was accompanied with a chuckle and a wink. Time and time again *Salt* kids suggested, "Why don't we do a story about rum running?"

But how? Who was going to talk? How could we expect anyone to trust us enough to speak for publication? How would they know that our aim was not to expose individual rum runners—far from it—but to try to make the spirit of an era come alive on paper so that we could understand it better?

Maybe it was inevitable that we should have to wait four years to get this story, that we should have to earn the trust of the people in the community before they would tell us the secrets of the rum running days, before we could share the comradely conspiracy that grew up along the coastline to outwit an unpopular law.

At any rate, last fall we had a break. During a public appearance of *Salt* in York, we told the audience about some stories that had stumped us thus far, among them rum running, soapmaking, widow's walks, and sea chanteys. Our remarks were published in a newspaper, and shortly afterward, we got a mysterious telephone call.

"If you want to hear about rum running, go see Henry Weaver in York," the voice said. "He can tell you all about it." We asked, "Who's

137. Rum running vessel pictured in a 1928 newspaper.

this?" The reply, "Never mind who this is. Get over to Henry Weaver, and he'll tell you about rum running."

We did go to see Henry, and there we found the rich vein of material we'd been after. Henry had been a fearless, tough, cagey, incorruptible federal agent during prohibition days. He had a scrapbook of clippings. He had some old photos. He had a code book he had taken from some rum runners. And he had a store of vivid tales that he told with verve and gusto.

After that first interview with Henry, the seven of us babbled with excitement returning home from York. "I can't believe it!" Keith Euler kept saying. "What a guy!" We recounted to each other the things Henry had told us with near incredility.

And it wasn't Henry's past prowess alone that impressed us. Now eighty-two years old, Henry had recently stopped working out with his punching bag, because "I broke it last week."

Henry gave us all the material he had, asking only one thing: that we not use the names of Maine townspeople who had been involved in rum running. "I wouldn't want to hurt anyone," Henry emphasized. "Those people have sons and grandchildren living there now, and I wouldn't want to embarrass their grandchildren."

We were quick to agree to Henry's condition. We have kept the names of local Maine people out of all the rum running articles (though Henry didn't care a whit if we used the names of out-of-state mobsters who operated in Maine, and we have used those names.)

Once the story began to break with Henry, we discovered other sources. A fellow with the nickname "Pirate," who was dredging the Kennebunk River, was telling stories about rum running around the wharf. Paul Jackson and Clint Robinson went down to see "Pirate" and convinced him to tape some interviews with them.

Then it began to seem that all our contacts had some kind of experience to add to the story. Herbie Baum's grandfather spent a year in the Coast Guard chasing rum runners in Massachusetts. "We never caught any," he said. "They was like a bunch of spiders in a nest. They all ran away when they saw us coming."

Reid Chapman told some tales about how the liquor was circulated to customers on dry land after it was taken off the boats. And a school teacher remembered going lobstering as a little girl—"and *never, never* catching any lobster." The boat was planting orders for liquor in the lobster traps.

In the months of working on the rum running story, we have come to admire some people on both sides of the law during those days, both those who were breaking the law and those who were upholding it. Both the daring, cocky rum runners and the tough, uncompromising lawmen like Henry who couldn't be bought.

We find that we have learned something about the relationship of laws to people in these months. Laws can't stand alone, elevated, separate from the people, not in our part of the world. We have seen that laws are kept alive only by the support of the people. Beyond that, we've heard one whale of a batch of good stories that are worth sharing.

P.W. with Gerald Dickson, Keith Euler,
Paul Jackson, Clint Robinson, Kelly Emery,
Kathi Preble, David Bragdon, Howard Doane,
David Durrell, Herb Baum, Ruth Kadra and Ellen
Daggett.

DARK OF THE MOON

"Rum running always took place on the dark of the moon, that is, when there is no moon at all. I don't think there ever was a case where we ever made a seizure unless on the dark of the moon," former federal agent Henry Weaver said. "It was always in the dark.

"It had to be a local pilot, a local fisherman who knew the waters. Of course, those fellows knew the navigation. They could go along the shore and tell by the surf crashing in. That's the way these pilots would operate. They never came in with any lights.

"That big ship we got in Seal Harbor, it was just as close as you," said Henry, glancing at the few feet between his chair and ours. "It was just like a ghost in the water. Foggy and snowing that night. These are some of the things I remember."

Henry Weaver was telling us all about rum running during prohibition days, when he was chief agent for alcohol control in charge of the state of Maine. Henry wasn't an outsider sent up to Maine. This is his home, and we were sitting around the fire in his house on a cove in York, eating his wife's cookies and listening hour after hour. (Later one of us said, "TV sure can't match Henry for excitement!")

Henry described "rum row" to us. "There would be fleets of boats outside the three-mile limit. They'd anchor there for weeks until they disposed of their cargo [liquor].

"Outside the three-mile limit [in international waters] they used the deep boats. They'd be mostly schooners, because they rolled pretty good. They could load them very heavily.

"Speedboats used to go out from the shore and contact the boats, and they'd load the boats." Sometimes this was done "by prearranged plan, by talking when they were ashore. But the real organized groups operated by radio. And they would load at the three-mile limit and start in.

"Usually rum row was off from Massachusetts, just three miles out," Henry told us. "But if they had a big shipment for Maine, if they were landing a lot up here, the convoy would move up here, outside the three miles.

"These big fellows, you understand, these ships were owned by syndicates, principally by big racketeers. It was all attached to big money. Money was paid outside the United States. A lot of this stuff that was

138. The rum running French vessel *Cherie,* seized in 1925 off Swan's Island, loses her cargo of liquor. Federal agent Henry Weaver (with back to camera) supervises.

brought in was paid for outside of the United States.

"On rum row, it was all good liquor. They had a big business in St. Pierre, you know, in the French islands down there. That's where the rum fleet, ninety per cent of the rum fleet loaded there, so it was a short run up here, ya know."

"Drops"

We asked Henry what would be a good place for a landing to drop liquor. "Well, first it would be away from houses, on a beach with no rocks. Big enough so a boat could come in and unload. But better than that would be a dock, a small dock they could tie up against.

"So there would be a quick landing, away from things, like I was telling you. They'd have three or four places designated where they would land this liquor. And those were called drops. They'd have a code name for the drops.

"And they'd go to the designated beach by code. On the beach they would have a crowd of local people come and unload the boats." Henry made it clear that he didn't blame local Maine people for unloading. "There are a lot of fine men that are fishermen. Back in those days some of them would work for a few extra dollars.

"They used to have a person in charge on the beach. Local fishermen would row out and pilot the boats in to the beach. It had to be someone local who knew the waters."

When Henry mentioned local Maine fishermen, he began to worry. "It's such a long story," he said. "What I'll have to talk about, I mean people in your very town that have been law enforcement officers have been arrested for participating in this thing.

"That was the reason why this law was not successful, because the people weren't behind it," Henry said emphatically.

Henry handed us a fat scrapbook crammed with yellowed newspaper clippings from prohibition days. Black, bold headlines screeched the news of cargos seized and trucks confiscated, nighttime raids, and highway chases. Often the name of "Weaver" flared in those headlines.

"I was going through some of those clippings," Henry said, "and there was somebody from Kennebunk there, a police officer that was involved in a rum transaction. If you come across any names in there, please don't use them because it would be a cruel thing to do.

"All along, you'll find there were many law enforcement officers arrested for violating the law—I mean protecting the rum runners. There was a case right here going into this harbor one night. The channel runs along that stretch of land there, and they came in above the bridge. We had advance information on 'em.

"We jumped them [the rum runners] down to the bridge there. And the buyers, they were in this yard, of *my* house! The two of 'em protecting the money were Gloucester policemen!"

Jumping Runners

When rum runners were caught, they were usually caught on land as they made their drops, seldom on the sea. There were two reasons why it was hard to capture rum runners at sea, we gathered from listening to Henry.

The main cargo ship could not be touched as long as it stayed outside the three-mile limit, in "safe" international waters. And the speed boats that brought the liquor ashore were lighter and faster than anything the Coast Guard had at the time.

Picket boats were used by the Coast Guard to keep tabs on the

139. Henry Weaver beside a high-powered car he drove to capture rum runners during prohibition. Inside is his hefty partner, Arthur England.

140.   Henry Weaver. (*Photo by David Bragdon*)

rum running operation, Henry explained. "The picket boats couldn't touch the rummy. He was in legal waters."

They could, however, monitor, survey, and picket the cargo ships, trying to be in a position to seize the smaller boats completing their connections. "They didn't have the luck they should have, because they didn't have the boats. About the early '30s they started getting little boats, and then they could run these people down."

So the best way to catch rum runners in the early years of prohibition was to nab them physically at the drops, Henry told us. "That's the only way you could do it. One night—to show you how crooked they were in Massachusetts—I got a call from the director one night, and he said, 'Henry, can you get a couple of men?'

"I said, 'I can get a couple of local fellows,' and I got Captain Hancock here, he used to be on the state police, and another deputy sheriff. The director said, 'I'll deputize them soon's they get in Massachusetts. So he met me there and outlined the situation.

"It seems down to Salisbury Beach it always had been a haven for those bootleggers and he said, 'I don't know, but I think the chief of police is in on it.'

"And he says the chief usually parks down on the road leading into Hampton Beach. He said, 'I think you got to leave your car and that's about three miles off.' And I said, 'That's all right.' So we parked the car in the woods and got across the causeway there into this section of cottages. It was the fall of the year, and it was closed.

"We knew just where we were going. We had prior information that there would be a drop there that night. Just before midnight, a police car drove up and it was the chief of police."

Henry said they heard the chief give the all-clear signal to the rum runners in one of the cottages. "'I just come from the causeway,' the chief said to them. 'I've never seen it so clear. You wait till you hear from me before you start out.'

"So he left, and about twenty minutes later the deputy chief come in and he says [to the rum runners in the cottage] that it's all right to start some of the trucks off.

"Then the truck came in, so we jumped the truck. There was two guys. They were tough. They was from that Detroit crowd. They were tough ones, but boy we sharpened them up. We took a gun from each of 'em. And I just called one of my other men to come around to go in with us because there was quite a few people in there in the cottage.

"I left one person in charge. A good big rugged fellow, my partner England, and it took a good man to get rid of him.

"The second I turned my back, there was a shot. And down went my partner England. And these two guys started right down behind the building, running, and there was my partner on the ground, just apparently in intense pain.

"Well, course I had nothin' else I could do. I took a bead on them and hit one of the guys in the knee, and the other guy fell on top of him. By that time my crowd come along and was able to arrest those two.

"And I sent the crowd in the house and I bent over England with my light. You might wonder why I'm laughing now," Henry said, as he began to chuckle. "You know I was tellin' you what a rugged guy he was.

"It seems that we had a leaky radiator, and we had to take some alcohol to pour in it, and England had this quart bottle of alcohol in his inside pocket, with his overcoat over it. And that shot hit that bottle of liquor and it shattered the bottle, and a piece cut his groin and the alcohol ran down between his legs.

"I took his trousers down and I started to laugh. And he said, 'You son of a gun' and up he jumped." Henry was laughing hard now. "I mean he wasn't hurt at all."

England was a huge, hulking man, but Weaver was small, wiry, tough, and fast. "Whenever we hit a place, I always seemed to be the guy that was first. And it was the big ex-prize fighter I was always up against.

"And I was the guy they took a punch at, because I looked like a minister," Henry laughed. "Then I got wise to it, and I made them put some of the big guys out front. But I was always the guy out front there for a couple of years.

"But I never got in any difficulty. Of course I knew what it was all about." Henry boxed and he taught Judo. "You have to know how to take care of yourself when you're up against the crowd we were up against."

Mobsters and Bathtub Gin

"The Maine coast was a tough one, with over two thousand miles of indentation," Henry told us. Having an unpopular law to enforce made it even tougher. "People who were robbing the bank would have been apprehended," Henry explained, but the public generally didn't want to expose smugglers and bootleggers.

"You could get liquor, if you knew how, in almost any city, small or large, in the state of Maine. I hate to say it but you could. I remember some prominent people in Portland would go down and buy it from the traffic officer on duty. I know because I arrested him."

But Maine wasn't the territory of mobsters, as were many parts of the United States. "In New York City, the syndicates operated. Certain streets belonged to a certain group and anybody who went on that street [to sell liquor] would get knocked off. I mean they'd murder them.

"They were set up with their radio men, with their truck drivers, with their speedboat men, and they had a real organization.

"To a small extent, some of this went on in Boston also," Henry said. "But usually there wasn't any violence. Some of them was hijacking. Occasionally some of these thugs would find out about a drop being made, and they'd get half a dozen thugs and go down and knock the whole thing off and hijack it.

"But Maine wasn't like that. No, Maine was with the locals."

Among the newspaper clippings that Henry gave us, we found a funny story that backed up what he had said about Maine not coming under the rule of syndicates. The yellowed clipping described how some local rum runners in Maine had bested out-of-state mobsters by beating them out of their merchandise and their money.

NEW JERSEY BIG SHOTS
FAIL TO COLLECT PAY FOR
ALKY HI-JACKED HERE

PROTECTED AT GUN POINT, BACK OUT OF
POOLROOM AFTER FUTILE DEMANDS AS
LOCALS EXIT BY WINDOWS

The New Jersey booze runners whose liquor was hi-jacked from a Capisic Street barn two weeks ago have attempted to collect from the local gang responsible for the theft within the last two days, this reporter learned from authentic sources Thursday night, with conspicuous lack of success. Heated words flew back and forth in a poolroom in the lower part of the city, where the encounter took place, but negotiations ended with the New Jersey crowd backing warily out, empty handed but protected at gunpoint, while the locals left precipitately through the windows, it is understood.

Rumors have flown about that the "big shots" in New Jersey weren't going to let the little fellows in Portland get away with the liquor and were going to collect for it, or else——. Two days ago the attempt to force a payoff came when two of the out-of-state crowd entered a poolroom frequented by local bootleggers.

Two of the local characters believed to have engineered the liquor theft were in the poolroom and between them and the New Jersey pair a sharp argument took place. Finally, the foreigners gave a sign, whereupon a man who had been waiting in an automobile outside, entered the room, both hands thrust deep in his coat pockets in an ominous sort of way.

The man with the bulging pockets broke up the party. The locals decided it was about to become too much of a good thing and tumbled pell mell through windows and out of the room and that, in turn, disquieted the New Jersey visitors. Fearful of possible results of the commotion, they backed from the room, the reserve member covering the retreat with his hands still thrust menacingly in his pockets, jumped into their car and rode away.

They were believed to have been in Portland as late as Thursday night but were still without their pay for the stolen liquor, as far as could be learned.

Henry told us that the liquor brought in by the sea was stowed in gunny sacks. "The cases were stowed in gunny sack bags." But the "bathtub gin" manufactured in illegal stills was stored in three-gallon sealed cans.

"You always got good liquor from the boats outside. But around New York, the mobs started to distill their own liquor. Chemists would imitate the best Bourbons, ryes, whiskeys, and rums.

Some Of The Liquor Seized In Falmouth

141. Gunny sacks of liquor seized in Falmouth.

142.   Stills making bootleg liquor.

"You've heard the term 'bathtub gin.' A good many times it would turn poison and kill people.

"There were some stills that turned out a good brand." The stills of this type had a big column and baggle plates that took out impurities. "A big still with a big column was a still that brewed darn good liquor.

"The alcohol would then go to a chemist who would imitate the various brands." Toward the end of prohibition, according to Henry, "They say you couldn't tell it from the real thing. It was putting the real people out of business."

We were curious about what was done with all the thousands of cases of liquor that were seized, along with the fleets of cars and trucks.

"We always had to take a sample of the liquor, no matter how much you took. Generally, it was more alcohol than bottles. Course, people became hard drinkers. It was 190 proof.

"One of the fellows would deliver it in person to our chemist. He was in Boston. He would analyze the liquor and return it to me. I used to have charge of the liquor room down there."

"If it was good liquor, we'd give it to the hospitals. I don't know how many hospitals we kept in alcohol during prohibition. If it was bad, the court would order it destroyed.

"The court decreed it to be spilt, and they had a big sewer opened up in the federal building and they'd spill it. The first time we did it, there was a half dozen onlookers, and they got intoxicated.

"You know, it was a closed room about half this size, and they got lit! Just from the fumes of the liquor. We learned a lesson there. We had to put in a ventilating system after that.

"The cars, we'd seize—probably thousands of cars that I've seen—and they would be forfeited to the government. And they'd sell them by auction, and those that were good, why we would use."

"Buying Weaver"

People were always trying to bribe Henry while he was chief agent in Maine. When we asked him if he gained a reputation as "a pretty tough cookie" in those days, he laughed and replied, "Well, I did.

"They knew there was only fifteen men [for the state], so it got so they had you under surveillance. Many a time I come out of my house down there, I have seen a car and without asking any questions, I reach in and take this guy by the nab of the neck and give it to him. And I didn't make any mistake, because it was one of these people.

"To show you how smooth they were, one of my best friends ran a big garage in Boston. And no matter how honest you were then, it was business for you.

"He took care of a fleet of rum runner cars and trucks. One of the big owners came to him, he knew he had been down Maine to college and all, and said, 'Do you know Weaver?' And Max said, 'Well, now I was his best man at his wedding.'

" 'Well,' he said, 'see if you can put the clicks on him, will you?' And Max said, 'I don't think so.' And he said, 'Will you do it?' Max said, 'Yeah.'

"So when Max came down, he said, 'Henry, I'm going to ask you something.' And he told me the fellow's name, and we all know him as a big shot. Max said, 'He wants to know if you would take a thousand dollars a week to let them know where you are on the dark of the moon.'

"And I said, 'Max, if it was anybody else, I would have knocked you down!' And then I said, 'I appreciate the position you are in.'" Henry added, "I never took a nickel from anyone, and none of my men did either.

"I had a fellow one time—he was a big-shot operator—and we hit lots of his cars. He came to a state trooper up here, a fellow by the name of Hanscom who was a good friend of mine and an honest person. 'What can you do with Weaver?' he asked.

"Hanscom was smart and knowing the games we used to play, he said, 'Will ya give me a connection with Boyer?' Boyer was the big fellow down there. Well they set up the meeting, up there in the woods, and Boyer told me he wanted to run a boat in. And he also said he had

PORTLAND EVENING NEWS

State Edition Portland, the Sunrise Gateway of America **State Edition**

VOL. 8. NO. 39   2   DIAL 3-1721   PORTLAND, MAINE, FRIDAY, NOVEMBER 16, 1934   THREE CENTS

Weaver Threatened In Big Rum Expose

Charges Officers Got $100 Nightly

MORE SENSATIONS ASSURED BY U. S. OFFICIALS HERE

Deputy Sheriff State Patrolman Packard Already Held in $5,000 Each on Convoy, Conspiracy Charges; Ace Investigator Weaver, Reporting Threats to Clifford, Given Assurance of Full Protection of U. S. Government; Political Influence Boasted by Man Warning Enforcement Officer

The initial thrust to shatter a huge, powerful and wealthy rum-running ring whose ramifications extend to Massachusetts and New York and which flourished while some members of the police and sheriff's departments either did not care or ignored its activities, Friday had been driven by the unrelenting hand of the U. S. government.

Two law enforcement officers, whose sworn duty it was to enforce the statutes, were under arrest in $5,000 bail on charges of convoying rum trucks and conspiracy. Other arrests of equal sensational character were predicted by U. S. Attorney John D. Clifford and Henry P. Weaver, ace investigator for the Alcohol Tax Unit of the Internal Revenue Department.

Meanwhile Weaver revealed to the Evening News that he was threatened with "everything from violence to loss of my job," if he went through with his investigation.

The arrest of Harry W. Irish, deputy sheriff, was published exclusively in The Evening News, Thursday afternoon. The News also declared that a State patrolman would be arrested later in the day. Gerald H. Packard, the trooper, was arrested at the Dunstan barracks of the State police by Weaver. He immediately gave his resignation to Adjutant General James W. Hanson and Capt. Joseph Young of the State police. Irish was picked up by Weaver in the rum room of the sheriff's department at the County Building.

Weaver declined to reveal the identity of the man who threatened him. He said, however, that the man boasted of "political influence" strong enough to have Weaver fired from his ...

said, his subordinates watched an tened from the hidden room.

Wanted To "Fix" Weaver

As the conferences proceeded, intimated that he would like to Inspector Weaver, the deputy al and asked him to serve ... ... ary ...

Seven Men Arrested For Alleged Attempts To Bribe Dry Agents

Four Walk Into Trap, Expecting To Pay, Three Have Delivered Sums, Two Officials Charge

Ir ... vere ... time, s ... tempte ... Federa ... investi ... that oth ...

She ... , ... a statement concerning the cleanup, ... he had known of the "gang" for a long time and that he had run for his office for the chief purpose of ridding the county of it.

Tuesday night, the enforcement officers allege, four men walked into the trap expecting to pay $1200 for light sentences in pending cases and future protection and found themselves promptly arrested instead. The other three had paid, it is alleged, while witnesses watched the t ... saction through a peep hole into the County rum room, and ... ere arrested on warrants sworn out by Sheriff Gilbert A. Powe ...

Those under arrest are Victor Pelosi, India Street grocer and alleged "Bag Man" for the others, Domenic Marino, Congress Street restaurant keeper, his brother, Joseph, Preble Street storekeeper, Charles J. McSwigin of 112 Center Street, Fortunat Nava of 36 Federal

PORTLAND EVENING EXPRESS

LAST EDITION

TELEPHONE FOREST 7790   PRICE THREE CENTS

The Weather   PORTLAND, MAINE, MONDAY, JUNE 29, 1931

VOL. 49—NO. 218

Weaver Reveals Rum Bribery

Tells Of Attempts To Enlist Officials In Smuggling Plot

Involves Fall River Liquor Runner In Conspiracy To Land 3,000 Cases Monthly On York Shore, Paying $2 A Case For Protection, Following Seizure Of Alcohol At Auburn

DRY AGENT Henry P. Weaver of York talked freely today in narrating how capture of two men, 1,158 gallons of alcohol, a truck and a couple of Auburn Saturday night followed negotiations to pay him and other officers for protection. Money was paid in two instances, Agent Weaver said. He notified District Attorney Frederick R. Dyer and gave the money into custody of John F. Knowlton, clerk of courts ...

143.

several hundred gallons coming from a still in Rhode Island. That was coming over the road.

"And he pulled out a hundred dollars and said to me, 'Your clothes don't look so good. Take this and buy yourself a suit of clothes.' And that was back in the '20s and I'm tellin' ya, a hundred dollars was a lot of money. And twenty dollars would have bought a good suit.

"Well, course he didn't know it, we had dug a hole right behind this bush, and England was in that hole. [Arthur England was Henry's partner.] England had been a telephone lineman, big, rugged, and strong. And he was my bull. All the way through.

"After this thing was over [arranging the 'deal' with Boyer], I don't know what the speed limit was, but I think I was in Portland probably in thirty minutes, right in the U. S. District office with a notation on that money. We put it right in the safe. Of course those were the things you had to do that way, in an undercover job.

"Well, Boyer came through with five cars two days afterwards. When the stuff reached its destination, we knocked the cars and drivers off and picked up Boyer. Then Boyer got a lawyer, and that lawyer was a good friend of mine in Portland. Boyer said to the lawyer, 'Look, I'm not afraid of this. I got this guy Weaver all bought up.'

"He says, 'Weaver? You got to show me before I'll believe it.' So the attorney talked to the District Attorney, who laughed and said, 'Yeah, I'll show you how he has Weaver bought up.' He opened the safe and there was the notation with all the money.

"There was a good many incidents like that, you know," Henry told us. "It got like they wouldn't get within a mile of me. After that they started to put the brake on coming down here. We started to get more men [federal agents]. They still came, and there's a lot of them we didn't get, but we got some of them."

Seizing the Narmarda

One thing that certainly made it easier for Henry to catch rum runners was to know their code. Henry showed us a code book he had captured that made it possible to seize a great prize, the rum running British ship, the *Narmarda*.

The rum runners sent messages in code by wire. When Henry got the code book, it was easy to listen in on their calls.

The code had a mixed alphabet. To signify the letter Y, the code would use T and vice versa. House, for example, would be coded DQXFZ or street, FYNZZY.

The alphabet, however, was not used as much as one might think.

Pages from a Rum Runner's Code Book

BRANDS

Rye	FOB
Atherton	FOC
Golden Wedding	FOD
Indian Hill	FOE
Old Crow	FOF
Old Kentucky	FOG
Biltmore	FOH
Wm. Penn	FOI
Pikesville	FEJ
Charter Oak	FEK
Scotch	FEL
Rum in cases	FEM
Rum in kegs	FEN
Gin	FEO
Alcohol	FEP
Champagne	FEQ
Brandy	FER
Cordials	FES
Malt	FET
House of Lords	FEU
Teachers	FEV
Lawsons	FEW
Ne Plus Ultra	FEX
Coon Hollow	FEY
Old Colonel	FEZ
Early Times	FEA
Old Log Cabin	FEB

ALPHABET.

Y	E	L	X	O	N	G	M	I	S	H	A	W
T	Z	V	U	Q	R	P	J	K	F	D	C	B

In using the above alphabet use the corresponding letters above or below the letters required.

Example: House would be coded: D Q X F Z

GEOGRAPHICAL

Boon Island	LGL
Boston Ls.	LGM
Briar Island	LGN
Cape Elizabeth	LGO
Cape Ann	LGP
Cape St. Mary	LGQ
Chatham	LGR
Gayhead	LGS
Graves	LGT
Half Way Rock	LGU
Highland Light	LGV
Isle of Shoals	LGW
Lurcher Shoal Is.	LGX
Marblehead	LGY
Metinicus Rock	LGZ
Minots Ledge	LHA
Monhegan Island	LHB
Montauk Point	LHC
Mt. Desert Island	LHD
Nantucket Shoals Ls.	LHE
Nauset	LHF
No Mans Land	LHG
Petit Manan	LHH
Pollock Rip Ls.	LHI
Portland Ls.	LHJ
Race Point	LHK
Sankaty Head	LHL
Seguin	LHM
Wood Island	LHN
Ringtown Island	LHO
Saybrook Gas Buoy	LHP
Red flasher off Castle	LHQ
Duck Island	LHR
Little Gull	LHS
Race Rock	LHT
Block Island	LHU

CITIES

Bangor	AFC
Barrington	AFD
Boston	AFE
Calais	AFF
Canso	AFG
Digby	AFH
Gloucester	AFI
Halifax	AFJ
LaHave	AFK
Liverpool	AFL
Lockport	AFM
Lubec	AFN
Lunenburg	AFO
Lynn	AFP
Meteghan	AFQ
Plymouth	AFR
Portland	AFS-
Portsmouth	AFT
Provincetown	AFU
Sacco	AFV
Salem	AFW
St. John, N.B.	AFX
St. John's, Nfld.	AFY
St. Pierre	AFZ
St. Stephen	AGA
Shelburne	AGB
Sydney	AGC
Weymouth, N.S.	AGD
Yarmouth, N.S.	AGE
Cape Sable	AGF
	AGG
	AGH
	AGI
	AGJ
	AGK

144 and 145.   Pages from a rum runner's code book

Rum Runner's Code Book

CUTTERS

75 footer ------LTA
36 footer ------LTB
125 " --------LTC
White ---------LTD
Four Stacker ---LTE

We are picketed by

75 footer ------LTF
125 " --------LTG
White ---------LTH
Four Stacker ---LTI

We have eluded the

75 footer ------LTJ
125 " --------LTK
White ---------LTL
Four Stacker ---LTM

Cutter following us to sea

75 footer ------LTN
125 " --------LTO
White ---------LTP
Four Stacker ---LTU

WEATHER

How is the wx -------LHV
The wx is clear -----LHW
Visibility good -----LHX
"   fair -----LHY
"   poor -----LHZ
The sea is smooth ---LIA
Rough but possible --LIB
Too rough to work ---LIC
Breeze --------------LID
Wind ----------------LIE
Gale ----------------LIF
Foggy but clearing --LIG
The tide is bad -----LIH
The moon is bad -----LII
Good wx to work -----LIJ
Bad wx to work ------LIK

VALUABLE PHRAS

Are you alright ------   Asparagus
Are you picketed -----   Almonds
Are any in sight -----   Apples
Come again tomorrow --   Apricots
Come soon as possible   Berries
Come to position -----   Blueberry
How many can u take --   Blackberry
How many did they take   Beef
How many left --------   Butter
Hw soon wl u be ready-   Broccoli
Hurry and get there---   Beans
I wl QSY to -- meters   Bantam
L. B. coming out -----   Beet
L. B. didnt leave bec   Currant
L. B. is -----------   Coffee
L. B. wl meet you ---   Cod
Let me know ---------   Catsup
QRX at --------------   Citron
QRX every hour ------   Crab
Report every half hou   Celery
Report every hour ---   Corn
What is cause of dela   Carrots
What is your course--   Cherry
What is your position   Cocoa
What time to be there   Cake
What time can u be th   Cereals
Wl let u know -------   Celerys
You QSY to -- meters   Cocktail
Has L. B. arrived ---   Diced
L. B. has arrived ---   Dills
Msg. decoded and unde   Eggs
Msg. decoded and not   Garden
How many did you take   Grape
Diff. L. B. wl meet u   Green

MVJ

Other Valuable Phrases.

Our fueloil is getting low.   Guava
Our lub. " "   "   "   Goose
We have fuel oil for only
        day more -----   Golden
Send fuel oil immediately   Herring
Our food is low ----------   Haddock
Send out meat, sugar, milk
            bread--   Juice
Send out water immediately   Jelly
Two L.B. will meet you ---   Lodan
Stay there till tomorrow--   Lima
Come in --milles--towards-   Lobster
L.B. wl meet you-after-dar   Lumber
Go to Lurcher and await or   Lilly
Go to --and await orders--   Pork
Flash light three times---   Pickerel
My receiver is working bad   Peas
My Xmitter " "   "   "   Peanut
We are having engine troul   Pimento
L.B.wl lv fr pos. immedia   Prunes
L.B. loaded and left, wl   Parsnip
On our way in, everything   Radish
L.B. alongside and loading
We can see L.B. coming --   Mackerel
L.B. will be on position   Oranges
We pos.nw but no L.B. yet   Olives
Watch for cutters and C.G   Pickles
STay outside the limit --   Plums
Conditions are hot here--   Peaches
May not want you in tonit   Pineapple
Come in slowly ----------   Potato
We are all ready here for   Preserve
Which drop --------------   Pike
Come to ----------------   Pumpkin
This last two way schedul   Pears

Many of the words that had to be communicated were assigned three letters that stood for the word. The code book words were grouped under brands of liquor, geographical locations, cities, compass points, and valuable phrases. For example, the code letters for Portland were AFS.

Henry's account of how the code book was seized was a good story in itself. "It was the first instance in which a direction finder was used" to track down a radio sending message, Henry told us. "That was back in the mid '20s."

Henry was called by the supervisor of the New England states to come down to Providence. There he met Johnny Hines, a wire expert. "I'll never forget him."

The rum runners' radio location seemed to be coming from the north, and the two agents began tracking it down. They got to Boston, then to Bangor, then "to a little place called Brookline, Maine.

"The thing developed much quicker than we expected. All of a sudden we were going through this little village and it would knock your ear off, it came in so strong.

"The idea is to try to get the operator. So we passed this house and there was a garage, with a window wide open upstairs. We knew it was there because it [the direction finder] would have knocked your head off.

"We rushed up there, and I went first. The fellow didn't hear us coming up the stairs and he was sending. So I got there, got a damned good hold of him and lifted him off his seat. And Johnny Hines took the key, and there was a message instructing us to come up to Seal Harbor by the next night.

"So Johnny, he took up the key and took the rest of the message. And boy, we were in!"

After Johnny answered the signal, he and Henry struggled with the two men in the upstairs apartment. They caught the two men and took them to jail in Ellsworth. Then they went to the Coast Guard and asked for a boat and men to help them.

They sailed into the November storm, after the *Narmarda*. "The fog was very thick, which made it almost impossible to see more than three feet ahead of you.

"All of a sudden, just like a ghost, this ship came right along side of us. Course we were waiting and we made the jump. And there she was laden right to the gunnels.

"I went with Hines right to the radio room. There was the radio operator trying to raise the shore operator. Of course the minute he saw us—well, he was a good sport about it.

"He said, 'Look, I want to know who the operator was.' He said,

'Yesterday when I talked to shore, there was a split-second interruption, and that seemed to tell me something. But when it was picked up . . . whoever picked it up did a beautiful job.'

"You see," Henry explained. "Those operators that talked to each other, they had a knack. They knew by the touch if there's anyone else that picks the key up."

In the radio room was the code book that matched the one Henry had taken in Brookline. "And there was all kinds of papers. In other words, we tied it all up and got the person behind it—the real leader of it—and he went down to the penitentiary.

"The *Narmarda* was seized. I think we had seven or eight thousand cases of liquor. We called that one of our prize cases."

The Top Guys

Henry told us that during prohibition he wasn't after the "little fellow" that had a bottle or two of bootleg liquor in his car, or the fisherman "who was getting fifty or a hundred dollars to help unload" the liquor.

"In the small places, you'd get calls from people that were on the side with the dries. I don't want to say too much on the dries, but I've got to use the term—they were so narrow minded. Somebody might have a home brew still, makin' a batch of beer. We didn't want that.

"I was a great one to try to get the person responsible, the fellows with the big money that were running the thing." One way he did that was to "put pressure on the people at the bottom.

"Like the boat fellows who used to repair the boats. There was always bills—some bill for a muffler or something to do with repair of a boat. The fellow who took care of the boat was only a worker. And then we put pressure on him and he'd lead us to who was giving his orders, see."

Henry told us about tapping telephone wires in those days to get information on rum runners. "It was years ago, and of course it would be illegal today. We used to use the information only, and nobody ever knew in Maine, probably until this article is published, that there ever was a wire tap used.

"They wore head phones, you know, those that are called 'sitting on the wire.' They usually knew shorthand, and they would take it over the earphones and then put it down in shorthand.

"I went over to the place [where they had set up a wire tap] which isn't customary for anyone who is known by them to do. Well, I took a chance and went in there anyway. I wanted to see how the thing was going, and he [the agent] gave me an extra ear set.

"The first voice to come over that phone was the chief liquor deputy for that particular county, Cumberland County. And the guy from Boston was calling.

" 'You know where that son of a bitch Weaver and his crew will be tonight?' he said. That was the first talking voice I heard, and I recognized the fellow's voice. He was a good friend of mine, the chief deputy!"

Henry told us about an undercover case he was involved in. "This case turned out to be a funny one. When I went on the force, there was a group operating out of New York. They wanted to develop a local customer in Portland. We knew something was taking place—the whole department did—and we finally got a break.

"We got a hold of a fellow who didn't want to go to jail, and he said,

Federal Agents Seize Malt And Hops

Federal agents removing between $1500 and $2000 worth of malt and hops from the Donahue Brothers' shop at 51 Free Street Monday afternoon. Thomas M. and John E. Donahue, the owners, were charged with violating Section 18, Title 2, of the National Prohibitory Law, which makes it unlawful to sell or possess for sale any preparation, utensil or contrivance intended to be used in making alcoholic liquor unlawfully.

146.

'I think I can tell you something.' He told us about this crowd and that they had three or four hundred cases of liquor they wanted to get rid of.

"We needed an undercover person, so I said, 'I'll take a chance.' So he introduced us to this wise guy from New York that had charge of the liquor. We made a deal for a hundred cases for five thousand dollars. I got in touch with Boston, and they wouldn't touch it."

Henry went to the bank and borrowed five thousand dollars on his reputation. The drop was to be at a garage out in Woodford. "They were going to deliver the liquor and this fellow appeared with a body guard. I said, 'Look, give me one man,' so I got my pal England up there. I said, 'When the truck goes by, I'll pay you the money.'

"So when the truck made its swing up, I paid him the five thousand dollars. He wasn't home yet, so England and I stuck right with him. Then the truck pulled in.

"I jumped him and he went right to his pants pocket. I took the whole pants pocket right off him with the five thousand dollars in it! And then the truck drove in, and sure enough there was this guy.

"I got him and put the screws to him—I mean the heat to him. And he said, 'All right, it's down to Laughlin's Grain Drop.' Laughlin's was a grain drop on the commercial dock. He said, 'You go on to the second floor and there is a trap door.' He says, 'It's camouflaged.' So we got four or five hundred cases there in all.

"By putting the screws to people, we got three more problem policemen and some of the ground crew.

"There was a very swanky yacht that they had loaded to drop that stuff, and it was standing outside with more liquor on it. We got in touch with the Coast Guard and they grabbed it. There were several thousand more cases on that. So you see what my five thousand dollars did!"

However, in Henry's report he billed the government for the interest accumulated on the five thousand dollars, and they wouldn't pay it.

Henry went on to tell us about another case. "I remember a fellow from Lewiston. He was a notorious rum runner. But he ran it on the road. We had a tough job getting him one night.

"It would always be one particular car that we used to knock off rum runners. We had a twin six Packard. What a beautiful car that was! Then we had a Lincoln that would outrun anything on the road. We had three hundred pounds of cement in it, a hundred and fifty pounds on each side to weigh the rear down.

"This fellow came down one night and we tried to stop him at the corner. He slowed down. He had running boards on the car and I jumped on the side. He put it in high gear and hit me over the knuckles with a jack handle and broke four of my knuckles.

"I couldn't hold on and down I went. I had a .32 caliber automatic and I put that gun on the rear tire and pulled the trigger, but the cartridge was defective. So it was so much for him that night.

The next time he came we were waiting for him. We got our new Lincoln and down he came one night. We knew it was him from advance information, and we tackled him on the road to Brunswick.

"Boy, he had an auto that could go! It was nearly twenty-two miles from here in Kittery to Brunswick, and he couldn't get away from me.

"I got in front of him just before Brunswick and hit his left front tire. He went into the bushes. We got him before he got out of the car. He went to jail for six to eight months. They found out he was an alien, and he was deported to Canada.

"To tell what a desperate fellow he was, he was in Canada for a short while and he had a big storage of liquor in his barn. And somebody was stealing it.

"He got his shotgun out one night, parked his car, and planted himself in the bushes. Shortly after, these two fellows came down the driveway. He let them load the car, then went in and shot and killed both of them. He was hung in Canada shortly after."

"A Bad Penny Always Comes Home"

Henry was born in New Hampshire. He lived there until 1911, when he went into the service. He fought in World War I, and came to York in 1919, where he married Gladys Young.

We asked Henry what he did when he got out of the Navy. "I went to the Department of Justice, went to law school—took a correspondence course to get in—and then they took us out to enforce the liquor laws. That's how I happened to get started with it."

Henry was involved in many cases from large to small, and became the agent in charge in many cases. "I loved my work," Henry Weaver told us. Since it was dangerous work, how did his wife feel about it, we wondered. "She was accustomed to it. She always knew I'd come back," Henry explained.

"I was sunk on a ship [during World War I] and the report came back the ship was lost with all hands. When she got the report, she felt that I'd come back. Some of us were saved in a boat.

"It was the same thing when I got hit over there during World War II. She said, 'He'll be back.' And back I came. That's the way it's been all the way through.

"She knew that a bad penny always comes home!

"Prohibition went out in '34 and then they established an alcohol tax

147. Henry Weaver at his home in York.
(*Photo by Gerald Dickson*)

unit and, of course, they had a head of the organization. I wasn't the
first head. There was an attorney by the name of Seth May, and he was
a politician. I was the second head, but I wasn't political."

Soon after that, Henry left the Justice Department to head the state
police. "Then the war came on and I had been in the first war. There
was a team of some of my F.B.I. buddies going to Italy.

"They called me from Washington and said, 'What do you say we get
you part of this team?' so I got it. I got hit over there in 1943, and I've
been retired since then."

"Seldom a Person Who Doesn't Take a Drink"

We began to talk about the prominent people in every town who were
good customers for the liquor that came off rum row, about the small
stills that operated in barns and garages, about the number of lawmen
involved in rum running.

One of the lawmen who helped the rum runners was the sheriff of
Cumberland County. "He had the most beautiful voice. He sang in the
choir at church. He was an awful good guy," Henry chuckled.

As we listened to Henry, it seemed to us that large numbers of people
in Maine were breaking the law during prohibition, either by buying liquor, selling it, transporting it, making it, or protecting somebody who
was. It seemed to be a law that only the minority was willing to abide
by.

We wondered how people would have reacted if someone had

Highlights of Dry Era

(By the Associated Press)

Here are the "high spots" of prohibition history at a glance:

Aug. 1, 1917—Submission of the 18th amendment to the States, voted by the Senate, 65 to 20.

Dec. 17, 1917—Submission voted by the House, 282 to 138.

Jan. 8, 1918—Mississippi became the first State to ratify.

Nov. 21, 1918—Congress adopted war-time prohibition, to go into effect July 1, 1919, and continue through demobilization.

Jan. 16, 1919—Nebraska became 36th State to ratify, thus completing adoption of the 18th amendment, to go into effect Jan. 16, 1920.

Oct. 27, 1919 — Volstead Act vetoed by President Wilson, but passed by both Houses over his veto.

June 1 and 7, 1920—Supreme Court declared adoption of 18th amendment valid and upheld Volstead Act's limit of one-half of one per cent alcoholic content.

May 22, 1924—Ratification of a treaty with Great Britain proclaimed, permitting the boarding for examination of vessels not more than one hour's run from the coast, although territorial waters extend but three miles.

April 1, 1925—General Lincoln C. Andrews named assistant Secretary of the Treasury to reorganize prohibition enforcement.

March 3, 1927—Bureau of Prohibition established in the Treasury Department.

March 2, 1929—Jones law, providing five years' imprisonment and $10,000 fine for violation of the prohibition act, signed by President Coolidge.

July 1, 1930—Bureau of Prohibition transferred to the Department of Justice, and department of industrial alcohol organized in the Treasury Department.

Jan. 20, 1931—Report of the Wickersham commsision made public, showing two of the 11 commissioners for immediate repeal, seven for revision of the 18th Amendment, and two for retention without change.

March 14, 1932—House defeated, 227 to 187, Beck-Linthicum resolution to restore to the States the right to abolish or continue the 18th Amendment.

March 18, 1932—Senate defeated, 61 to 24, amendments to legalize 2.75 per cent beer.

Dec. 5, 1932—House, by 272 to 144 vote, failed to muster two-thirds majority to pass Garner repeal resolution.

Dec. 21, 1932—House adopted, 230 to 165, the Collier bill modifying the Volstead act to legalize beer of 3.2 per cent alcoholic content. (The first "wet" victory in Congress in 15 years.)

Feb. 16, 1933—Senate, by 63 to 23 vote, voted to submit repeal of the 18th Amendment to State conventions.

Feb. 20, 1933—House, by 289 to 121, concurred in Senate submission resolution.

148.

predicted that before long the government itself would be in the business of buying and selling liquor. We decided it would be more impossible to believe than television or flights to the moon. The State of Maine selling liquor?

We asked Henry how he felt in 1934 when the prohibition act was repealed. "I was all for it [for repealing the act]. It was a mockery. As

149. Henry and fellow agents hold bottles of French liquor seized from rum runners.

I've said before, it was an unpopular law. That was the reason why this law was not successful, because the people weren't behind it, and a greater part of the law-enforcement agencies were crooked—or wouldn't enforce it.

"I was glad to see legal liquor come back again," Henry said. "That's why I told you some of these stories. To try to give you an insight of what this thing is all about, so you would never vote for prohibition again.

"Well, there's seldom a person who doesn't take a drink once in a while. And I tell you, I had a feeling that if a man didn't take a drink, then watch out for him."

PIRATE

by Paul Jackson and Clint Robinson

Photography by Paul Jackson

After school one day, we decided to go down to Government Wharf to see if we could talk to Pirate. Pirate is the captain of the tugboat that is pulling the dredger on the Kennebunk River near where we live in Kennebunkport.

When we shouted across the river to ask Pirate if we could talk to him, he got in his punt and paddled halfway over to us. He sat there backpaddling. He was reluctant. "I don't want any publicity," he said.

"I was a notorious rum runner on the high seas," he yelled. "I don't want any newspaper publicity." We yelled back that we were students for a school magazine, not reporters. "We won't even use your real name, just your nickname," we promised. "We just want to hear some of your stories."

That seemed to do it. Pirate said he couldn't talk to us then because he was waiting for a radio telephone call. But he agreed to meet us the next day.

So the next day we went back down to the wharf. Pirate was waiting for us in his car (the license plate said "Pirate"), and he began to tell us about himself.

"I never done anything too bad, that is, illegal. As far as I was concerned, out on the high seas I was covered by international law, and there was nothing wrong. I got orders to pull off Maine and New York and all kinds of places.

"But I was outside the continental limits of the country, and what went on inside there was none of my business, you know. What I did was outside on the high seas. Of course, I did get a lot of notoriety. There's plenty of records of it, but nothing serious. I mean nothing that I did that's too bad.

"Everybody was doing it in those days. Even some high officials in every town were connected with it, you know, during prohibition.

"I remember years and years ago—way back in '30 or '31, I had to

150. "Pirate" talks to Clint Robinson of *Salt*.

make positions off the coast of Maine. But I never came into the Kennebunk River because it was a foreign vessel and it drew eighteen feet of water.

"I always stayed out on the high seas. What I did out there was no law. Nobody, not even the Coast Guard, could grab me. As long as I was outside of the continental limits, there was nothing they could do. But if they saw a boat leaving the side of her and she was an American vessel, then they could seize her anywhere. But foreign vessels were protected by international law.

"As long as the ships stayed out of the limits, there was nothing they could do. They can't arrest you. They can hinder you, stay near you, so no contact can be made."

The Cargos

"On some vessels we carried ten thousand cases, and of course it would take a month to discharge it. Towards the end of it [prohibition] there was other ways of getting rid of it, you know. We didn't sell over the rail, so it took a while to discharge it all."

We asked what other ways there were of getting rid of the liquor. "Did you load it onto smaller boats?" we suggested.

151. "Pirate's" car.

"No, we stopped that because of so many hijackers. There was a great deal involved. There was hijackers that would come in and try to get you, and it did happen in a couple of cases.

"So people started to run the outside vessel right in. In a certain type of weather, they'd run right in, unload it and go straight back out again, and nobody ever knew it. It took a long time before anybody caught up to it, and then it was just about over. This was just at the tail end of it, and prohibition was over in 1933 I think. [It was actually repealed in 1934.] I think it was '33 when President Roosevelt got in there, and he abolished it completely."

Then Pirate explained how he knew his customers when they tried to do business with him. "When I made positions off Maine here, the local people that were doing business—the ones that purchased whatever was aboard—they would come out in small boats.

"Who they were I didn't care, as long as they had the proper credentials. And it was developed that we would have a code. The people that would buy would have half a dollar bill, and we would have the other half, and whatever matched, we knew they were the right ones.

"So long as we got the other half of the bill and it matched our half, we knew it was the right people and to let them have it."

"Proceed to St. Pierre"

Placing orders for the liquor was often done by radio (though one of our contacts described orders placed in lobster traps, see next section of this chapter). "Different ones used different things, different ways of doing it. A lot of them were caught that way, using the radio, which is illegal. You can't use a transmitter like you can today without a license, you know. And of course they were operating illegal, so it didn't make much difference anyway whether they operated an illegal station or not.

"There was codes that were made up, and it took a long time to make them up and each trip you thought of different things, you would put them down.

"Today even, I'll say that the smartest man, decoder, the government has, or anybody, there is nobody that could decode those messages. See, they think they can and they will give you an argument. They came out with that argument because they don't know what it's all about. The transposition code of any kind, where you were spelling out something, eventually you would finally do it, see.

"I'll give you an illustration. There is no technician, not anybody smart enough to decode this. Say for instance I want to tell you your position for today is eighteen miles south of Kennebunkport. All I send is A, B and I'm off the air in one second and you acknowledge it.

"Well, you look up in this book A, B. There's only two of the books and you've got one and I've got one. The smartest man in the world if he picked up, now how could he signify your position for today is eighteen miles south of Kennebunkport? There isn't a bird or a government man that could decode that.

"Say for instance we were all done on the high seas and we came on and asked where they wanted us to go—Halifax or St. Pierre? And they would come back on and they might say Z, I, and you look in your book and Z, I would be 'Proceed to St. Pierre.' See, there's nobody that could decode that!

"If you use a transposition code, you're on the air much longer when you spell out every letter. Therefore, a guy getting a bearing on you, he could go to work and have more time. But with this other code, it was just a matter of seconds and you were off. Before he could start the rig up and get a line on you, you were gone and off the air.

"So you licked them both ways, see what I mean. There's all kinds of tricks that were done, that were applied [to fool] some of the top agencies in the country."

Hijackers, Murder, and Money

Hijacking got to be a problem, Pirate told us. He stopped unloading onto smaller boats "because of so many hijackers. There was hijackers that would come in and try and get you, and it did happen in a couple of cases.

"In those days, things were kind of slow and we were riding in a

152.   The tugboat *Jovi* beside a dredger *Major Mudd*.

depression, and on top of it some of the smartest guys couldn't find anything real hard to hit. So they figgered that they could hit a rummy. What they called a rummy would be a rum runner. Sometimes rum runners had a lot of cash on board because some used to sell over the rails, see.

Nobody ever tried to hijack Pirate, "but there was a ship somewhere near me, in the same area, that was hijacked. And there was another one that they found the dead bodies floating around, and they could never find out what took place.

"Everybody on the inside thought it was a hijack job, and the Coast Guard has records of it. I'm trying to think of a name—the *Thomas Dwight* was a schooner and she sunk in Vineyard Sound and they found bodies floating around. And there was signs of tragedies taking place aboard.

"Of course all the tough things—it was just like today. Thieves and holdup men go into and hold up a bank, or they will hold up a Stop and Shop store.

"Well, they'd come and get a boat, try and take it, and of course just like all holdup men they didn't hesitate to shoot anybody. All they were after at any cost was the cash or all the cargo that was on board.

"I had the crew killed on me once. I was inshore helping a friend out, in another boat. My ship came into Newport Harbor and it was thick-a-fog. It was so thick she came into the river and listened for the buoy. She drifted up beside a 75-footer and they cut loose with a machine gun and they killed everybody. That was one of the worst things that happened in the annals of prohibition. It was too bad it happened.

"The country got in an uproar. They testified for the crew that it was downright murder, and so many agencies got into the deal. Even the minister preached on it in the pulpit that Sunday morning.

"The Coast Guard did a wonderful job and they still do today, but during prohibition they had such a hard time of it.

"Most of the people that operated didn't resort to murder. It was a legitimate business. They handled it that way. It was just another way of making money.

"They got so much a case. I had a vessel—I finally got one of my own. I got so much for each case for transporting it from one port to another, from where they wanted me to pick it up to where they wanted me to deliver it. It was purely a matter of business. Other than that I didn't get involved.

153. Could this abandoned boat, the *Comet*, be the same rum running boat named in one of the old clippings loaned to *Salt* by former federal agent Henry Weaver?

"I got a lot of notoriety in the London papers when I smuggled out of Tangiers. It was a free port. I was just hired to run the ship. I went into a port, loaded it, then cleared for the high seas. Nobody knew where I was going. Whatever cargo was on, was taken off.

"I've been mixed up with the water and many other things, too." We asked Pirate if he had ever had any close calls with storms at sea.

"Yeah. Hell, I've ridden out all kinds of storms, even when I was fishing. When I came out of the Navy, I got mixed up with trawlers, fishing trawlers out of Gloucester, and right here in Rockland. General Sea Foods had big trawlers, and they worked out of here [Maine] to go clean to the Grand Banks. Heck, I lost four years of my life off the Grand Banks.

"The average fisherman today fishes around the shore. A lot of them never even seen the Grand Banks. When you fish down there, the nearest port was St. John's, and it was 150 miles to go to St. John's. So, if a gale came up, you would get caught. Well, we'd just stay there and ride it out, that's all, and then when the weather got good, we'd go back fishing again. That was part of the deal, see."

Nickname of "Pirate"

"I got the nickname 'Pirate' from another country. The towns we used to go to were tough everywhere—the small towns. Well, hell, most of the men got good pay. So we would hire a band and everybody would come. Well, we would have a dance and we would supply all the booze, so we would get friendly, and we got pretty well known everywhere. So different ones [of the crew] got nicknames."

Pirate seemed to be pretty proud of his nickname. Not only did he have it on his license plate, but he had a card made up for himself with the nickname on it.

"Now here's the card they made up for me. This was put on there for me because the old pirates used to go ashore and make the other guys dig the hole for the chest, and then they shot them, see, so they'd be the only one to know where the chest was buried, see.

"There was three notorious women pirates. Ann Blythe, she was known as the G string pirate. And there was Mary May and Anne Bonny, three of them."

Pirate explained that he wanted the woman pirate Ann Blythe on his card. "She didn't care for gold or silver, but jewels . . . emeralds, rubies, diamonds, oh boy, she ran. The crew could have all the silver and gold that was aboard, but anybody that was caught touching the jewels, they would have to walk the plank or they would have their

154. "Pirate" designed this calling card for himself.

heads cut off.

"She had knives in her boots and a sword in her hand with blood dripping off of it. She had her own ship and everything. She used to work out of Monaco. She came down to the Caribbean and she raised hell around there with a Spanish galley. They say she hung around with Blackbeard for a while, but they had a disagreement and they broke up and she went her own way.

"I was in the restaurant the other day, and a lady saw 'Pirate' on my license plate, and she asked me if I had anything to do with the Pittsburgh Pirates.

"I said, 'No, I'm just plain Pirate!'"

LOBSTERING FOR RUM

by Paul Jackson

A school teacher in southern Maine recalls her childhood experience with rum running during an interview with Salt.

"Well, it must have been when I was about ten. My next door neighbor had a big barn and he made lobster traps all winter, although his prime business was a large automobile agency. He had a summer home in Winter Harbor, Maine, which is on Frenchman Bay.

"And he had a large lobster boat. Theoretically, he was a lobsterman. He also had a crew that worked for him out of the harbor, where he had his home. His daughter was my friend.

"We were taken on the boat early in the morning, in the lobster boat, and I thought it was strange that in hauling and baiting the traps there were no lobsters. But I didn't know enough about it, so I didn't ask any questions. And we were a considerable distance from the mainland and a considerable distance from the area of Winter Harbor.

"That night we had a lobster feed even though we had not brought home any lobsters, and I really didn't dare ask any questions. I just felt I better not.

"And when I got home I told my parents what had happened, and they were upset, because they had some idea of what was going on, and yet they couldn't be sure of it.

"The actual fact of the matter was that he would go out in the morning and leave a note in the traps, and then the rum runners from Canada, the black-market people would come down and fill the orders for bootleg booze during the night.

"His crew, they were lobstermen, and they did lobster. But they also were the ones who moved the cargo [liquor], and this is why we saw no lobsters and couldn't understand what was going on.

"In the front of his barn, there was a big wire cage filled with homing pigeons. Sometimes there would be many, many pigeons in the cage. Many times there would be very few, but they always came home to roost. We would have to assume what they did, carrying messages to the Canadian side of the border, to send a shipment. There was no proof. They never caught him, and it was very strange.

"Just at the end, when you didn't need the black market, he stopped building lobster traps, and the next thing we knew all the pigeons were gone.

"He was a very, very wealthy man."

BOOTLEGGING

by Ellen Daggett, Ruth Kadra, and Herbert Baum III

"When I was drinking and they sold alcohol, this fella in Sanford, he's a pretty nice guy, he made a little store in South Sanford, and he said to me one day, he calls me Chappy, he says, 'Chappy, my bootlegger's

156. "Wanna hear a bootleggin' story?" asks Reid Chapman.

coming. Do you want a gallon?' The bootlegger had been coming there
for several years and it was good stuff. It came in gallon cans, and I
said yes."

Reid Chapman, a West Kennebunk farmer who is an old friend to
Salt, had heard we were doing a story on rum running during prohibition days. He offered to tell us how the forbidden liquor was bootlegged
around town.

"I went up town all day peddling my green groceries, that's what
they call it in Canada—green groceries. And so when I come back I see
that his face looked sober and he'd bought quite a little and his wife
was dead against liquor.

"So he told the bootlegger, just like he always did, to leave it in the
back shop, and he paid him the $330. So when he came to look [at the
liquor] and get a drink out of the alcohol, every one of them had
water in it. The bootlegger figured, he came from Massachusetts, he

didn't figure to ever come back there. This man was awful mad. Oh Jesus, he'd shot him if he had a gun, if he'd come back. He'd paid him $330!

"There used to be a bootlegger who came around here, and, ah, he sold to the prominent people of Kennebunk. He sold to—I ain't gonna mention his name—but he was a priest. And so he sold to him, and the priest drank a lot. He preached a good sermon. I went to his sermon once. So this bootlegger come around, and my wife, of course I didn't let my wife know that I bought alcohol, and I hope you kids never do it.

"Well, you've got a lot to learn, and I loved everything that wasn't good for me. So he'd come around once in a while, about two or three times a year. He was all dressed up, nice car, so he'd say to my wife, 'Where's Mr. Chapman?' Oh, nice kind of guy and she'd say, 'He's somewhere,' then he'd find me. And he would have some good whiskey that would be about fifteen dollars a quart.

"And he'd come year after year and I couldn't afford much of that, but once in a while I'd buy a gallon off him and he wouldn't deliver it. He would tell me where he was gonna put it and where he put it for me was down behind a juniper bush in Trottin' Park, there he had one marked. And when I wanted, I went and got it.

"But he wouldn't deliver it, because he was afraid I might squeal or something. But [to] some of the noted men he'd deliver it, see? He delivered some to the dentist, some to a grocery man, and one or two more. I knew where he delivered some, and I don't like to mention names, see.

"Well I'll tell ya another one. There used to be a bootlegger, had a big nice car and a chauffeur, and I never bought anything off him, but my brother I guess had.

"So one day he [the bootlegger] drove in here and he had a whole load in this big Packard car and I was busy and he said to me, 'I want to put this, leave it here. They're kinda after me.' So I said, 'Okay, stick it over there in the corner and here's a blanket to put over it.' And there was a whole bunch of it. I wouldn't know, probably four hundred dollars' worth, or more, and I never touched it. One day he came back and got it.

"Well, Harry knew him, my brother, he lived across the street, and he came over and said, 'What's he doing here?' I said, 'He left a whole load here about a couple of weeks ago.' He said, 'Did you get some?' I said, 'No! I didn't touch it!' He said, 'Didn't he give you some?' I said, 'No! He didn't give me a darn thing.'

"But what I come to find out, if they'd [the police] come here, I was perfectly innocent, and if they come here and seen all that stuff, I'd be to blame, and they'd of pulled me in. I didn't think anything of it at the time. And it stayed here two or three weeks in the corner, and nobody touched it.

"The bootlegger was pretty smart to know that I wouldn't tell somebody up town Sanford. Course, I had been there for years, and somebody had told him I was pretty damn honest and that's probably why he left it in the corner. Now you see how smart they were."

Home Brew

"I'll tell ya, in those days they all made home brew. Did you ever hear of it? And it was pretty good stuff—powerful. You know what they used to put in it? Potato peelings. And all that kind of stuff, vegetable stuff, oranges. And they had it in a jug, and they would drink it before they bottled it up.

"But it was kinda raw. See, that's probably the trouble with my stomach today. Every few houses [on his vegetable route] somebody would say, 'Chap, you gonna have one?' See? And they'd dish that out. It tasted good, but it wasn't aged enough, see? And ah, so I used to have hard work keeping sober, and I had a good trade.

"And I'm gonna tell you something. Nice customers don't like to buy off ya if ya smell of it on your breath. Sometimes I'd have to not drink any to get by certain women who would give me a talkin' to. 'Cause I was a nice young man.

"I'll tell ya, I had a fella, he was a big man, worked in a cloth mill. Well, this fella was a big man in a mill, and everytime I come—and he ain't the only one—he'd have a jar about that big, a pickle jar or something, of this moonshine, with the potatoes and oranges and stuff. You could make some more after you'd had one started, you could keep adding to it.

"Once I was driving home along toward night, and I always picked up everybody if people were walking along the road. I come down from South Sanford and around through Wells. They didn't have a road up here then, and I had this old tan truck and I had a heater in it. It was pretty warm in the wintertime.

"Well, I see a fella walking with a little bundle in his hands and I thought he lived down South Sanford somewhere, so I had this bottle of moonshine, right near the seat. So I stopped and say, 'You want a ride?' And he got in and I said, 'Where do ya live? I thought you might live somewhere down below there.' And he said, 'I don't live nowhere.' He said he came in a truck towards Sanford and he was trying to work his way back to Boston.

"Well, I never was afraid of anybody, but I watched him pretty close.

I was all ready to slam him one in the face if he tried to hold me up. And I said, 'You want something to drink?' He got talkative, and I hadn't touched it [the bottle on the seat] you see. And so I told him to take some and he said, 'Boy, this is good!'

"It was powerful stuff. So he slopped it. So I had to go to Wells and I think that was about twelve miles from Sanford to Wells, and I pooped her right along. I see he was getting feeling pretty good. All of a sudden he commenced to take stuff out of his pockets. You see, he had been to some stores and he had picked up all kinds of junk, you know, pens and pencils and candy in a ten-cent store, and he put it on the seat. I said, 'I don't want them' and he left them there. And I let him out at Wells Corner.

"It was awful comical. He staggered over to the telephone post and leaned up against it and I never knew what happened to him. He couldn't hardly walk. You see, it took us a half to three quarters of an hour to get there and that booze had gotten to working.

"Well, of course I was full of Old Scratch, and I laughed about it. I never did know where he landed up. There wasn't much left in that bottle. It was powerful stuff. He got out just before the corner so that I could go right through. So I started and he got over to the telephone post, and I went off laughing.

"Everybody used to make home brew in a crock, and everybody used to steal each other's. They came in one day when I was away, or to the beach, and I'd have the crock hidden in the greenhouse or in the barn somewhere, or upstairs in the house. They'd start to come with a pail and a dipper and dip it all out before I'd got it.

"And that's what they used to do in them days. You didn't call it stealing when you stole their booze. I never stole any, no I never did, but they stole it from me.

"You could want a drink awful bad, and all you had was an empty crock."

Sea Moss Harvesting and Sea Moss Pudding

HARVESTING

by Kim Lovejoy and Mary White

A man on the beach is collecting something with a pitchfork and loading it onto an old truck. The man is Arden Davis of Kennebunkport, Maine, and he's collecting Irish sea moss. What is sea moss? According to Arden, not too many people know.

In the ocean, the moss is comparable to a small rusty-brown tree or flower swaying in the wind, but on the beach it's dried and shriveled. It has lost most of its beauty. "It grows on rocks in the ocean just like grass grows on the lawn." It also grows on ledges and shelves. "When it comes, you get it, bring it home, you got to spread it, rake it up, you got to turn it, you gotta bring it in the barn, pick it, bag it an' it makes a long, long process."

When asked where it grows best, Arden Davis replied, "Of course now we don't get the amount of moss here that they get down along Bailey's Island, around Rockland, oh, they get a tremendous amount. Also down along Nova Scotia and Canada they get tremendous amounts." Why? "There's ledges . . . a different bottom down there. It grows thicker and bigger."

The moss comes up on the beach from rough storms. The water tears it off the rocks. Arden mosses every day possible. His favorite "mossin' holes" are anywhere from York to Biddeford Pool, a distance of ap-

157. Arden's son Kirk shows us what the sea moss looks like "right out of the water." (*Photo by Ernest Eaton*)

proximately thirty-five miles. Sometimes he doesn't have to travel that far.

"When we have a storm, there's generally moss on all of 'em, and you have enough right near home. But when it gets scarce, there's some beaches where it floats in when it's calm, a little bit at a time, and so we travel more when it's calm weather. If we drag, we generally stay around Cape Porpoise, Turbot's Creek, and Biddeford Pool, and go draggin' in the water."

During the fall he gets more up on the beach than in the summer, but in the winter it's only 40 per cent moss. In the summer, it is 60 to 70 per cent usable moss. The unwanted scrap is used for fertilizer. In quantity, the collection ranges from only a few bags full to a couple of truckloads, depending on the weather.

Collecting on the beach is a simple process. "We pick it up with a fork, load it in the truck, and haul it home." Collecting in the sea is more complicated since it involves dragging. When he drags for moss, Arden uses an iron frame with a billowing net attached. The frame settles within the ledges and in the holes. It is pulled up and emptied, then used again.

The tide is an important variable in dragging. "You can only drag at low tide. After it's in a couple o' hours, you've got too much water—too deep to drag." For a while, some companies would buy it "wet, right out o' the ocean." It eliminated raking, spreading, drying, etc.

In addition to earning money on moss, Arden occasionally finds a ten-dollar bill, or a one, or half a one-dollar bill. Other odds and ends such as gloves, Band-Aids, and cans are found.

More times than not Arden is able to drive his truck right up on the beach. His son, Kirk, helped to explain why. "You can't have a fairly decent truck to go on the beach with; the salt water just rusts 'em out." We found this true, as Arden has many old model trucks.

After the moss has been collected, it's ready for the spreading stage. It must be spread out thinly so that it dries. For spreading, Arden and his son use places called pits. These are usually old abandoned roads. The best pits are asphalt and tar roads. "The tar draws the sun and heats the moss, drying it quicker and better." It is spread about two inches deep. The top part is dried, then he turns it over with a rake in a back-and-forth, swishing motion, and allows it to dry more. "The minute one load is dry, we have another load to go in its place. We keep rotating until we run out."

Drying is an operation which depends on the weather. If it is sunny out, it dries fast, but if it's raining, drying will take longer. When it doesn't rain and there's no sun, wind will dry the moss. If it snows, that's a different story: "There's only one place you can dry it then; it's on the sand on the beach.

"We let it dry on top, then we flop it over and let it dry. When it's thorough dry, it gets all crispy." Most of the moss turns white because of repeated contact with water. If it gets rained on two or three times, it becomes bleached.

Some companies built big dryers that could dry a ton at a time. They would buy it wet from the mossers for three cents a pound. Arden built screens and used portable heaters to dry his moss in poor winter weather. In his back yard, he has a large cylindrical wooden cage surrounded by wire. "What is it?" we all asked him. "It's a dryer that I started to build." It is run by a large motor, and has all sorts of pulleys and shafts. "But I never got it finished . . . takes a lot of heat and

158. Arden rakes and turns the drying moss, along with Kirk (background). (*Photo by Jay York*)

power . . . It saves a lot of time, but it isn't payable" unless he.has a lot of moss.

Arden and his son rake the moss, spread and dried, into a pile. The moss has reduced about four times in weight while it has dried. They pitch it with a fork into their truck. Then they drive home, back into the barn. The load is pitched into a heap in the corner of the barn.

All the moss has to be sorted by hand. They remove the biggest weeds on the beach when a load is gathered so it dries better. A stormy day is a good time to pick out all the weeds, because the moss wouldn't dry if he collected and spread it on a rainy day.

"Seaweed an' stuff" is Arden's description of the foreign matter mixed with the moss. They clean the moss in both the drying pit and the barn. "Lots of times in the summer when it ain't quite as dirty, why, we pick a lot of it right in the road." The scrap is piled in the yard and sold for fertilizer. Arden says the stuff they pick out "makes wonderful fertilizer!"

The two men built a table which facilitates packing the clean moss into burlap bags. "All it is is a piece of plywood with a hole cut in it. You hang your bag right in here on those nails and then you can pitch it right full, see, pound it in there."

"I was out here baggin' at quarter t' six," Arden told us when we met him in his barn. Each burlap bag holds between twenty-five and thirty-two pounds of dry moss. Sometimes it takes two or three weeks before a pickup load of about forty bags is ready for the buyer. A certain moisture content and a percentage of small weeds that they don't pick out is allowed. The purchasing agent for the Stauffer Chemical Company in South Portland currently pays seventeen cents for every pound of dry sorted moss. The cash value of a bag containing thirty pounds is approximately five dollars. The average load of forty bags yields slightly over two hundred dollars, for up to three weeks' labor.

Arden spoke about the buyer, who lives nearby: "He'll take all you can get. He'll take any amount. You can't get enough of that." Stauffer Chemical is one of the largest companies in the world, with many, many branches, he said. He described the process that the company uses.

"What a thing to see! They grind this all up, and they process it through liquids, alcohol or something. When that comes off the wheel before it's completely finished, it's just like tissue paper, white, pure white; it comes rollin' right out of them rolls. Then it's ground, and it comes out like flour, a white powder."

Arden had a question for us: "You know what it's used for?" We didn't, so he told us that it is used for "anything that needs thick'nin'. In the line of food, mostly food, like canned milk, instant puddings, ice cream, cheese, all o' these things: it's used in that and the product that

159. The sorted moss is packed into burlap bags, each weighing about thirty pounds. (*Photo by Seth Hanson*)

comes from this is carrageenan," pronounced kare-u-geen. He said that we could find it marked on evaporated milk cans.

"There's thousands of products . . . all your pie fillin's that need thick'nin'. Now cheese . . . I used to sell to the Kraft Cheese Company for many years, and they used t' have t' process cheese and age it, before it was stiff so they could cut it. Now they put a spoonful of that powder in it an' in a week's time or a day's time the cheese is ready. You know, all your strawberry milk and chocolate milk is a little thicker than regular milk. It's the powder from this moss that makes it that way. Also, the poor grade of this is used in fingerpaints, and all kinds o' paints, I imagine.

"A lot of these people that lived down the seashore here used to make puddin' years ago. You can make your puddin' from this moss." Bleached moss is best. "You take a cheesecloth, and you put that in a quart of milk and bring it to a boil. When it gets to the boiling, you should squeeze that cheesecloth and get the juice from that, and you put chocolate in there, or vanilla or whatever, put it in the icebox and you've got jello." He calls it "sea moss puddin'."

As we learned how sea moss is harvested, other questions arose. Kim wondered if any particular season of the year is best for mossing. Arden answered, "The best part of the season to accumulate moss in more

160.   A forkful of sea moss.

quantity is always October. Some years in September it's real good. We could have a heavy storm, it rips off everything, and it brings it all in together in a bundle." The peak period may run through November and into December.

"At this time of year [fall] there's a lot of it. But now it's hard to dry it and it's awful dirty. Makes the pickin' hard." The rough water carries tons of moss back into the ocean. One or two days must pass before the ocean calms, washing the moss on the beach so Arden can collect more.

Sometimes in the summer there is a week, even two or three weeks at a time, when it doesn't come in. Four or five bags full would be all he'd get from a whole day's work. In this situation he might go out in the water with a boat and drag for moss. Dragging involves many hours and seldom results in a full truckload.

Arden's experience suggests that the annual yield of moss has not decreased through the years. "There isn't too much difference. There used to be a tremendous amount of moss when I started mossin', but there weren't so many mossin'," he reflected.

"Some years you get plenty, other years you don't. Depends as I say on the weather, the warmth of the water, and the growin' of the moss."

Arden thinks that it grows faster in warm water. The yield increases in years with warm water because the moss is fully grown before cold weather arrives.

"Now this year we've had a poor year," Arden told us, but it had nothing to do with the water temperature. "We haven't got as much moss this year as we did last year because it just weren't there! It's there, but you can't get it. You can see it on the rocks out there, but you can't rake it off, or, then there were no storms to push it off till now.

"This storm we had the other day put in a mess of it, but we have to drive all the way across the beach to get that moss. The length of the beach is about two miles, right out next to the water. It's forever an expanse with these trucks." We too saw evidence of the strain the driving on sand with heavy loads puts on his truck.

Yet it seemed that Arden wouldn't exchange his way of living for a more leisurely trade.

"I've been working with sea moss thirty years. We don't depend on it too much in the winter. The main thing is the weather. If you've got good dryin' weather an' you have moss, you can produce a better living. You could make a good week's pay in a week. But if it dribbles in, you can't try to make a living at it, just that alone.

"One thing about it, don't nobody tell me how much to get nor when to get. I'm my own boss. And I don't think you could find much of a job that had any more fresh air."

I (Kim), for one, am convinced that mossing is a good life. Arden Davis may have initiated a future mosser, earning a living by the edge of the sea.

SEA MOSS PUDDING

Story by Suellen Simpson
Interviewers: Suellen Simpson, Margaret Welch, Sandy Frederick
Photography by Sandy Frederick

On a sunny Sunday afternoon, we learned, with the help of Mrs. Marion Webber of Kennebunk, how sea moss can be turned into a delicious white pudding. For this recipe, Mrs. Webber used the white type of sea moss (more commonly called Sea Moss Farina) that had been completely dried out. (The process of drying usually takes about two weeks, and can be done on an ordinary sheet of newspaper.)

Before beginning to cook the pudding, Mrs. Webber soaked the sea moss for fifteen minutes in water, and then washed it. After soaking, she explained the simple process:

"I'm going to put a quarter cup of sea moss into two and a half cups of milk in a double boiler, and this has to cook for thirty minutes. I'm going to wait 'til it comes to a boil, and then the heat will be lowered so it won't cook so fast. Now we've just got to wait thirty minutes."

Instead of putting the sea moss directly into the milk, it can be put into a small cheesecloth bag and then into the milk. Either way, the mixture should be stirred occasionally to prevent sticking.

Thirty minutes later, Mrs. Webber removed the milk and sea moss mixture from the heat and strained it to remove the remaining pieces of sea moss. We were surprised to find that there was not much of the moss left after it had been strained from the milk. Mrs. Webber went on with the process:

"Now I'm going to add an eighth of a teaspoon of salt and three fourths of a teaspoon of vanilla. I put in a teaspoon because I think it needs it, then stir it up. Now, we're going to pour it into individual molds that have been dipped into cold water. This is supposed to serve six.

"There, it's all done. Now we have to put it in the refrigerator for three hours."

After forty-five minutes of patiently waiting for the pudding to chill,

161. Mrs. Marion Webber of Kennebunk.

162. Dried Sea Moss Farina.

we looked at it to find that it had set nicely and that it was ready to serve. (We decided that it set faster because it was put in individual bowls, and it would take approximately three hours to chill in a large, single bowl.)

The finished product was snow-white in color. To remove the gel from the bowls, Mrs. Webber dipped the bottom of the dishes into hot

163. Strained Sea Moss Farina, after cooking thirty minutes.

164. The cooked moss-and-milk mixture is poured into bowls.

water and outlined the edge with a knife. She then garnished our servings with cream and sugar, and it was really great!

Sea Moss Pudding

¼ cup sea moss
2½ cups milk
⅛ teaspoon salt
¾ teaspoon vanilla

Soak moss 15 minutes in cold water. Drain and pick it over. Tie in a small cheesecloth bag and put it in a double boiler with the milk. (You can also put the moss directly in the milk.) Cook this for 30 minutes and then remove the moss. Strain into mold or individual molds, which have been dipped in cold water. Chill for 3 hours (45 minutes in the individual servings) and serve with cream and sugar.

Lighthouses

*Looming into the sky, a lighthouse hovers over a harbor filled with
fishing boats. Curling waves pound against the rocks where it stands. A
stray seagull flutters across the horizon, squawking in frustration as the
wind immobolizes him. His shrieks pierce the sky, then echo against a
distant mountain that bleeds snow. Wet seaweed clutches the moon's
gold, glowing as it fingers the temporary loot. Now the circling lighthouse beacon tilts with a moonbeam, forming a crisscross on the sea. A
fisherman steers home, his ears tuned to the sounding bells, eyes trained
on the path of dark, bobbing buoys.*

Stephanie Wood

These are the sights and sounds of a North Atlantic seaboard whose
sentinel lighthouses stand guard over great frothing stretches of craggy
coastline. Swathed in fog or etched sharply against the sky, the lighthouses cast a spell of mystery and romance for most of us. What ships
have foundered beneath them? What wrecks have been narrowly missed
because of their warnings? What manner of men and women have lived
on them, kept them going day and night?

Their splendid isolation intrigues us and we wonder about ourselves.
Would we have the guts to live alone on one of them, away from the
rest of the world? Would our inner resources be snuffed by the sea, or
would its ceaseless movement renew us, revitalize us? Would our family
ties grow stronger, or would they fray from too much rubbing against
each other, too little outside exchange? Would our eyes grow weary of
the vast gray churning sea, our ears tire of its unending beat, or would
the sea give us new vision and flow a better rhythm to our life?

As we began to consider writing a series of articles about lighthouses
for *Salt*, these were the kinds of questions that fed our interest. We
wanted to explore the mystery and romance that surround lighthouses,
and ultimately we wanted to explore ourselves, though this was an

165. Portland Head Light. (*Photo by Mark Emerson*)

unspoken want. In talking with lighthouse keepers, their wives, and
their children, and in visiting the lighthouses, we could measure our re-
sponses.

Perhaps, in the end, this is the secret to the strong primal tug that the sight of a lighthouse gives us. It strikes to that core of self-knowledge we might wish to have about our own inner fortitude.

And so we bring you some stories about lighthouses. We let you see lighthouses through the eyes of a fisherman who depends upon them. Then we let you hear about living on lighthouses from two wives of lighthouse keepers. Next we talk to two people who spent much of their childhood on lighthouses. And, finally, we lead you through the daily routine of a lighthouse keeper. After you have shared these lighthouse tales, we wonder if you will in the end agree with Mrs. Earl Benson:

"It sounds exciting about all these storms that happen and all that kind of stuff goes by. That's gone. But you take the other days, you got all them other days to keep goin'. It wasn't so much the exciting things that happen. It's how the people live on 'em."

Stories by Stephanie Wood
Interviewing and photography by
Stephanie Wood, Anne Pierter, Jay York,
Herbert Baum III, Karen Eames, Anne Gorham,
Fran Ober, Mark Emerson, Sandy Frederick, and Mark Serreze

"WE KNEW ALL THE SOUNDS"

"Speakin' of how important those lighthouses are, we knew all the sounds from all the different ones. You hear them all your life, and you could tell 'em—the ones inshore and everywhere.

"One night in the summertime—it was getting just about dark—this fella comes in. He had been hanging around all day. He had blood poisoning in his hand, and the worst of it, if he didn't get to a doctor in Rockland that night, he probably would've died. He come to me just at dark, and my boat was hauled up over there. I was having it painted. And his boat was there, and he said, 'The compass ain't right on it.' But we started. It was just dark when we left.

"I got the best bearing I could on it—the compass, of course. And

166.   Matinicus Rock Light.

I'd time it [running the motor] and keep shutting off and listening, and I only made it just by picking up whistles and bells that I knew. You see, his compass was way off, but I knew I had to get him in to that doctor. I was some uneasy, but I made it in there perfect."

Pausing a moment to remember the incident, Willie Ames of Cape Porpoise set his elbows on the armchair in such a way that he looked as if he were steering a boat. A lobsterman who lived much of his life near the lighthouse at Matinicus Rock, Willie was telling us how fishermen feel about the lighthouses that save many a boat from wrecking along the rocky shore line. He also told us of some of the vessels that didn't make it.

"A big ledge—Malcolm's Ledge—picked up a good many boats, that ledge. Before my time I heard them telling about a big mackerel seiner out there. It was thick-a-fog and rough, and they were jogging it—running it back and forth. The crew was down forward playing cards, and one fellow was on watch, standing watch. But he was watching the card game, and they run her ashore. And on that ledge, course, the tide covers it in high water. And then the vessel stood and there they were on the ledge. They all piled off of her except two of them that didn't quite make it. Then the vessel slid off [the ledge].

"One got into the yawl boat [lifeboat] and lost his oars, and he couldn't help them [the men left on the ledge] as the tide rose. They fished him up in the bay sometime afterwards.

"And the other fella crawled up on the mast. And he watched all the rest of them drown, was all he could do. By God, he was up there I guess a day or two. The fog cleared up and someone on those neighboring islands down there, I guess it was Seal Island, saw the mast sticking up, and sent them down there to see what was happening. And he had froze right to the mast. They had to break his hands loose from the mast, he had a death grip on it, he'd been on for so long. That was before my time."

Willie sat up in his armchair and thought back even farther. "If there was a death message, somebody died, or something they wanted serious [at the lighthouse], they'd blow the whistle constantly in calm weather and everybody knew something was wrong, and they'd go down.

"Down there it was unmerciful rough at times, and if it was so rough that they couldn't go off the slip, they'd throw a bottle overboard and it'd drift off with a message in it. The men on the lighthouse, they'd deliver their message that way.

"Abbie Burgess, how old was she?" Willie asked his wife as he embarked on another lighthouse story. "Sixteen or seventeen? Well, anyhow, her father was a lighthouse keeper, and he had to go out, had to row out to Matinicus [Island near Matinicus Rock] to get his supplies.

"She knew how to run everything. I think her mother was an invalid. There was a terrible gale, one of the worst gales we ever had on the coast, and that girl was down there and they thought it was going to wash the towers off. She kept the light and everything going while her father was gone. That's been written in a lot of stories. I think she married a lighthouse keeper afterwards.

"After they changed the lighthouse service over to the Coast Guard, they [the Coast Guard] didn't do too good. They drowned a boy down there. Landed when they had no business landing. It was too rough. If there'd been the regular old lighthouse keeper down there, they mightn't of landed that day. You see, I think this boy come from out Midwest somewheres and probably the rest of them [Coast Guard] did. That was just needless because they didn't know exactly what they were doing.

"Course, those fellas [lighthouse keepers before the Coast Guard], they must've come from Down East somewheres, Jonesport or Deer Isle. Boy were they able. They were great fellas for lighthouse keepers, real good men on the water." Willie Ames' wife, Elizabeth, walked in from the kitchen to agree with Willie about the kind of people who ought to run a lighthouse.

"It's no place to fool around if you don't know what you're doing."

"YOU HAD YOUR OWN WORLD"

"It's the way that the people lived there, what they had to put up with, and yet I bet there wasn't one out of fifty that wouldn't do it over again. There was something that was different, and once you got out there, everything else was away. You know? You had your own world."

A wife of a lighthouse keeper, Mrs. Earl Benson of Biddeford Pool, has lived on lighthouses at Duck Island, Portland Head, Wood Island, and Bear Island. "It sounds exciting about all these storms that happen and all that kind of stuff goes by. That's gone," she said.

"But you take the other days, you got all them other days to keep goin'. It wasn't so much the exciting things that happen. It's how the people live on 'em."

As she described her lighthouse experiences, Mrs. Benson suggested that we go to see Ada Foss. Ada, she told us, had lived more years on lighthouses than any other person in our area. Ada's name was not new to us, because we had already met her earlier when she demonstrated how to make bait bags.

Ada was sitting on her plant-filled sun porch when we pulled into her driveway, but she beat us to the back door. Tall and thin with upright bearing, she spoke in a low, gentle voice that grew enthusiastic as she remembered her twenty-seven years as a lighthouse keeper's wife on Libby Island, Goat Island, Blue Hill, and the Cuckolds.

"I really loved the lighthouse service," said Ada. "I guess I was about nineteen, twenty when I went there [to her first lighthouse on Libby Island]. Just young, but I loved it. It's really interesting.

"I enjoyed watching the boats come in and knowing what they were doing and how they were making out fishing." With her husband, Justin, "We knew every boat that went out of this harbor; we knew when they came in.

"Course, I suppose the fishermen were all pleased that someone was watchin' for them. And in the night we used to sleep on the harbor side."

As a young woman, Ada went to her first lighthouse with two small children. "We had our two girls when we came, and after we'd been there, we had two boys. So they grew up in the lighthouse service. And they all liked it.

"I always remember when Justin, he was named for his father, when he was little, we was so afraid that he'd get away and he might fall over the cliffs. We used to keep him tied in front of the windows. And we'd give him a box and some nails, and he'd stand and he'd pound nails all day long. And whenever he'd see a vessel, he'd throw his hammer and he'd holler some day he was going to be captain of one of them boats.

"I know we were all happy. They seemed to be happy. I really don't know of anything that was unpleasant, you know, living like that. It was really okay by me, in every way.

"There was three families on Libby Island. We were there fourteen years, and then he got transferred to Blue Hill Bay, and that was just him and I. So we did the work together. We'd get up in the morning and first we'd do his work and then we'd do my work. It took the month of May to get the house in shape so we could relax a little."

On a three-family lighthouse, like Libby Island, the men stood watches at night, Ada said. "One would have from six till ten, and then the other one would have from ten till two, and the next one would go on. What we used to do—the three women—in the evening, we used to get together and knit and crochet and do things like that to pass away the time. Libby Island seems to be closer to me 'cause it was the first one I'd been on.

"Every Sunday we used to take the kids and go on a picnic. We'd have dinner, and then we used to play ball. We'd all get together. Course, with three families we can have quite a little ball team. Oh, they [the children] loved it there.

"When they were small, we had a teacher that used to come and she'd stay with us two weeks. And then she'd go away to another station. And there would be eight weeks we would have to keep the children up in their studies until she got back."

Later the three families hired a teacher "that stayed right there" on the island. "The government paid so much and we paid so much. But then that didn't work out so well, so we boarded our children with my father. Course, they were all gone all the time, and we didn't like that too well. So then after a while, we got a grant and I moved ashore and stayed with them while they were in school and then go back in the summer."

Ada pointed out an old wooden rocking chair in her kitchen which she and her husband had rescued from a shipwreck. "One morning it was so thick with fog and it was cold. I looked out of the window and the fog had begun to lift. Well, over on the next island, we called it Big Libby, I could see these stakes sticking out. Well, I knew there was no stakes there, so I kept watching, and as the fog lifted, we could see it was a vessel.

167. Ada and her prize chair salvaged from a wrecked ship. (*Photo by Jay York*)

"The vessel was a total loss, she was just pounded to pieces. When the tide went down so we could get over, we all walked over to see what was going on." In the wreck was a heavy oak chair, bolted to the floor. "I said to my husband, 'Oh dear, I'd love to get that chair. Do you suppose we could get it?' And he said, 'We'll try.' And we carried it across, oh, it must've been a half a mile from one island over to the other. But we carried it, first him then I."

Carrying the chair brought to mind the time when Ada had tried to carry a horse that had fallen in a gulch. "We knew an old lady by the name of Katie and she was lame. So that's how Katie [the horse] got her name, because Katie was lame and she was lame. They both had a funny way of walking, on the backs of their feet.

"Well, old Katie was a horse that they used to haul the coal from the boathouse up to the engine room. Well, the way she moved her feet, she couldn't put her hoofs down the way a horse does. They would be up more, so she'd be kind of walking on her heels. Well, my husband used to take care of her, and nights he'd put her in the barn because he was afraid she would fall in the gulches. So one morning he didn't feel very good, he had a cold. Well, evidently he forgot it, and he didn't put her in.

"Next morning he [another lighthouse keeper] came and he said, 'Justin, old Katie's gone and we can't find her anywhere.' So Justin said he'd get ready and go right out. Course, we all went hunting for her, and the poor thing had slipped and fallen in a gulch. But there was nothing we could do to get her out, so we called the Coast Guard.

"They came over and they made a cradle out of canvas and they put it down and tried to lift her up. But she died when they was lifting her out. And, of course, we all cried and we all had a terrible time about it, because she was just like one amongst us, you know. Well, that was the story of poor old Katie."

Sitting in Ada's pleasant sun-filled kitchen, our thoughts naturally drifted to lighthouse food. "We used to go over on an island called Tinker's Island, and that's where we used to pick the blackberries and raspberries. There was old houses there and they'd all tumbled down so these little cranberries grew up. They call them Highland cranberries. They were delicious. There were loads of them there. We used to pick them and have all we wanted to eat. We used to can them, you know, for the winter, and they were awfully good with hot biscuits.

"Oh, I used to can everything. We raised our own beef and we raised our own pork. Late in the fall my husband would kill it so we could keep it good. Then I used to can the pork and the beef, and I always used to can chicken. He'd go fishing, and I'd can fish. I used to can mackerel—canned mackerel is awfully good. We'd have all those nice things in the winter.

"We had a cow; we had a pig; we had hens and ducks. Course, we'd raise chickens so we'd have them to can. And our cow was beautiful. We made all the butter, we had all the milk, cream—we had all the eggs. So Libby Island was really the nicest one we were on because it was a big place and we could have all the things that we wanted. We raised the garden, and that was always lovely except potatoes. You couldn't raise potatoes because they got too soggy.

"Our inspector [whose job it was to inspect the lighthouses unannounced at regular intervals] came in the fall, and I had just got through canning. I had six hundred jars full of everything, jellies and jams and preserves, well, everything. I had taken the children and gone down to the boathouse because there was nothing there I had to stay there for while he inspected.

"So when he came down, he says, 'Mrs. Foss, I went down in your cellar, and if I'd had a suitcase, I'd have filled it up!' I says, 'Well, that's all right. If you give us a transfer, you can have everything there is in there.' He laughed. Well, it was only a while after that we got our transfer. Course, it wasn't on account of that, but that's when we was transferred to Blue Hill Bay."

Even though Libby Island was the nicest lighthouse station, in Ada's opinion, her favorite was Blue Hill Bay. When we asked her why, she smiled and said, "Well, it was just him and I. We had it to ourselves."

None of the lighthouse stations, however, brought critical comments from Ada. Not even the Cuckolds, which was just solid rock rising out of the sea. Didn't she miss having soil around her, taking long walks?

"In front of our kitchen windows there was a wide place and my husband and I used to take out dirt. We brought it out in buckets on a boat [from the mainland], and we made ourselves a little flower garden. That was kind of pretty."

Putting in plenty of provisions was important for lighthouse families. We asked Mrs. Benson if she ever opened her pantry and found it empty. "No, it wasn't our business to," she replied, "because you would've had to suck on your thumb!"

Ada said, "We used to plan six months ahead. We used to buy onions, one hundred pounds sacked. And we used to buy flour at that time in a barrel. We used to buy one hundred pounds of sugar, and we would have salt and soda and spices. You really had to buy in quantities in order to have plenty. We used to buy our potatoes six hundred pounds at a time. We raised our own vegetables, but that's one thing, potatoes you couldn't raise too good. It was the soil. They would all be like a bag of water, so we used to buy most of our potatoes. When we'd see it would be gettin' low, we'd buy the same amount again. And we always knew that we had plenty."

In Ada's kitchen was a fish tank with a plastic lighthouse to guide the goldfish. They circled the lighthouse closely, but once in a while they would make an abrupt turn and circle the opposite direction. Sometimes they got too close to the lighthouse, darted away and continued circling. They knew their area well, and we found that this applies to lighthouse keepers, too.

"We knew every boat that went out of this harbor. We knew when they came in. I really enjoyed watching the boats come in and know what they were doing and how they were making out fishing.

"Course, I suppose the fishermen were all pleased that someone was watchin' for them, and in the night we used to sleep on the harbor side," said Ada. "You slept with one eye open all the time, cause you had to have that light on your mind all the time," explained Mrs. Benson.

"One night I couldn't sleep," Ada remembered. "I don't know what the matter was. Oh, it was a beautiful moonlit night. I just couldn't sleep and I heard voices. Of course, out on a place like that and you hear talking, you want to know what's going on. So I got up and listened. Well it was a big yacht and they had run ashore on the island.

"The tide was going and they couldn't get her off. So I told my husband, 'I think you better find out what's going on.' He went down and

168. Rockland breakwater lighthouse.

she went right in between two big rocks so she sat right up there. She didn't go over either way. After they got everything taken care of, they came over to the lighthouse.

"Well, he told them, he said, 'We don't have much room, but you come up to the house and we'll make you comfortable as we can. So they all came and slept on the floor. They didn't want to go to bed. They just wanted to lie there on the floor because they was awful nervous about the boat. Well, the next day on the high water they got her off. The Coast Guard came over and got her off. So she was all right. I don't think she was damaged at all. They were lucky.

"Of course, it used to get awfully rough, but unless it was a terrible storm, it was nothing to hurt you. Like on the Cuckolds it would really be bad. But you always thought: I can get in the tower if anything should happen, and it would take an awful lot of pounding to pound that down.

"We were in the Cuckolds in the 1938 hurricane. The seas would come all around it, so that it would bring the rocks and seaweed right up to your door, it was such high seas. That was in the night, and I don't like anything like that after dark. In the day you can see, but of course they took care of everything at night. The boathouse, closing the

169. "I have seen so much rough water." (*Photo by Anne Gorham*)

doors and things like that to be sure. They would always close the doors and then they would nail boards. If the sea did happen to break anything down like that, it would take longer to do it if you had them protected like that.

"I have seen so much rough water that I'm telling you, I don't like it at all. I love the water, yes, to a certain extent, but I know it is dangerous and I wouldn't take any chances."

Part of Ada's knowledge about the sea came from her father, who sailed out of Beals Island. She says she learned a healthy respect for the sea at an early age. How did her sea captain father feel when she and her husband became lighthouse keepers? "Oh, he was very pleased."

Their first experience with lighthouse keeping implanted a lasting sense of caution, however. "It happened when we first got to Libby Island. My husband, of course, he didn't know nothing about the rules and regulations of the light. The head keeper went ashore that morning. They were going visiting, him and his wife. So the other lighthouse keeper came and asked my husband if he would like to go out fishing. And of course he went.

"I hadn't been around the station to see anything at all because we had only been there a week. So the first assistant's wife came over and she said, 'Ada, would you like to go out and look around a little?' And I said, 'I'd love to.' Well, we was walking up from the island and we was lookin' around and then we went up in the tower.

"And just as we got up in the tower and was lookin' right around, I saw my husband on top of his boat and the other fellow was gone. And I said, 'Oh dear!' So she [the assistant's wife] took the baby and I hustled right down out of the tower and ran for help. It was wartime then and we had patrol boys that was stationed there. I told them that my husband was on top of the boat and he was calling for help in the water.

"There wasn't any other boat on the station except a peapod, they call them. Course, I had everybody on the telephone to get help from the Coast Guard. Well, my husband said that he thought it must have been a heart attack the fellow had, and then fallen on the side of the boat. My husband didn't know anything until the boat was going right out from under him.

"The boats dynamited all that afternoon. They had tried to raise his body, but they couldn't. Later on he was found and he wasn't bitten or anything. They said he was perfect, but he was so black.

"I really didn't get over that for a long, long time. That was my first experience in the lighthouse service," Ada said. And Mrs. Benson said something that summed up Ada's experience. "It's those kinds of things that doesn't draw any beginners there."

We wondered if the fishermen had ever let the lighthouse keepers know if they were appreciated. Ada thought and remembered a fisherman's wife who had been glad to have her there.

"Did you ever talk to Hartley Huff? He was an awful nice man. And

170. Owl's Head Light.

he used to fish in this little old dory, oh my Lord, she was awful! And all you could see was the top of him, he'd be down in her so far, you know. And every night, just before he would come in, his wife would call, and she'd say, 'Have you seen Hartley Huff?' I always remember the poor thing. She used to get so nervous, you know, if he didn't get in just when he was supposed to. But he always made it."

And then our question reminded Ada of something else. "We used to have a fisherman from Gloucester. *Cigar Joe* was the name of his boat, and I used to know that boat. And every time they came in by the light, I used to salute him with the bell. He always used to give us fish and shrimp, and he'd always say to his crew, 'Now when we get in to Cape Porpoise, we've got to give Mrs. Foss some of those shrimp.' And he always did, always.

"I came ashore one day and he was there. And he said to the man with him, 'That's the only woman on the coast that knows how to salute a fisherman when he goes by!'"

"NOBODY EVER WAS SICK"

A brilliant sun burned the patch of grass near the door of the white clapboard house where we stood. Overhead, hungry seagulls circled, trying to spot a meal dumped overboard by nearby boats in Cape Porpoise Harbor. "You again!" called Arnold Stinson as he walked briskly to the door in his bare feet.

Half-knit bait bags formed a sort of carpet in one corner of the sun porch where Arnold had been working. We stepped over a lobster buoy to the comfortable wicker chairs he motioned us into. A familiar sign hung on the wall: "Old Fishermen Never Die—They Just Smell That Way." We had visited Arnold before to talk about lobstering, but this time we were here to talk to his wife.

Hearing a yell, we knew Kay Stinson was coming to join us. Kay had grown up on lighthouses, the daughter of a lighthouse keeper. After her marriage, she and Arnold learned how to run the lighthouse so that they could replace her father during his vacations. Kay's father also taught the couple to make sails for him, Arnold cutting and Kay stitching. It seemed fitting that the table beside Kay's chair held a miniature lighthouse made by her grandson.

"Off here on Matinicus Rock, you wouldn't believe, but I learned to play ball," Kay told us. Matinicus Rock is an island of pure ledge rising out of Penobscot Bay with a lighthouse and living quarters for the keepers and their families. "I was twelve years old then," Kay said.

171. Arnold Stinson. (*Photo by Jay York*)

172. Kay Stinson. (*Photo by Herbert Baum III*)

"We had workmen come up, carpenters, to repair the buildings and they taught us. Took all of us kids together, you know, and taught us.

"They didn't allow the children in the lighthouses. We might mar something up, you know. We just had to help our parents to keep the house clean. Someone had to do the beds, somebody else had to clean the lights, those kerosene lights, and opening up a coal fire, we had to burn coal, and there was always gettin' the wood.

"My father was at Matinicus Rock from 1926 to 1933. It was under the United States Lighthouse Establishment. He had to keep the whistle goin' and the bell, so if there were any boats that went by, they'd know where they were because of the whistle or the bell.

"He'd keep lookin' out the window to see if the light was goin' and see if the fog was comin' in. Had a certain distance to look to see if the fog was comin' in or a snowstorm. He had to see to it that light was cleaned every day. You see it ran on kerosene and, naturally, they had to wash it every day. And he had to keep the lighthouse all cleaned out.

"Dad kept the house in perfect repair, painting and varnishing every year. That would last probably a couple months, in the spring and in the fall."

Fremont Ridlon backed up Kay's memories of a lighthouse in shining good order. Fremont is a Cape Porpoise lobsterman who has "been going it since I was twelve years old. And I'm still going. Yup, I hauled a

173. "Lighthouse keepers had uniforms with brass buttons on them. Lighthouses on them."

174. Lighthouse on Deer Isle.

hundred traps today. And I'm almost seventy-eight—be seventy-eight my next birthday."

Fremont's grandfather, Brad Wakefield, was lighthouse keeper on Goat Island for thirty-seven years. "He was very fussy, my grandfather was, about that lighthouse. There's nobody got in there unless he was there. Gee, now that floor there, he used to have that waxed, and nobody ever walked on it with shoes. That was one of his prides, yuh."

Another memory Fremont has of visiting his grandparents on Goat Island is eating sea moss pudding. "Boy, we used to live on that. They always made that moss pudding. We called it ice cream. They used to go right down and get it, and come up and cook, make it right off."

Kay explained that lighthouse keepers and their families could have a month's vacation each year. "And we always took ours in August. Stayed the whole month visiting our relatives ashore.

"It's funny. We were there two years and a half on Matinicus Rock. Nobody was ever sick. There was no nurse to get, no doctor. If you did need a doctor, you had to go to Rockland, twenty-five miles by boat. But no one was ever sick."

Abruptly ending her story telling session, Kay Stinson turned to us and declared, "Well, that's all I can tell ya."

175. Goat Island Lighthouse. (*Photo by Steve Bragdon*)

GOAT ISLAND LIGHTHOUSE

by Jeff Bonney
Photos and interviewing by Jeff Bonney and Steve Bragdon

Martin Cain is the lighthouse keeper at Goat Island light station in Cape Porpoise Harbor. Martin belongs to the Coast Guard, and has been running Goat Island since October. He lives out there with his wife Cathy, and their ten-month-old baby, Martin J. We asked Martin how he became lighthouse keeper at Goat Island.

"In October I was relief keeping at Squirrel Point lighthouse when I got a telephone call asking me if I would like running the lighthouse at Goat Island. When I got done relief keeping at Squirrel Point, we came down here to look the island over. My wife summed it up in her own words, and she said that she would like it, so October 31 we took over the island out here.

"When we first came out here, my first primary function was to familiarize myself with the island. Learning the life out here was different.

"Like I know where every rock is out there. I know that at a very high tide I can cut right across there. Not only did I have to know this, but I had to teach my wife also.

"Would you like to go up to the tower?" Martin said. "We can go right up there and take a look."

We proceeded down the covered walkway, and at the end of the hallway was a winding staircase. Martin showed us the controls for the light. "This is one of my master control panels to run my light. I have a large system, two relays and two timers. These are back-up systems. This is my master power source to turn my light on and off.

"The light is turned on fifteen minutes before sunset, or if you lose visibility of the buoys, and fifteen minutes after sunrise it's turned off.

"We have a buoy out there that is 1.9 miles out, and if I lose visibility of that I have to turn the light and the foghorn on. Now the two-mile buoy is my guideline. It's after Old Prince buoy. It is a lighted buoy, and at night you can tell if you lose visibility.

"This right here is a dumb compass. It is used to take the angle of a

176. The rockbound coast of Goat Island makes it necessary to use a ramp for landing boats. (*Photo by Steve Bragdon*)

buoy to see if it is in the ranges, because a buoy has different ranges to be put in. Latitude, longitude, and depth of water."

We asked what type of light bulb the lighthouse used. "These are quartz iodine lamps. It's a type of light that if you're not careful with it, it could explode. So you have to have warnings, be careful."

Hanging on the wall was a face mask and Martin explained. "These are just some of the precautions in changing a lamp. I have to wear a face mask and gloves. If it does actually explode, my face is protected."

When we were on top of the lighthouse, he started pointing out the buoys and explained how he could tell the different conditions of the water. "Being out here you learn to judge the different surf by different buoys, like Old Prince buoy out there.

177. The light in Goat Island tower.

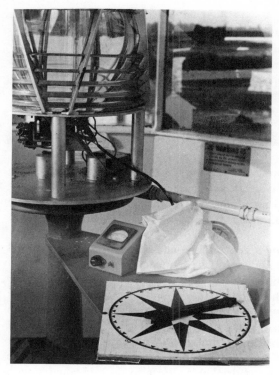

178. The dumb compass.

"If she is sitting nice and calm, then the seas are calm, but if she starts rocking around—and having worked around buoys you can tell the size of buoy—then you can judge if the sea is one foot high and you can judge the sequence [of the waves] also."

Martin took us back down the tower and into the yard where he showed us his generator house. "This is my generator house; this runs on diesel fuel. This is my emergency generator. In case we lose power, this will come on at any time, even in the middle of the night so that the light does stay on. The diesel engine is always warm because of the preheater on it.

"In an emergency you want it to go to work right away, so you don't want to wait for the oil to warm up. These are battery sources for starting, and then my electrical control boxes. It's an electric starter so it needs twenty-four volts to turn it over. As it turns over it will switch the load and carry the whole island power automatically.

"We've had minor emergencies out here, losing power to the island, the light getting stuck in one position, bad relays due to the cold up in the tower. In the tower it's very cold in the wintertime, and moisture might get in. This is why we have back-up systems.

"There is one thing that happened to me once. I went to put the fog-horn on one day and it wouldn't work. So immediately I had to send messages to the district that something was wrong. I didn't know if it was serious or minor. The district sent someone out and the problem was something really minor. It was a bad fuse, which I probably should have known about.

"Now I know. You learn by your mistakes, but thank God nobody was hurt from it."

Martin explained the process of getting fuel to the island. "For us to obtain our fuel, a [Coast Guard] buoy tender has to come up. I request help. I go out, bring two men ashore, and then I go back out to the boat, pick up another man and move into the rocks as close as we can get.

"With one man throwing a heaving line and with us dragging the fuel line, I have my line already in and we connect hoses and fill up my fifteen-hundred-gallon fuel tank."

Martin told us how they collect their rain water. "We collect our rain water for drinking water as the water runs off the roof down into the gutters and right into the basement. Then it goes into my tanks. I have a filter chlorinator before it comes up to us. It's a cone-type filter and chlorinator. I have to send water samples twice a month to the state to make sure that my water is drinkable. We also do our laundry with fresh water and our dishes also. Our sewer system is run by salt water."

Martin explained their daily routine at the island. "I have a certain routine. The first thing I do in the morning is to turn the light off. I don't have to do it all the time. My wife can do it sometimes.

"Also, I have to put the flag up. I have to make daily soundings of my water supply, and Mondays and Thursdays I have to make my fuel soundings.

"We have to check the weather four times a day, 9:00, 12:00, 3:00, 6:00.

"We also have to monitor our buoys. I have to look for debris, check the generators.

"I have to make a daily mail run, so you can keep up with all the re-ports you have to send out. I have loads of paper work, typing and writing quarterly reports on the island. I have to make reports on how much fuel and water we use.

"I also have my own little projects, like caulking windows or paint-ing, working on the water tanks, cleaning and scraping them down.

"See, out here I am a little bit of everything. I am the electrician out here, I'm the damage-control man, I'm the engineer, I'm the radio man, I'm the bosun's mate, and I'm the yawl man."

179. "I know where every rock is out there." (*Photo by Steve Bragdon*)

180. Martin and his family.

We asked Martin about his budget. "Yes, I have a budget. It is based on a one-year period. It is broken down into categories, maintenance, household, fuel for the boat, fuel for the island, buying little things like light bulbs, recreation, communications, utilities, electricity. I have to send everything out in a purchase order."

Leading us into his office, Martin pointed out shelves of manuals. "These are my group instructions, my commandant instructions, search manuals, and paint codes.

"See, we can't paint anything out here just any color we want it. For instance, blue designates electricity, yellow designates fuel or danger, light blue would designate fresh water, green would designate salt water, red would be danger or caution.

"You can't just call the local fire department if you have a fire, so throughout the whole island I have fire extinguishers handy. Upstairs we have fire ladders in case we do have to get out.

"This is my weather station . . . my barometer and my tidal charts. This log is kept every day four times a day, and at the end of the month it is sent to Portland."

Martin told us about how he and his wife get along on the island.

"You have to be compatible to live out here, more so than usual, because the normal husband and wife . . . well [the husband] can say, 'I'm going to go to my job today,' and they can get away from each other for a little time.

"If we do get mad at each other, one goes to one side of the island and the other goes to the other side and talks to the seagulls."

Martin's wife told us that she comes from a farm in the Midwest and likes living on the island better than being cramped into a city apartment, as they were before they moved from Portland to Goat Island.

Both of them told us about their plans for the spring and summer, which included "a big garden" and scraping down and repainting the lighthouse tower, as well as remodeling the inside of the old house, whose sloping floors they proudly pointed out to us.

While we were talking, Mrs. Cain kept a sharp eye on the boats coming in and out of the harbor. "We always know which fishermen have gone out and which have come in.

"The fishermen have been real friendly to us," Martin said. "Like they've told us if there's a real emergency, the baby needing a doctor or something, they'd help us out. I try to help them out, give them the driftwood and lobster traps that wash up on the island. Sometimes they give me a few lobsters."

It was a fine sunset as we sped back in the Coast Guard boat to Cape Porpoise Pier. We shielded our tape recorder from the spray to catch Martin's voice above the roaring motor as he told us more about "my island." We may not have caught all his words in our tape recorder, but we sure caught the way he feels about the island.

Two weeks later, our local newspaper ran a large news story announcing that Goat Island lighthouse will be closed down as a manned lighthouse. It will be automated, the Coast Guard said, because the living quarters are in "deplorable shape." But Martin Cain's story has a happy ending after all. The poeple along the coast here, especially the fishermen, objected so much to losing their lighthouse keeper that the Coast Guard changed its mind.

"We need him there," the fishermen said. And so Martin Cain, his wife, and baby will stay on Goat Island.

The Land

Ida

Story editing:
  Anne Gorham
  Anne Pierter

Interviewing:
  Herbert Baum III
  Mark Emerson
  Anne Gorham
  Anne Pierter
  John Wood

Transcribing:
  Gwen Page
  Anne Gorham
  Herbert Baum III
  Kristy Bunnell
  Anne Pierter

Photography:
  Mark Emerson
  Anne Gorham

Ida . . . you have to meet Ida. That's what the people of The Forks said on our first visit to the tiny logging town in northwestern Maine. So we did meet Ida. She's a tough, plucky little lady of eighty-two who stands up for her own rights even though she is only four and a half feet tall.

Ida built log cabins in the wilderness of Maine. She could swing an

181. *(Photo by Anne Gorham)*

ax as well as any man until she fell off a ladder a while back. She hauled her own water, even after she reached her eighties. Ida grew up with wild animals as friends. You touched the fur or feathers of one of her friends, and you were in for trouble, as her brothers and husband found out.

Ida Allen is still standing her ground. The power company would like to take over the land near Moxie Falls where her small store and hunting camps were built. "They'll have to take me out in a box first," Ida vows. Then she chortles, "And it'll be a little box!"

"We Lived Pretty Poor"

"My father was a settler. He come from Canada when there were no roads or nawthin'. Mama came from not far into Canada, the second town I think in Canada. She come over to be with her sister who was sick.

"Now there was a big hotel in The Forks. It had ninety-some rooms, pretty near a hundred. She worked there, and they kind of liked her. They called her their daughter, and they used her awful well.

"Papa was a hostler, you know, at the hotel. They had nawthin' but horse carriages and horses, and he took care of that stable. Well, so Dad and Ma got to courting. They [the hotel owners] didn't like that very well, 'cause they thought she was better 'n he was, but nobody's better than anybody else.

"After they got married, the common lands, you could get all the land you wanted. They called it settlers' land and you pay fifty cents an acre, and these were eighty-acre tracts of land.

"So they moved in, and he cleared a little. He cleared this little piece of land, built on that, and then all these children were born. There was thirteen in the family."

Ida's not too sure how old she is. "They had a midwife. But this woman forgot to put in my name, see, on the birth certificate. I don't know how they got it down in Augusta with no name. After a long while I wrote into Augusta. There was no name on it, but it was a girl, so it must of been me.

"Well I thought I was eighty-four, but I ain't. I thought I was two years older than I am. So I got two more years to live.

"We lived pretty poor, everybody did, because there was no way to get things. They lived hard. They didn't live [to be] old like they do now. Men used to work. They'd go with lanterns, that's all there was, was lanterns, and they'd go out to work. So as soon as it come daylight they'd be in the woods and working. Then they wouldn't come in until long after dark, you know.

"So Dad worked in the woods and they only got . . . well when I grew up enough to remember, they were getting one dollar a day. But then [earlier years] they only got sixty cents a day.

"But Dad used to work. He'd be gone a whole week [working in the logging camps in the woods]. He'd have to come home Saturday night —he'd walk down from Indian Pond in the winter when they were logging—and then Sunday morning he'd have to walk out for grub.

"He'd take a pair of snowshoes and go to The Forks with a pack on his back and bring in enough grub to last until he'd go out again. And just a pack basket. It was six miles. He could snowshoe good. He could do it about as fast as you could walk.

"Dad had a permit to kill what deer he needed. So we had deer all the time. I have et moose meat. I never had bear meat. He'd get flour. Flour was only three dollars a barrel and sometimes he'd get a big bar-

182. Ida's store in Moxie Falls. (*Photo by Mark Emerson*)

rel, two hundred pounds. People going into the woods would haul it for him with an old tote team going into the woods.

"We made our butter and cheese—like cottage cheese. You couldn't buy much 'cause you didn't have any money, you see.

"You know, people was different, though. If you had a potato, you'd give half of it to your neighbor. If he'd come in, whatever you had was welcome to him, whatever you could give.

"We had hens. They wouldn't lay all winter. When I was little, the first egg they'd lay, I'd stay in bed and cry 'til I got that egg! After a while they'd give it to me." Ida chuckled as she remembered.

"Well, those times is done. Thank goodness. Everybody thinks it's hard times now. There ain't hard times now.

"The first music I ever heard was on an Edison Phonograph. My brother worked for five dollars a month in the woods. He came out of the woods and he took his money—two months' wages. And he bought this, and he came out of the woods with it Saturday night. We was all

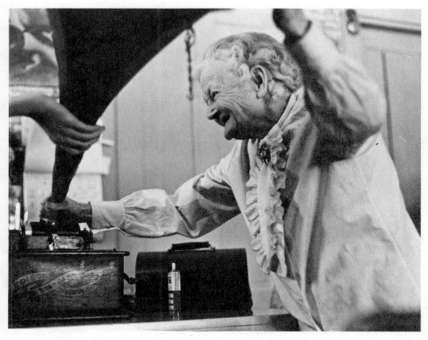

183.   (*Photo by Mark Emerson*)

a-bed, us kids. I never forgot that because they made us all get up and they put on their record."

What kinds of games did you play when you were a little girl? we asked Ida.

"Tag, horseshoe. Tag was a mean game. Rock would hit you right in the leg. You put an old boot on a rock, you see, and everybody has a rock to try and knock the boot. When you knock the boot off with a rock, then they all run.

"And if you catch one of them, he'd have to be the next tag man. So you gotta be smart or get jumped, or else you'll get it. Sometimes the rock don't go where it ought to. Yah, it was a funny life, all right.

"The women didn't get out any, hardly, in them days. Well, they used to come in sliding parties with sleds, slide right in back of where we lived. At night we'd get with either a shingle or anything you could find and go down over that hill and have a big fire outside. That's the way it was.

"At first we were taught right in the house, just the family. That's all there was, but there was quite a family. There was thireen in the family. A teacher came to the old house there and Mama and Pa, they boarded the teacher.

"Some of the bigger boys had never been to school before. We laughed at them, us younger ones. Then we went out to The Forks for school. The teacher stayed right at the house first, and then we had a school house.

"I used to go with Dad. He used to call me his girl, you know. Oh, I used to go with him [along the river] all the time. You see there was a dam, a wooden dam. There was nawthin' but wood then. And three miles down there was another dam.

"So they'd put these logs out of here and this dam held them back. Down below, it would be pretty near two and a half miles down to the falls, Moxie Falls. So when they sluice them out of the dam there, if they catch on something, and get crossways, all the other logs coming down pile right on top of that. There was logs forty and fifty feet and as big round as that chimney. So that's what his job was, to walk down [and unjam the logs].

"And he'd always come round to the house and take me down. We'd go down and if the logs didn't come to the top of the falls, you see, he'd know they were jammed up somewhere.

"He'd say, 'My girl, I got to go. You set right there now 'til I come back,' and he had to go this two and a half miles to have them shut down, because all them logs was piling up. So I'd sit there watching upstream waiting for him to come back."

Sam and the Woods

Ida married Sam, a big man "but not fat" as she is quick to point out, who knew the woods and streams so well that he was a hunting guide most of their life together. "Sam was quite an entertainer. He used to throw his voice. He could sing and play the harp."

But when they were first married, Sam worked in the woods along with the other men, logging in the winter and river driving in the summer.

"We built a little house, a good little house, and the boys [her brothers] helped, you know. It got struck by lightning and the cat, too. The lightning came down, come off of the telephone. We had one line by that time for fire and stuff, and it come in on that line.

"My husband was a fire warden and he'd been up where there was an awful fire. It rained hard, so he came home. This night I was stayin' down with my father and mother in that bigger house, so we went up home.

"In the morning the black storm come up, and he was working in this little house putting the laths on. And that lightning come in, come right down that stove funnel and the cat was under the stove.

"I was washing dishes right in back and had a handful of knives 'n' forks, old-fashioned steel. Sam was sitting back on a trunk.

"When it came down, I guess that's what saved me—the cat. Struck the cat. And it went both ways, right out through the house in two places. We had a small cellar under the house and poles, just trees, to hold it up. It went down through that, followed the grain of the tree, and went out through the house.

"It blew right across from the stove where it came down the funnel, went out and blew a hole right through the house. Went right across the road and into the brook in those rocks. So that was that."

The lightning struck Ida's feet. "It went along in that steel and blew up [my boots]. Blew the tops. I never kept 'em, no. Tops blowed right off. I hollered. Sam was on the trunk—it knocked him down off the trunk.

"I hollered, 'I'm kilt!' He said, 'No, you ain't. You couldn't talk.' So he jumped up and grabbed me, took me outdoors in the rain. And the boys got up from the house, headed for the doctor.

"My body weren't burnt, just my feet. Couldn't walk or nawthin' for a long while. So he'd lug me around, 'cause both feet, you see, were burnt. So he said, 'I'm glad you're small.'

"After that, we finished it up, the house. Kept working on it. And then we went up cutting hay, old back farm where they used to cut hay. It was Willy Clark in Caratunk. He used to keep horses and cattle. There was nawthin' but horses then. So we went up there and cut the hay.

"The men was up there pressing it. And I suppose some of them in the morning were smoking. So I was close to the house. I took the grub after the men. I was eating breakfast and I heard my sister hollering.

"I ran out and she said, 'Ida, your house is all afire!' And I had a little horse and two cats, one with me and the other was in the house. So I rushed up, and Mama and Dad was hollering, 'Don't go near there!'

"The horse, I knew the horse was in the stable. So I ran around and you know the cat was sitting on the window. And just as I looked at the cat, he fell off. I just struck the window glass and broke it, reached in, took the cat and put him on my shoulder, and ran right around the house to the barn.

"The barn was full of smoke. And she was a young, nice little horse. She knew me well. She was standing up, so I went inside and opened the door. She had a halter on with a snap, and I pulled her down, you know, and unsnapped her. She backed right out and ran to the woods. I shut the door because she would of went right back in.

"So, it hadn't got cooled off before we started building. After the house burnt, we started keeping people."

Ida has a yellowed clipping from a May 4, 1922, newspaper that tells about it. "Into one of the best hunting and fishing sections of the state, a new sporting resort is being built," the newspaper reported. "The owner is Samuel Allen, an experienced guide and jolly good fellow, whose years of experience have thoroughly prepared him for the needs of the sporting world."

Sam took out hunting parties, and Ida kept them fed. "They took good food. We fed them good. It didn't cost like it does now. People weren't like they are now. They don't have no guides now hardly.

"I had a pet skunk, and I had a cat, oh, a beautiful cat. I called him Yella Belly. He was as big as this dog and he was yella. And the cat and this skunk used to eat together out the back door, you know.

"The men would have supper and about time they got done eatin', I would feed some to the cat. So after they'd eat, they'd go in the settin' room. If they couldn't set in chairs or nawthin' they'd set on the floor.

"There'd be probably—well the table held ten. Sometimes it would be full, you know, and I would feed 'em and then they'd go in there. Sam would tell all these big stories about fishin' and huntin'. And fishin' season, it was all fishin'.

"I don't know what happened to the cat and the skunk, but the skunk spew on the cat. I heard this noise, you see, and I opens the back door. And when I opened the door, in comes the cat. He can't see—his eyes is, you know, by the skunk. Yella Belly comes in the house and right through the settin' room.

"Well, you ought to see the men's faces. And Sam says, 'Get that cat out of here.' I said, 'Get that cat out of here? If you don't like it, let them go to their camp.' I said, 'And you get a towel, too. And you put it in some water and bring it here 'til I wash his eyes out.' And I hid the cat in my arms.

"You ought to see them men get up and get out of there. So Sam got the towels, and the cat couldn't wash that off, you know. He couldn't see. I was cooled down some, and Sam said, 'Ida, if you let the cat outdoors, nature will take care. He can go, and he'll come back in a little while and he'll be all right.'

"Well, I says, 'A car might hit him or something.' He said, 'It won't. He'll be all right.' So I let him out. And you know it was about an hour and he come back and there warn't no scent on him at all.

"But the men didn't come back that night!

"Sam said, 'And another thing, the skunk will kill all your hens.' I said, 'No, he won't. I'll feed him enough, he ain't gonna kill nawthin'.'

"But Sam went out to milk the cow one night and the skunk had my

184. (*Photo by Anne Gorham*)

hen. And the skunk had a breast tore right off. He rushes in and he says to me, 'Ida, get the shotgun and the shells.'

"So I go and get the shotgun and a shell, and he went out and he shot the skunk in the barn, see. He didn't kill the skunk. He rushes in again. He said, 'Get me another shell.' I said, 'What are you doing with them shells? What are you killing?'

"He says, 'I'm killing your skunk.' I said, 'You're killing my skunk?' He said, 'Yes, he had a hen almost dead. I've got to kill him. He tore the breast all off of her!' Well, I couldn't say much, you know.

"So that was the end of the skunk.

"I was awful small, you know. And you take in a big crowd, I can't see nawthin'. Well, we went to a circus down to Waterville. Jess Willard, the prize fighter, he was there, and there was a big fat man. He weighed five hundred or something; he was an awful fat man.

"So we went there, Sam and Mama and Papa and I. First we went to the hotel and got a room. Then we went over to the circus grounds, and it was muddy and the horses couldn't haul the wagons, you know. They mired down. So they took the elephants and put the elephants behind the wagons and them elephants would push, push them right along.

"We bought a ticket and went in. I couldn't see Jess Willard, but I could see this small man and the big man up on this stand. They had them up on a stand so that the crowd could see over the other people.

"I made a dive for that stand. There's steps going right up, and I goes right up. And I'm standing right on that stand between the fat man and the little man. And the big fat man—I wish I coulda got a picture—he looks up at me and he laughs, see. And so everybody was laughing. They knew I wasn't supposed to be there.

"So Sam looks up, he sees me up on the stand. He comes over and says, 'Ida, what's the matter with you?'

" 'Well,' I says, 'I wanted to see Jess Willard, so I come down [and climbed up on the stand].'

"When they had a circus, we was sitting back four or five seats, because everybody's scared. The lions and tigers, you know, for fear one of 'em would get out.

"It weren't near enough for me. So I jumped up and went down to the front seat and set down. And a man's puttin' these tigers through a burning hoop. So he sees me there. After he puts them through, he comes out and sits down aside of me.

"He says, 'You like animals, don't ya?' And I say, 'Yah, I do.' "

Does anybody else in your family love animals the way you do? we asked.

"Not that way. Not to be foolish about.

"Oh, I love everything. You couldn't live back in the woods like that

185.   *(Photo by Mark Emerson)*

unless you did. Everything knows if you're going to hurt it. I used to set for days 'til I got this woodchuck so tame.

"They got so they didn't pay no attention to me. They'd come out. One day I thought I'd make a prisoner of one. There were four, so I takes an old coat and I throw the coat over one. I put him in a box and took him down to the house.

"That little woodchuck, he got out. I watched him when he got out of that barn. The rail of the fence cast a shadow down on the ground. He gets out and he goes right along in the shadow of that fence and when he got pretty near his place, boy did he leap up to that hole! He never came back to the house.

"Well, a little bear, you know they're cute, the little bears. We had a crab apple tree. And right under this crab apple tree, there's a big ledge, you know. And my brother was picking apples from the ground." Ida began to chuckle.

"He didn't know a little bear was up the tree. And I suppose the bear got so scared up the tree he fell. He fell right out of the tree. Here's Charlie, and the bear falls right onto this ledge, right aside of Charlie.

"And the bear went, 'Aaaauuuugh.' And the bear gets up and he runs. Charlie weren't scared or nawthin'. Couldn't scare Charlie. Geez that was funny. He grunted awful, the bear.

"I had my brother cut down the hollow cedar. And in it was four little squirrels. When he sawed up the log, he didn't know squirrels were in it.

"He took and cut a block off it and he cut the tail right off of one of those little squirrels. He didn't know it then. And so the dog was smellin' around this log and I told Johnny, I said, 'Geez, there's something in that log. Don't saw anymore on that log 'til we find out.'

"So I said, 'Bring the log in the house.' So he brings that into the kitchen. And there's woodpecker holes in it. You know how they make the big holes.

"And so out pops these little squirrels out of this hole, see. So I got some milk. They was young and I give 'em some milk. They'd run along on the log and then they'd go back in the hole.

"But soon they got too big. They was all over the house. They could go anywhere. And they got so big and so tame I couldn't do nawthin' with 'em.

"So a fellow was logging up here. I asked him, I says, 'Could I buy a bag of grain from you?' He said, 'Well, I've got a bail of hay, and I've got a bag of grain. I ain't gonna feed it to the horses.' And so he took the log and the little squirrels up and put 'em in there [in the woods]. They had that bag of grain. It would last 'em all winter, see.

"And I used to go up, it was about a mile up, and they was all right. They'd run around. And one come back down. I knew him, because 'twas the one without the tail! Yup.

"I ain't been down to Moxie Falls for a long while. I fell in down under there once. Gee that was funny. Sam and I were fishing, you know. We was always doing something.

"And I a standing on a rock and there was the spray. And the rocks was kind of slippery. So Sam says to me, 'I'm going over to the other under there once. Gee that was funny. Sam and I were fishing, you side down below and cross over.' And I says, 'Well, all right.' But anyway, he kept fishing a little longer, where he was.

"I pulled in a fish and I give it a yank and my feet went out from under me. I went in. And I hollered, 'Quick, Sam!' He took me by the hair of the head and pulled me up part way, but left my legs in the water, 'n' my feet.

"I says, 'Pull me out!' He says, 'Well, set there a little while and drain off.' Well, he done it 'cause he knew I was scared, probably. He said, 'Set there and drain off.' I'd a drownded if he'd a went on the other side.''

The Mill and Back Again

"The same year that Sam died, I went to work. So that would be twenty-two years ago. [Ida was about sixty then.] I worked down in Skowhegan. They made shoes. I made box covers. I liked that job.'' She chuckled, "I made them covers walk!

"They used to say, 'Why don't you slow up a little?' It made the others mad because you know—after you made so many covers, you got so much more. Well, I used to make them ahead, a lot of them, and I wouldn't put 'em in, 'til some days that it was mean or something. And I'd put in the extra ones, see, so the other girls wouldn't get mad.''

She worked there two years. "And then I went out to Connecticut. My brother lived there. I worked in the yarn mill. The mill, it was an old mill, built over a brook. Oh, it was the handsomest place!

"It was South Coventry, a little town. There weren't too many people there. Awful nice people.

"It was something like here. Fences made out of rocks, you know, rock fences, and it was hilly and then this brook.

"When I got started in the mill, making the yarn, I made a lot of mistakes. And I got it tangled up and everything else. But the boss was awful good, a woman boss. You've got to be quick. You had to have a pair of shears and there's a way you hold 'em. You have 'em in this hand and you've got to cut it coming off.

"And they put a woman on to show me, see, and, oh, she was hateful! I was always wrong. So I stood it for quite a long while and I knew I was right, see, so one day she said, 'That's wrong.' I said, 'Look, I ain't gonna make another mistake.' I said, 'I'm not making any mistakes any more.' So she didn't do it [criticize Ida] any more.

"The sister of the boss, she worked where they made thread in another mill. And that mill shut down, so she come over to work in this mill. They put this hateful woman to show her, and she done just the same to the sister of the boss that she done to me. So he fired that woman.

"Old Squire, he was the head of the mill. He was a mean ol' scamp. He wouldn't let them mill workers talk back and forth. So there was two old ladies in there, and they liked me awful well, those two old ladies.

"So when I go in, in the morning, I'd say hello to them and speak to them, you know. So Claire, she was my brother's wife, she worked there, she said, 'You can't talk.'

"I said, 'What are we? What are we in, Russia or Germany? This is a free country, you got a right to talk to whoever you want to.' Well, she says, 'You can't talk here.'

"So old Squire, he come and he put a woman on with me to show her how to do what I done, see. I said, 'All right.' But I didn't tell the woman nawthin'. She let the thread come off. He come back after a while and he said, 'But this woman ain't doin' it right.'

"I said, 'Look, Mr. Squire, I ain't getting no money for teachin' that woman.' And I says, 'That woman is as smart as I am. I ain't gonna tell her nawthin'.' He didn't say anything, you know, but he didn't put nobody else on for me anyhow. He kept me on because everybody knows how to do things when they learn. You see, I told him.

"And then he had a boss in there, a pet, a man boss. At night he had to clean up. But he'd always leave work for me. So I just told him, I said, 'Look, I ain't gettin' no extra money for doing this. You're the boss. You've gotta do that.'

"After four years of working, I thought, 'Well, maybe I can make a living and stay home.' So I left Connecticut. I got my license to sell beer. They was awful good to me out there at the dam [Harris Dam]. So they bought a lot of beer. I had to not sell beer during the daytime, because the men worked. So at night they'd come in. Then I got the store in."

When Harris Dam was completed, Ida bought the buildings the men stayed in. She started taking in people again.

186. (*Photo by Anne Gorham*)

187.   Moxie Stream. (*Photo by Anne Gorham*)

She hauled her own water and chopped her own wood " 'til I got sick. Well, I fell, you know, painting. It hurt me awful, and then I got that virus. Old age ain't what it's cracked up to be!

"I was painting the windows on the piazza there. Puttying them and

then painting them, see. I was on the step [ladder] and the window
sloped, so I was reaching out quite a ways. I had on a little woolen sort
of a sock, they're loose like. There was a nail and when I was reaching
over, I went to make another step and the yarn caught on that nail.
That paint, it was in my hand, you know. You oughta see that paint.
Whew! [She gestured to show the paint was slung everywhere.]

"Did you ever read Rachel Carson? Well, everybody knows she's right
now, but they didn't then. The world is so greedy. Now they've been
doing what she wanted them to do. But it's too late now. They've killed
off everything. They've murdered all the birds and fish and everything.
There's nothing to stop the bad stuff now.

"You know these big red-headed woodpeckers? Well they sprayed for
them bud worms on these trees. That's what the woodpeckers live on,
this stuff they get out of the trees, see. They don't make a hole in the
tree unless there's something in it, worms and stuff. Well they sprayed
the trees, they killed the woodpeckers off. Handsome they were, with
big red tops on them.

"They sent a man from Washington to see if I had seen any of these
red-headed woodpeckers, or if I see any I'd notify him. But I didn't see
any. But my brother said he saw one. I don't know if they're coming
back or not.

"Two eagles was up on Bald Mountain here. It was Mosquito
[Mountain] right across from here. The eagles used to scare me because the dog was so small. He'd go outdoors. If they'd start coming
down, I'd always run out and grab the dog.

"Well anyway they used to hatch up there. After they sprayed awhile,
they didn't hatch no more, and then I don't know what happened to
them. But there ain't any up there now.

"No more eagles up on the Mosquito. You see nawthin' now like you
did. Everything was right around."

And then Ida began to tell about her battles with game wardens.
"They do some funny things, the wardens. I used to get in some awful
binds with 'em. Well they had the stream closed after the fifteenth of
August, and the warden lived right there. You know when the game
wardens first move in they're harder to get along with. They've got to
know everything.

"That new one, he used to come up and open the door and look in
the 'frigerator. There wasn't nawthin' in it that I care about. So I let
him do it once or twice.

"The next time he did it, I went out and I said, 'Look, you ain't got no
right to go into my 'frigerator. If you wanta look in my 'frigerator, you
can come anytime and look in it. I don't care. But,' I said, 'by law you've
got to have a warrant to look in my 'frigerator. That's mine, private.'

188. (*Photo by Anne Gorham*)

"He said, 'There's men in the camp—they put their fish in there. I thought I could look and see how many fish there was in there.'

"'Well,' I says, 'you can. I don't care about that. But I want you to know that I know the law.'

"They didn't put no signs up on the stream. Well, if I went to Massachusetts with you and if a stream didn't have any sign on it or anything, and it was fishing season, I wouldn't know. So out-of-staters would be in the camp, and others would come in with them.

"They'd go to fish, I seen them, and the warden would wait. He'd be in the bushes with a pair of glasses. I had a pair just as good as his. I could see him in the bushes.

"So I'd run down, as soon as I'd see anybody stop there. I'd go and tell them, see. But sometimes he'd get there before I would and arrest them. So I sent for the chief warden. I called him on the phone.

"I was *mad*, you know. And he said, 'Well now what's the matter, Ida?' I said, 'Well, the matter is I want you to come up here. I've got a bone to pick with you.'

"And he didn't come for two or three days. Then he come, and when he come I asked him, I said, 'You give me a cooling off time didn't you, before you come?' He says, 'What's the matter, Ida?' and I told him.

"I said, 'Look. The people have come here from out of state. They pay for a license and some of them parties you get four or five hundred dollars, the state does, out of what people comes to my camp. They don't like to be in a camp here and see a warden come down and arrest anybody.

" 'Why don't you put a sign there?' I said. 'Well,' he said, 'we can.' And I said, 'Another thing,' I said, 'you should have a sign on every brook. Why don't you put a sign on every brook so they'd know?' He said, 'We couldn't. We couldn't send wardens into the woods.'

" 'Well,' I said, 'you send them in when they go to catch them. Why don't you send a sign along?' He didn't say nawthin'. They never say nawthin'.

"But they put up a sign here. Oh yah, they *had* to or I'd put it up!"

When we visited Ida in February, the seven shelves of her store were almost empty. The cans were dusty. When we returned in April, the shelves were freshly stocked. Ida and the store were ready for the summer customers.

189.   (*Photo by Anne Gorham*)

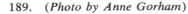

Snowshoe Making

by Anne Gorham and Anne Pierter

Snowshoe making is an intricate art, as we found out from our visits with Walter York of Caratunk, Maine. A logger who began making snowshoes in his spare time thirteen years ago, Walter is not the first in his family to master the craft. "Course, my great-grandfather before me was a guide [hunting guide]. And he made snowshoes, lots of them."

Proof of his great-grandfather's skill is hanging on the wall of Walter's small workshop: a pair of finely woven moosehide snowshoes made more than a hundred years ago. The workshop, sitting on the banks of a mountain stream that is tame in winter, raging in May, was put together by Walter York and his three lumberman sons. "We built the sections and then raised it all in one day. We had us a workshop-raisin'," Walter jokes. Two pieces of equipment dominate the shop—a wood stove with a homemade steaming box to prepare the bows of the snowshoes for bending, and a vise used in filling the snowshoes.

White ash planks for the bows are drying in Walter's barn, which joins a rambling frame farmhouse that is much like the neighboring houses in Caratunk, a town of about a hundred people. In Caratunk, Walter York wears many hats. He is a town selectman and assessor; he is the lay minister of the Presbyterian Church; he has served on the school board; and he is an active member of the Volunteer Fire Department (we saw him drop his work twice during our interviews to snuff out brush fires).

Snowshoe making is a family activity for Walter and Leona York. It

190. The view from Walter York's shop in April. (*Photo by Anne Gorham*)

takes the two of them to bend the bows around the forms, and in past years Leona coated the rawhide filling with varnish. In more recent years, Walter began filling the shoes with a durable rubber synthetic called neoprene rather than rawhide.

The Yorks make three kinds of snowshoes designed for different

191. The pair of snowshoes on the right are the last pair of rawhide snowshoes made by Walter York. The pair on the left are bear-paw style and are filled with neoprene. (*Photo by Anne Gorham*)

types of terrain. For going through brush, they make a long narrow shoe Walter calls "the hunter" that slides along easily without catching. It is twelve inches wide, forty-eight inches long and has a three-inch toe rise. For mountainous or hilly terrain, Walter makes "a flat shoe which I call the old State O' Maine shoe." With the unraised toe, the shoe can be driven into the snow when climbing uphill.

A third type of shoe Walter York makes is a good all-around snowshoe that can be used over fields, through brush, and up hills. It is a shoe designed by Walter himself: "I have what we call a modified bear paw. The common bear-paw shoe (an oval-shaped shoe, see photo 191) had the tendency to flip up and strike you in the back of the leg when the snow was right. They would catch in the snow.

"So I came up with this idea to balance the shoe, and the men that's used them said that's overcome all the flippin' on them. So we call it the modified, not the bear paw, the modified bear paw." The heel of the shoe is elongated and "it has an inch to an inch-and-a-half rise in the toe." The type of shoe the Yorks are making in this step-by-step demonstration is a modified bear paw.

"I begun in '63 in a small way. What sort of brought this about, probably, was a man that lived in Solon was quite a snowshoe maker. He was a genius. He was an electrical engineer, but he had made a lot of snowshoes, and he came up here in the spring, I guess of '63. And he wanted to know if we wouldn't get together and form a company and build a snowshoe factory on this street.

"Well, one of the boys, my son William, and I went down one day and talked with him, and he thought that 'twould be—anyone could make it a large business to build a snowshoe factory here, and have an' old-fashioned water wheel and different things, you know, the old way. Well, we figured the factory that he talked about would cost us somewhere in the neighborhood of $80,000 to build.

"But I got four men—well, three besides myself—together, and he came up and we talked about it, and we sort of planned the thing out. Planned the building and different things, and I told him, I says, 'I guess that we'd better sort of sleep on this for a while.' We met, I guess, two or three times together and finally two fellows dropped out.

"It left my son and me, and we bought some hides and cured them and started in sort of a small way to do it. Well, about that time my son built the mill down here [Caratunk], so that was the end of him. He dropped out of it. So I didn't get discouraged, I kept on myself.

"I had lumbered all my life, well for a good part of my life, and I was still lumbering. I had to be in the woods nearly every day, but I had some spare time. So I had some of this rawhide that we got and I

192. Walter York. (*Photo by Anne Pierter*)

started trying to make snowshoes.

"Course my great-grandfather before me was a guide. And he had made snowshoes, lots of them. And I started that winter. Well, this man in Solon, he came up and gave me sort of two lessons on the steaming and filling and everything. And he was here just as I say, I guess, possibly oh, four hours all together and I took it from there.

"And I sort of puzzled the filling and everything out. I had done quite a lot of carpentry, and so the wood work didn't bother me too much. And I don't know, the first winter, possibly, I made fifteen, twenty pair in my spare time. The next year possibly I doubled it.

"I still was lumbering. I had to be in the woods a lot. I guess I possibly doubled the number that I made.

"I stopped the lumbering. I was at the age I should retire I thought anyway. Then I went into it sort of full time. I built another shop and bought quite a lot of machinery, a planer and different things that I had to have, and the tools."

Making the Bows

"The main part of it is the ash tree, white ash, and, of course, I have to select some white ash that is quite straight—although I do take them that has some kind of a bend or crook in them, and that does come out, when I steam 'em. They go through quite a few steps in the process you see.

"Now I take the log itself and I cut smallish ones, oh eight, ten inches possibly—on the stump see—and I paint the ends of 'em, the log itself, with paint and that stops 'em checkin' [cracking or splitting]. Ash is the worst wood for that.

"And I take those to the mill and have 'em sawed out [into eighty-four-inch lengths for the modified bear paw]. You want to be sure, as I say [to cut them], seven feet and then you've got plenty to go and come on if they check.

"I cut them a little longer because, you see, the wood checks back in as it dries. If they check back in the end of the bow, they don't look good and they'll split. They're sawed out into inch boards, but the edge is left on to dry. I usually have a year's supply ahead. I like to have it air dried.

"I run 'em [the boards] through what we call the table saw which I have, a saw that turns up awful fast. I follow the grain of the wood through the saw, and I follow the grain even if it's crooked a little. Now an awful lot of your shoes that are made for the big companies, they don't pay attention to this. They cross the grain, which makes them break easily. That's where we get the strength.

"Now you notice that I stay right by the edge of this bark [he trims that off first]. I don't have any gauge, I just do it with my eye. Four and five is about the limit [the number of strips he can cut from each board].

"Now I got some of the heart. The heart is the grain where it comes together in the tree. Most of the larger ones [boards] have a little brown heart, and I don't get into that. I throw that out.

"And when I strip out thirty or forty bows like that, I go on to the planer, and I plane down three quarters of an inch square. And years ago they shaped 'em with a shave, which you can use instead of a planer. You can also use a finish saw blade on your table saw or a band saw.

"You have to thin so many inches [three quarters of an inch] in the middle of the shoe—what we call the toe of the shoe—and the back in order to bend 'em without breaking 'em you see. I thin the toe and thin the heel down as they come off through the planer so I don't have to touch 'em with a shave or anything like that."

Before Walter steams the bows he marks the center on each one. It makes it easier for him when he puts the steamed bows on the forms.

"Well, when the water is boiling good, when the steam is in good

193. Using a table saw, Walter trims off the bark of a white ash board. (*Photo by Anne Gorham*)

shape, I leave them between three quarters and an hour. I have steamed 'em, if I know everything's working good, a little over half an hour. But I intend to leave them about, well nearly an hour, just about.

"We have forms to bend the shoes on after they're steamed. They have to be bent round and wedged solid so the wood won't twist. And I have bent as many as eighteen pair of bows a day, and put them on the forms. I guess I've never steamed and bent any less than ten pair at a time.

"Well, the shoe that has the turn on the toe, I have to leave 'em on the forms about a week. If I don't, the turn will gradually weld with the shoe, you see. So, I have ten pair on the forms. When I take them off, I take 'em all off." Prior to removing them he marks where the toe and heel bar go.

"Four of five pair I take to the bench, and I mortise the sides of them where I put the toe and heel bars in. It's very simple. You put them [bows] in the vise. I use a three-quarter-inch chisel and a quarter-inch chisel. The mortise hole is a quarter of an inch deep in the bow. The toe and heel bars are shaped with a planer rasp to fit into the mortise hole.

"I'll mortise those and what I call 'rivet 'em up.' I put the heels together and rivet them right up. There's two-inch ones and there's three-inch ones [rivets]. I use the two-inch ones for the modified bear paw.

"Well, I'll do that whole bunch you see, like that and then next comes the drilling. The toe and heel bars have to be drilled for the filling." Walter also drills pairs of holes in the bow. Between each set of holes "I gouge them out there so the string will set right even with the wood, so it won't weather." [See diagram 208 for places and number of holes.] "I will carry that through the ten pair you see."

Walter drills holes in the toe, toe bar, heel, and heel bar. He uses a $3/16''$ drill, but a $1/4''$ can be used. On the toe he drills eight sets of $1/4''$ holes that are approximately $1/4''$ apart. The first set is $1\frac{1}{8}''$, measured on the outside of the bow, from the top of the toe bar. The measurements are to the center of each set. The second set is $1\frac{1}{2}''$, the third is $1\frac{3}{4}''$, the fourth is $2\frac{5}{8}''$. The process is repeated on the opposite side.

The toe bar is drilled only on the side nearest the toe. There are six $1/4''$ holes. The distance between the holes from center to center starting on the left-hand side: hole one is $3/8''$, hole two is $3/4''$, hole three is $1\frac{3}{4}''$, hole four is $2''$, hole five is $1\frac{1}{2}''$, and hole six is $2\frac{1}{4}''$.

On the heel section of the bow, he drills six sets. The measurements are taken on the outside from the back of the heel bar. First set $2''$, second set $2\frac{5}{8}''$, third set $3\frac{1}{2}''$. The process is then repeated for the other side.

194. Planing the strips down to ¾"
square. He then places the strips on
a planer board. (*Photo by A. Gorham*)

195. The planer board is a pattern
that makes the center (toe) and
ends (heel) ⅜" thick. (*Photo by A.
Gorham*)

196. In steaming, Walter inserts
the bottom half of this into his Atlantic stove. He then pours water
into the main hole. The smaller can
is used for refilling once the steaming box is in place. (*Photo by A.
Gorham*)

197. (*Photo by A. Pierter*)

198. The steaming box in place above the stove. It is approximately 10'×6"×6". (*Photo by A. Gorham*)

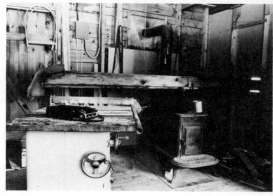

199. Leona York removes the steamed bows one at a time. Forms are in foreground. (*Photo by A. Gorham*)

200. Walter places the center of the bow on the toe of the form, and together they bend the bow around the form. The bow must be wedged tightly to prevent splitting. (*Photo by A. Gorham*)

201. Prior to removing the bows from the forms, Walter marks where the toe bar, heel bar, and the heel piece go. (*Photo by A. Gorham*)

202. A modified bear paw on the form showing wedges in place. The forms are made by Walter. (*Photo by A. Gorham*)

203. (*Photo by Anne Pierter*)

204. Walter marks the mortise hole for the heel bar, then cuts it out with the ¼″ chisel. (*Photo by A. Gorham*)

205. Pounding the heel bar in place. (*Photo by A. Gorham*)

206. Drilling the holes for the rivets. (*Photo by A. Gorham*)

207. Using a ¼″ drill, he drills the toe bar. (*Photo by A. Gorham*)

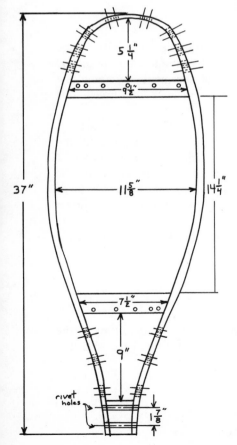

208. (*Diagram by A. Gorham*)

209. With a planer rasp, Walter smoothes the edges. This photo also shows the heel piece and brass rivets in place. (*Photo by A. Pierter*)

On the heel bar, the holes are drilled on the side nearest the heel. Please note that all the holes drilled in the heel bar and toe bar are drilled ¼″ in from the edge. From left to right the measurements are: hole one is ½″, hole two is 1⅜″, hole three is 2″, hole four is 2″, and hole five is ¾″. This completes the drilling.

"And then it's the sanding. I sand them all over. Then the varnishing. I'm using this neoprene now," a rubber synthetic that he uses to fill the snowshoes with. "When I used the rawhide, I filled the bows before I would varnish. They had to have three coats of varnish. With the neoprene I have to varnish the bows first, which takes two or three coats. We use the varnish and a little paint thinner in it to thin it down so's it goes into the wood.

"So, in order to tell you how long it takes me to make one pair I couldn't.'"

Filling the Bows

Walter has switched over from rawhide to neoprene for the filling of the shoe because snow doesn't stick to the neoprene, it doesn't rot, and it is much easier to work with. It is also stronger.

210. Some of the tools Walter uses. Left to right, needle-nose pliers, awl with ends bent over to form a hook, and end-cutting pliers. (*Photo by A. Gorham*)

211. Walter starts the filling with the middle section. Before he can fill the bow, he marks where the hitches will go. The first mark is made three inches from the toe bar. The next six marks are 1¾" apart from each other. He does this on both sides. Now he marks the toe bar. Measuring in from either side of the bow, the first mark is one inch from the bow. The second mark is three inches from the bow. After he does the same thing on the other side, the marking is finished.

The type of neoprene he uses is a rubber synthetic with nylon fibers sandwiched in the middle. You can obtain it from Portland Rubber Co., in Portland, Maine, or any distributor of Goodrich Rubber Products.

Neoprene comes in long rolls about three feet wide. Buy a 14′ length. You then have to cut it into strips. You'll need three strips 14′×½", for the middle section, four strips 14′×³⁄₁₆" for the toe and heel, and two strips $14' \times \frac{5}{16}''$ for the toe cord and toe wrap. This will fill one bow.

"I had a man in here, he's always beaver trapped in the winter. Well, I hadn't made this type of shoe [modified bear paw with neoprene] long, before he came in here one day, and he said, 'I want to order a pair with the neoprene.'

"So I made him a pair, and I made a sort of special pair for him. He weighed nearly two hundred pounds. I made his shoes a little heavier. I didn't plane the bows down quite as much; these are planed to $\frac{3}{4}''$. I left his a little larger. I made them an inch wider all around.

"And he was one of these fellows that start right off, and he wouldn't turn for brush or anything in the woods. He'd go right through if he could, you know. Therefore, he used the shoes hard. Since then he has said, 'One pair of neoprene shoes will outwear three pair of the rawhide.'"

212. "The first hitch is a simple splice. A split is made near the end of the neoprene with end-cutting pliers. You put the split end of the neoprene behind the first mark on the left-hand side of the bow."

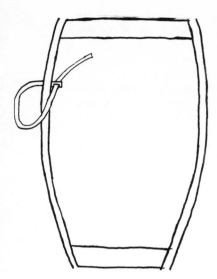

213. "Then you take the opposite end and put it through the slit." Pull tightly.

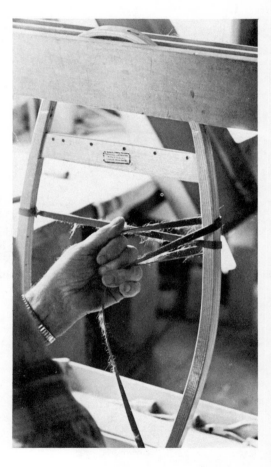

214. "This will be the first strand of four across the bow. You have to keep a strain on this all the time to keep it tight. It's the only way you can have a shoe filled right so it'll be solid, tight, when you get done."

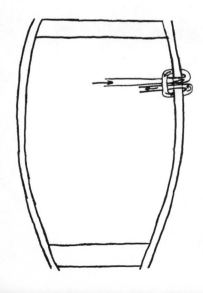

215. "This is an odd hitch. I go from the inside out so both strands come through a loop. I don't know if there's any name for it. It isn't a half hitch, that's the main thing. If you put in a half hitch, you can't draw 'em tight."

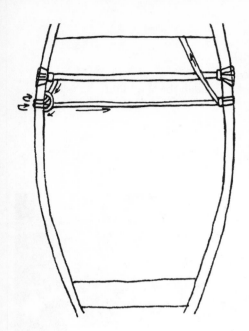

216. "Now I go back over to the left side. Another hitch. I do that four times ending up on the left-hand side of the bow." These four straps are now called the toe cord, and all the single straps going across are called the cross strings. Starting on the left-hand side of the toe cord, bring your string down to the first mark below the knot. Make your knot.

217. Bring your string across to the right side and make your knot. Bring your string up to the first mark on the right on the toe bar, staying over the toe cord. Take two twists around the string.

218. Bring your string behind the toe cord and between the bow and string. Bring the string down to the heel bar, staying behind the first cross string.

219. From the heel bar, go up to the toe bar, staying over the first cross string, the toe cord, and the toe bar. Bring the string down, twisting it twice around itself. Stay behind the toe cord, and over the strand from the heel bar to the toe bar, and behind the first cross string. Make your hitch at the mark.

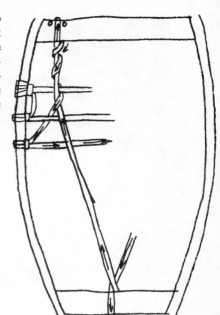

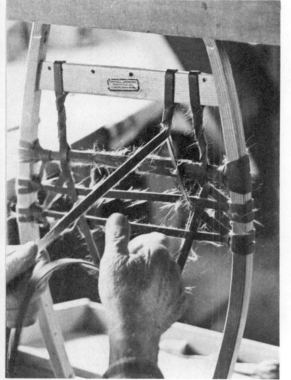

220. Go to the right side, staying under the strand from the heel bar to the toe bar, and over the strand from the toe bar to the heel bar. Make your knot. Go up to the toe bar, staying under the strand from the toe bar to the heel bar, and over the cross string.

221. When it's necessary to splice on another strip, use the end-cutting pliers to make the slits.

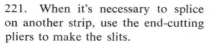

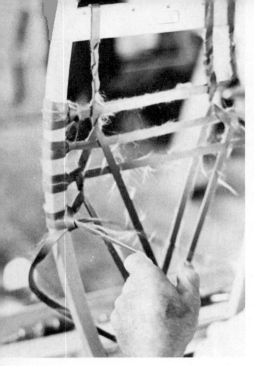

222. When you bring your string down to the heel bar, stay behind the toe cord, over the strand going up to the toe bar and behind the cross strings. From the heel bar bring your string up to the second cross string, bring it around itself, and make the first knot of the third cross string.

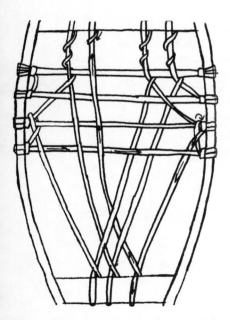

223. When crossing over to the right side, stay under the three strands from the heel bar to the toe bar and over the three strands from the toe bar to the heel bar.

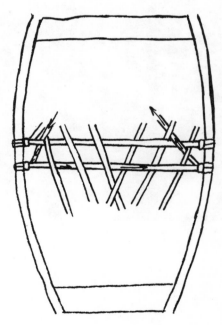

224. Making the fourth cross string.

225. After making your knot, weave up to the toe cord, twisting the string around itself and staying behind the first three cross strings, over the first string from the heel bar to the toe bar, under the fourth cross string, and over the two strings from the heel bar to the toe bar.

226. Bring your string up from the heel bar to the fourth cross string, twist it around itself, and make the first knot of the fifth cross string. Then bring the string up and around the fourth cross string.

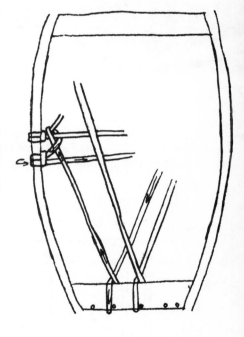

227. Staying under the strings from the heel bar to the toe bar, and over the strings from the toe bar to the heel bar, weave your way across to the right.

228. From the knot, go up and around the fourth cross string and down to the heel bar.

229. From the heel bar, weave up to the toe cord, staying under the strings from the toe bar to the heel bar, and over the cross string.

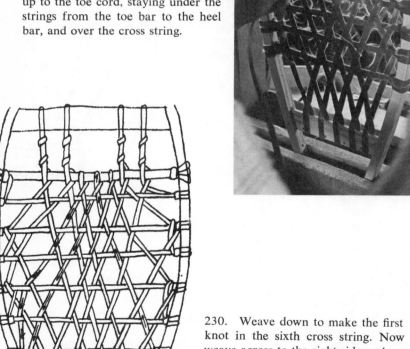

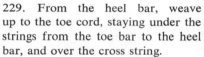

230. Weave down to make the first knot in the sixth cross string. Now weave across to the right side and up to the middle of the toe cord and back down to make the last knot. After making the last knot, nail down the little flap of neoprene.

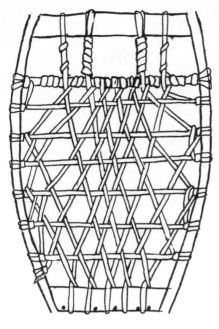

231. You now take one of your wrap cords ar ʌ, starting on the left, wrap it around the toe cord. Take the wrap cord up and around the two strings on the inside that go to the toe bar, then tie it off.

232. Now you fill the toe. With your ⅛" cord, make an overhand knot in the hole in the toe bar nearest the left side of the bow. Slip the short end under the wide cord next to it. Now take your cord and slip it through the top hole of the first set of holes.

233. Now bring your cord back through the bottom hole.

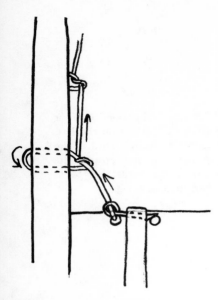

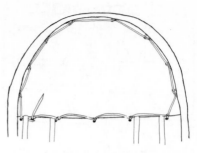

235. The completed lanyard.

234. Make an overhand knot and go up to the next set of holes.

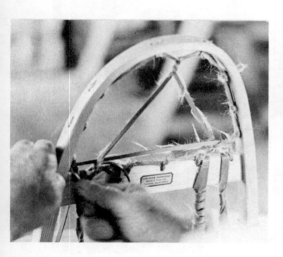

236. Bring the string up to the center of the bow, then from behind bring the string through the lanyard, twist it once around itself, and bring it down to the toe bar.

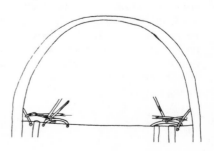

237. Close-up of lower left and lower right of the toe.

238. When making the second triangle, go up and through the knot, the same as before only through the knot. Now go down and through the first knot on the right-hand side of the bow.

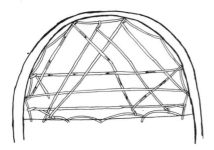

239. When crossing over to the first knot on the left-hand side of the bow, stay over the strings coming down from the toe, and under the strings going up from the toe bar. An awl with a bent tip helps to get the string through the knot.

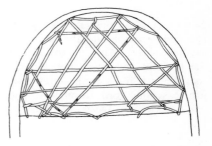

240. Make sure you get that cross in the lower left corner.

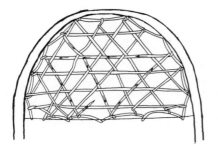

241. Make sure you get the cross in the center.

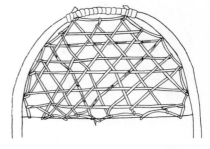

242. When you have finished, just make an overhand knot around the lanyard. Now take your second wrap cord and wrap it around the toe. This offers protection to the thinner wood in the toe.

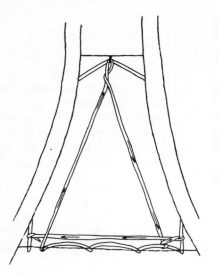

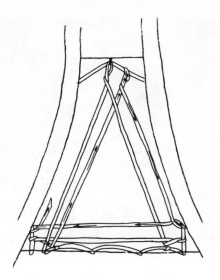

243. Get a ¼″-diameter ⅗6 screw eye and screw it into the center of the tail piece. Make a lanyard for the heel the same way you did the toe. When you get to the screw eye, just pass the cord through it and don't take any twists or make a knot.

244. The twists go through the first knots up from the heel bar.

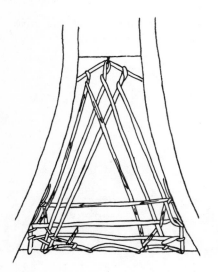

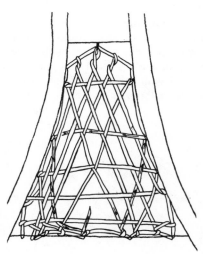

245. The twists from the third cross string go on the lanyard between the first and the second knots of the lanyard.

246. Make sure you get the cross in the middle of the weaving below the third cross string.

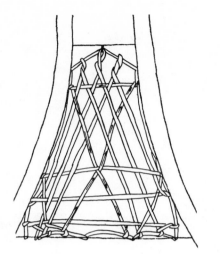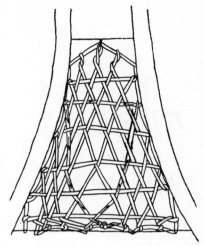

247. The twists from the fourth cross string are at the second set of knots.

248. After you've finished, tie off at the lanyard and try out your snowshoes.

Flintlocks

*by Mark Emerson, Anne Gorham,
and Laurie Astrowsky*

"My father always liked guns. He never had too many, but he liked 'em pretty well, and so I guess maybe that's why I got interested in 'em.

"He just had a couple of shotguns and a couple of rifles and maybe a revolver around the house. I'm probably lucky to even be here because . . . I remember we had an open chamber in the house where I was born. There was a room finished off up there, and I remember it had a big deer skin on the floor that he shot. In the corner was a couple of shotguns and a rifle and a great big box of reloading stuff with powder, 'n' shots, 'n' bullets, 'n' pliables, 'n' everything.

"I was warned on the penalty of death never to go up there an' touch that thing. So I guess that was the first place I peregrinated to.

"This old shotgun was standin' up in the corner and it always fascinated me. It was a great big thing, ten gauge, so I guess.

"I was just a little kid and I reached down an' cocked one of the hammers—gee, I got it cocked an' I didn't know how to get it down. So I reached in and I started pushin' on the trigger—and pretty soon SNAP! Geez that was fascinatin' the way it snapped! So I cocked it again and snapped it again. An' I kept doin' that till I broke the hammer on the gun.

"So then I quietly went out an' shut the door an' just didn't say anything about it an' then actually forgot it. I probably wasn't over five years old.

"That fall my father got ready to go huntin', there was a broken hammer on the gun. I don't think he ever figured out till the day of his death how that hammer got broken."

249.

This is Monty Washburn of Kittery Point, Maine, recalling how he
got interested in guns as a child. His interest grew to the point that he
began making guns himself, not only modern guns but flintlock guns
from earlier days. Monty spent several afternoons with us sharing his
knowledge about how to make flintlocks.

250. Mark Emerson fires Monty's flintlock. (*Photo by Sean Riley*)

251.

Before we got into the actual making of flintlocks, we found ourselves wanting to browse through Monty's collection of books about their history and design. We discovered that they were invented in 1630, that the finest flintlock rifles were made in Central Europe, and that the Pennsylvania Dutch brought both their flintlocks and their advanced gunsmithing skills with them when they settled in America.

Finding the European rifle unsuited to frontier use, they changed it to meet the needs of a new country. The barrel of the American flintlock was lengthened to allow long-range shooting of game. The rifle was also simpler, with less adornment, since it was built by frontier people with more interest in utility than style. These rifles were called Pennsylvania rifles. Later they came to be called Kentucky rifles after Andrew Jackson's Kentucky riflemen used them with such success to win the Battle of New Orleans in 1865.

Many different versions of the Kentucky rifle existed, Monty told us. "The smaller caliber rifles were known as squirrel rifles, and the larger caliber rifles as deer rifles and bear rifles and so forth. They went up to sixty caliber. The squirrel rifle and the bear rifle are both Kentuckies, except one was smaller than the other. Smaller in caliber and shorter. The real old Kentucky rifle that Daniel Boone and those people lugged was probably a forty-five- to fifty-inch barrel, where my squirrel rifle here is a thirty-six-inch.

"Of course back in the days when they made these things, each gunsmith had his own particular version of what a gun should look like. They made some with straighter stocks, some with more drop, some without the patch box. There was no set pattern to these things. It was all in what the gunsmith decided he wanted to make, 'cause these things were all handmade."

The flintlock Monty made is a squirrel rifle. A squirrel rifle (or youth rifle, as it sometimes was called) could range in caliber size from .31 to .43. Monty made a .38-caliber rifle with a barrel length of thirty-six inches and overall length of fifty-one inches. "This is a full stock," he explained, "because the wood goes the whole length of the barrel."

The tools he used to make a squirrel rifle were not all store bought. Monty is a skilled machinist who made two of his tools, the reamer and the rifling machine. Other tools he needed were various files, a drill, chisels, and a drawknife. Several of the steps involved welding, which can be done at a commercial welding shop if you don't own the equipment.

Supplies needed include a piece of steel $\frac{7}{8}''$ in diameter and at least 36" long (Monty's had a .38 caliber hole already bored in it); two pieces of sheet steel, one of which is $\frac{1}{8}''$ thick and the other $\frac{3}{16}''$ thick (at least a square foot of each); a piece of maple or other hard wood

252.   Monty Washburn.

2½″ by 6″ by 53″; two sheets of ⅟₁₆″ sheet brass (the amount will depend on how much ornamentation you want to use); several pieces of spring steel; and an oak rod or dowel for a ramrod, at least 38″ long.

"The first thing you have to have when you make a rifle barrel is a piece of steel with a hole through it," Monty told us. "If it doesn't have a hole in it, you got to put one in." This is called boring out the barrel. The bore of this rifle is .38 caliber.

Some of the flintlock barrels were round while others were octagonal. "This one was round when I got it," Monty said. "Took me three days to put that octagon on there by hand, with a file.

"A round one shoots just as good as an octagonal. I don't think there was any purpose for it. No more than there was of making ornate designs on furniture. It was just that it seemed to look better.

"So after you put the hole through it, it's got to be real smooth." The process you use to make it smooth is called reaming the barrel. "This little gizmo here is one of the oldest types of reamers that was ever invented." The handmade reamer that Monty used has a file that has all the teeth scraped off. He used the file because it is hard steel. On the bottom side of the steel file is a half-moon shaped piece of wood. (See diagram 253.)

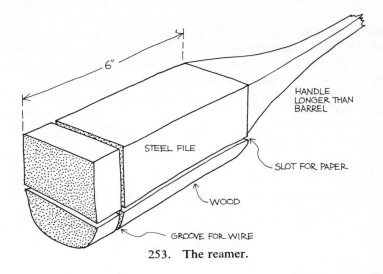

253. The reamer.

The steel and wood were notched at one end so that Monty could tie the two together with wire or rope. The other end of the wood was free so he could slide slivers of paper between the wood and the steel.

"Take little slivers of paper and put them between the piece of wood and piece of metal until you can just barely put the reamer in the barrel. The two file corners then will come in contact with the bore of the barrel, and the wood will come in contact with the other side of the bore. [See diagram 254.]

"Then very slowly you turn the barrel and run the reamer through it, and this will burnish or ream the inside of the barrel. Then you take the reamer out and put another piece of paper in with the first one, and

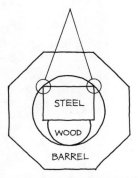

254. The corners of the file reaming the bore.

you continue to put pieces of paper in between the wood and steel until you have a very smooth bore. Like a mirror inside the barrel.

"After you get this all done and you've got a nice smooth bore in the barrel, it's got to have spiral grooves cut in it." The spiral grooves in the bore give the ball a spin when it is shot. The spin gives the ball gyroscopic stability. This means that the ball will go in a straight line.

The machine Monty made to put the spiral grooves inside the bore is called a rifling machine. It is simply a square rod that is pulled through a square hole. Welded on to the square rod is a round rod with a cutter at the end. (See diagram 255).

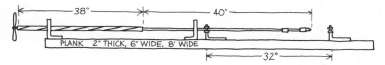

255.   The rifling machine.

"There's a handle attached to the other end of the square rod. The handle is much like an old tire pump handle. You can spin it like a propellor." Now the square rod has a twist in it, one turn for forty inches. As you pull the cutter through, you hold the handle straight and the whole thing will turn.

256. The handle on the rifling machine is attached to the twisted square rod.

The cutter is the part that cuts the groove in the barrel. "By turning a screw, you can raise the cutter up a little bit at a time. You adjust this cutter until it barely brushes the bore. Then give it just a little turn with the screw driver, and pull it through.

"So you pull that through and it gives you one groove. Then you knock this pin out and turn the whole plate, one notch or two, depending on how many grooves you want.

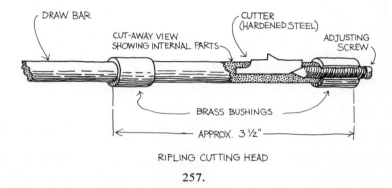

DRAW BAR

CUT-AWAY VIEW
SHOWING INTERNAL PARTS

CUTTER
(HARDENED STEEL)

ADJUSTING
SCREW

BRASS BUSHINGS

APPROX. 3 ½"

RIFLING CUTTING HEAD

257.

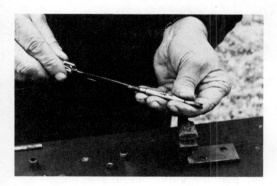

258. Using a screw driver to adjust the cutting head.

"This plate here has eight notches or eight holes so you can get either a four- or an eight-grooved barrel out of it. It isn't really that important to have eight notches over four. The only thing is that if you have four grooves in the barrel and if the grooves are narrow, then you have lands that are very wide. [Lands are the spaces between the grooves. See diagram 259.] The bullet wouldn't accept the rifling so quickly as it would if you had narrow lands and many grooves.

"Now, many of these rifles were rifled with seven grooves or five grooves—an odd number of grooves. But the only reason I rifled with

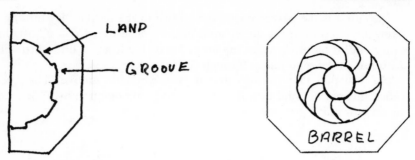

259. If you had lands that are very wide, the bullet wouldn't accept the rifling so easily.

260. The plate on this rifling machine has eight settings on it, so Monty put eight grooves in his barrel.

eight grooves was that I had a disc in my rifling machine that was set up so that I could rifle it with eight.

"You turn the plate one notch and pull the cutter through again. Bring it back and turn it one more notch and pull it through again, until you've gone all the way around the plate on the same setting with that cutter.

"Then adjust the cutter out a little and repeat the process. You go all the way around again, and that gives you the assurance that each groove is of equal depth.

"You can tell just by lookin' through here just how neat your grooves are. If they satisfy you . . . good."

The rear end of the barrel has to be plugged. The plug is called the breech plug. "The plug is made from a round piece of steel. And when

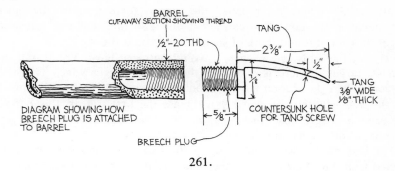

BARREL
CUT-AWAY SECTION SHOWING THREAD

TANG

½"-20 THD

2⅜"

½"

⅞"

TANG
⅜" WIDE
⅛" THICK

DIAGRAM SHOWING HOW
BREECH PLUG IS ATTACHED
TO BARREL

⅝"

COUNTERSUNK HOLE
FOR TANG SCREW

BREECH PLUG

261.

this thing is first made it looks much the same as a bolt. The tang is welded on and polished off so you can't see where it's welded." (The tang is a piece of sheet steel that helps to hold the barrel on the stock.)

Monty now makes the trigger and lock mechanisms. In making them, he said, "First I drew them out full scale. Then I pasted the drawings on a piece of sheet steel. Then I took a prick punch and tapped it all the way along, so when I took the paper off I had a series of prick punch marks. Then I sawed it and filed it out to the punch marks. And that gave me the configuration of it."

Monty uses a double-set trigger. The reason for using a double-set trigger is accuracy. "In a double-set trigger there's a screw that adjusts the pressure that you have to apply to the front trigger in order to fire

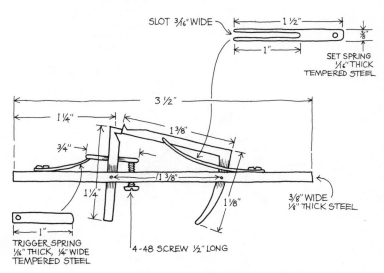

SLOT 3/16" WIDE

1 ½"

⅜

1"

SET SPRING
1/16" THICK
TEMPERED STEEL

3 ½"

1 ¼"

1 ⅜"

¾"

1 ⅜"

3/8" WIDE
⅛" THICK STEEL

1 ¼"

1 ⅛"

TRIGGER SPRING
1/16" THICK, ¼" WIDE
TEMPERED STEEL

1"

4-48 SCREW ½" LONG

262. The double-set trigger mechanism.

it. If you set it and just touched the trigger, there wouldn't be much movement in the gun. You can get it down so fine that you put your finger in front of it and think of shootin' and you'll shoot.

"If they had only one trigger, it would pull real hard. You'd pull the gun off target." There is a bar on the second trigger which is spring loaded. When the second trigger is pulled down, the bar fits in a notch on the first trigger. And when you release the first trigger, this bar on the second trigger hits the release on the hammer. This way you are able to get off an accurate shot.

The lock mechanism is made up of the lock plate and the parts connected to it. On the outside of the plate are the hammer, flashpan, frizzen, and frizzen spring. On the inside are the sear mechanism and the mainspring. Monty explained how the lock mechanism works on a flintlock rifle. When the bar on the second trigger is released, it strikes the sear bar releasing the sear mechanism. Connected to the sear mechanism by a rod is the hammer, which is released simultaneously with the sear mechanism.

As the hammer is released, the flint hits the striking plate of the frizzen, causing sparks. The frizzen is forced back, uncovering the powder in the flashpan. The sparks then fall into the powder and ignite it. Flames from the ignited powder in the flashpan pass through the flash hole, setting off the powder in the barrel.

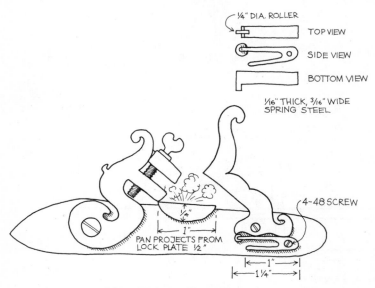

263.   The outside of the lock.

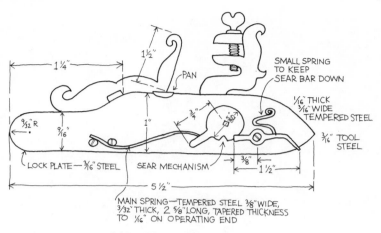

264.   The inside of the lock.

265.   When the gun is ready to fire, the hammer is up and the frizzen is down.

"The funny part of it is you can get that puff in the face first before the gun goes off, and this is where the expression 'flash in the pan' came from," Monty explained. "Flash in the pan is a dud."

After Monty cuts out the lock plate from sheet steel, he makes the flashpan. He takes a small piece of steel shaped like the end of your

266.   After the gun is fired, the frizzen is forced back, uncovering the pan.

thumb and bores out the inside. He then cuts it in half lengthwise, welding it on the lock plate and filing it off.

In making the hammer, the vise part is pounded out flat so that the flint can be held in its jaws. (See diagram 267.)

Now Monty makes the frizzen. The frizzen is a pivoting L-shaped arm. It has a large flat surface called the striking plate which the flint hits to cause a spark. At a right angle to the bottom of the striking plate is a smaller plate that covers the flashpan and keeps the powder from falling out.

After cutting the frizzen from sheet steel, Monty welds the striking plate to the pivoting arm. (See diagram 268). Because the flint won't spark on an ordinary piece of steel, the striking plate has to be case hardened. When you case harden the frizzen, you give a skin hardness to the metal.

Monty does this by heating the striking plate until it is red hot. Then he dips it into a commercial product called Kasenit. Next he dips the striking plate into water and the coating of carbon falls off, leaving a hardened surface a few thousandths of an inch thick. The composition of the surface of the metal has been changed by adding carbon to it.

What the old-timers used to do instead of case hardening, Monty told us, was "to take a little thin piece of metal that was real hard and solder

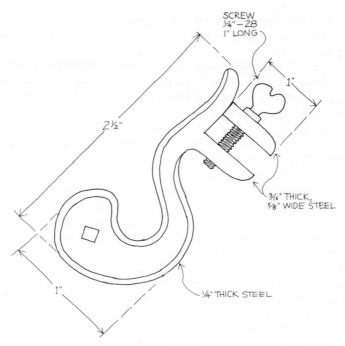

SCREW
¼″ – 28
1″ LONG

1″

2½″

3/16″ THICK,
5/8″ WIDE STEEL

¼″ THICK STEEL

1″

267. The hammer.

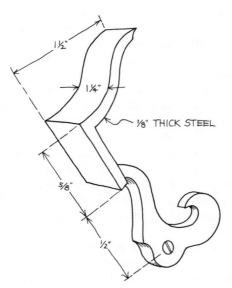

1½″

1¼″

⅛″ THICK STEEL

5/8″

½″

268. The frizzen.

it right on these things an' keep on using them."

Next the frizzen spring is attached by screws to the lock plate, preventing the frizzen from spinning more than 90 degrees.

While he was working with the outside parts of the lock plate, Monty told us about flints. The flint is made out of natural rock and it can be used eight to ten times before resharpening. To sharpen the flint, "I take the back of a jackknife and hit the flint on the edge, just bang it. This chips off pieces of flint and gives you a new sharp edge to it.

"There's a trade in itself, making flints. They call these people 'knappers.' The only place in the world now that these flints are made is Brandon, England. That is, the good flints."

After the outside of the lock plate is completed, Monty works on the inside. He fashions a small rod about ¾" long that is round in the middle and square at each end to prevent slippage. Then he attaches the tumbler to the rod with a screw. Next he screws into place the two screws which will hold the mainspring.

Now the tumbler on the sear mechanism has to be notched to keep the hammer cocked. Monty figures where the two notches on the tumbler will go by cocking the hammer and marking the position they will need to be in to link with the sear bar. Last, the sear bar is attached to the lock plate by a screw. A small spring is also attached to keep the sear bar down.

At this point, Monty began to tell us how to make the stock of the gun. The stock can be made from many types of wood, such as curly maple, walnut, or any other hard wood that suits the gunsmith.

"They made some with straighter stocks, some with more drop, some half stocks. This is a full stock because the wood goes the whole length of the barrel. Most of the half stocks were known as Hawken rifles. These were the plains rifles they took out across the West. This was back in the 1850s and 1860s."

We asked Monty what he meant when he said, "rifles with more drop." "Well," he replied, "if you took this rifle of mine and laid it on the floor upside down and measured the distance from the back of the butt to the floor, that would be the drop.

"Most of those old Kentuckies had a terrific drop in them. You didn't even have to lower your head to look through the sight. You could bring her up to your shoulder and look straight over the sight barrel. This is the drop." When we asked if the amount of drop in the flintlock was for easier and quicker firing, Monty agreed that "probably that was what it was for."

To make the stock, Monty first draws an outline of it on a plank 2¼" thick and at least 16" longer than the barrel. The butt end is 14" to 15" longer than the barrel. On Monty's gun the butt was 15" and the fore

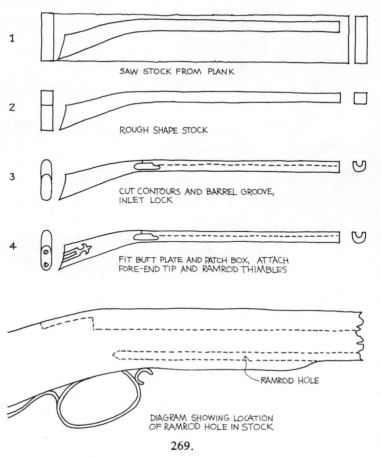

1   SAW STOCK FROM PLANK

2   ROUGH SHAPE STOCK

3   CUT CONTOURS AND BARREL GROOVE,
     INLET LOCK

4   FIT BUTT PLATE AND PATCH BOX, ATTACH
     FORE-END TIP AND RAMROD THIMBLES

RAMROD HOLE

DIAGRAM SHOWING LOCATION
OF RAMROD HOLE IN STOCK

269.

end 36″, so his plank was 51″ long.

Then Monty makes a groove to fit the barrel. This is done with hammer and chisels. When the barrel will nearly drop in its groove, files are used for the final fitting. The barrel tang is inletted, or grooved, at the same time.

Now the lock plate, with all its parts removed, is fitted into the side of the stock. To do this, the outline of the lock plate is drawn on the stock, then inletted with hammer and chisel. The same thing is done with the trigger plate, which is placed on the bottom of the stock.

When Monty positioned the lock plate and trigger plate, he made sure the rear trigger bar would hit and release the sear mechanism.

Next, the groove for the ramrod is chiseled on the bottom of the

270. With the lock removed from the stock, you can see one end of the ramrod and the flash hold going into the barrel.

stock, with a ramrod hole drilled parallel to it. "Boring that hole takes quite a lot of doing . . . and not have the drill come out through some-wheres. So what I did, I made some little drill guides that would fit the groove just the same as your ramrod thimbles. And I clamped them right on to the wood. Then I took a long extension drill—actually, it was a drill I welded on a piece of ordinary rod $\frac{5}{16}''$ in diameter. Run the drill right down through these guides and that keeps the hole straight" as the drill goes down in the stock.

Next the ramrod thimbles are fitted. The ramrod thimbles are made of brass and are short tubes through which the ramrod will fit. They are attached by a wedge lug and pin. The ramrod is made of oak and is two to three inches longer than the bore. The barrel is attached in the same way as the thimbles.

To make your rifle fancier, you can make escutcheons. They can be made from brass or silver, and are inletted into the stock. Monty made his by pounding out silver dimes.

After lock, stock, and barrel are assembled, Monty drills the flash hole. It is a hole $\frac{1}{32}''$ in diameter, and is located above the center of the flashpan. The flashpan leads to the powder in the barrel. The hole is drilled so that sparks can go through it to ignite the powder in the bar-rel.

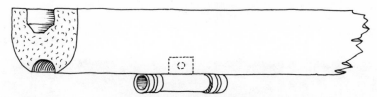

INSTALLATION OF RAMROD THIMBLES

THIMBLE PIN

RAMROD THIMBLE (3 REQUIRED)
TURN FROM BRASS, WELD OR SOLDER
LUGS ON THIMBLES FOR THIMBLE PINS

271.

RAMROD — MAKE FROM WHITE OAK.
1/16" SMALLER THAN BORE DIA. OF RIFLE
AND ONE INCH LONGER THAN DEPTH OF
BORE. TIP WITH BRASS FERRULES

272.

FRONT SIGHT

REAR SIGHT

DOVETAIL SLOT

FILE DOVETAIL SLOT
AT FRONT AND REAR OF BARREL
FOR DRIVE FIT WITH SIGHTS

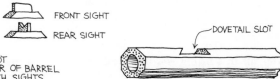

WELD

WELD

BARREL WEDGE—
STEEL OR BRASS

METHOD OF ATTACHING BARREL WEDGE LUG
TO BARREL (3 LUGS REQUIRED)

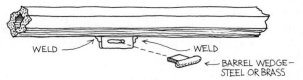

STOCK

ESCUTCHEON

WEDGE

BARREL SECTION SHOWING BARREL WEDGE
INSTALLED WITH STOCK

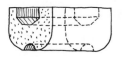

BARREL END FITS OVER
THE END OF THE STOCK

BARREL END
FABRICATE FROM 1/16" BRASS PLATE

273.

274. The fore-end tip, thimbles, and the barrel wedge.

After all this fitting is completed, it is time to make and fit the patch box, butt plate, and trigger guard. Monty told us what the patch box held. "Patches and an extra flint perhaps. The patches were pieces of cloth or buckskins." The patch box and butt plate on Monty's gun were made from sheet brass, as was the trigger guard.

Finally, the stock and its fittings are smoothed to a good snug fit with a file and plenty of sandpaper. Before final assembly, the steel has to be "browned" in the manner of the guns long ago.

"Browning" is taking the shine off the steel on the gun with chemicals. It is actually a controlled rusting process. "This was done in the days of the flintlock so that when hunters were in the woods the sun's reflection on the gun wouldn't frighten the animals away."

Browning Formula

225 cc. distilled water
225 cc. pure grain spirits, alcohol
Mix in order given, apply with a swab and let stand in a warm dark place until rust is formed: in warm weather, 10–12 hours; in cold weather, 15–20 hours. Card off rust and clean with a cloth free of oil. Repeat until color pleases.

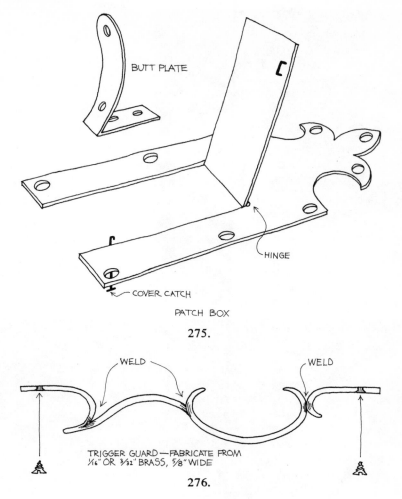

BUTT PLATE

HINGE

COVER CATCH

PATCH BOX

275.

WELD

WELD

TRIGGER GUARD—FABRICATE FROM
1/16" OR 3/32" BRASS, 5/8" WIDE

276.

Monty offered to let us load and shoot his squirrel rifle. As we loaded, he told us about the black powder that was used in flintlock guns. "This powder I use is F.F.F.G. This signifies that it's very fine powder. You can get four F.G. or five F.G. And the more "Fs" you have in front of the "G," the finer the powder is. For the smaller caliber guns you use a small-grain powder.

"I use thirty-five grains of powder, usually enough to cover the ball when held in your hand. Then put a patch on over the end of the barrel. You put the ball on top of the patch and push it down flush with

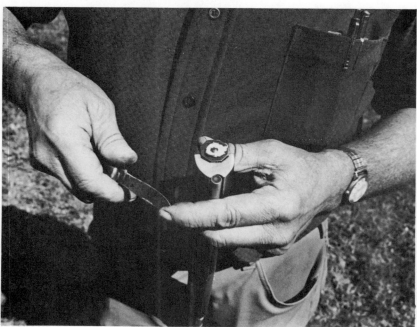

278. "You put the ball on top of the patch and push it down flush with the end of the barrel. Then take your knife and cut the excess patch off."

the end of the barrel. Then take your knife and cut the excess patch off. That leaves a little round patch around the ball.

"Actually the lead ball doesn't touch the bore at all. The patch takes the space between the diameters of the ball and the bore. The ball is approximately 15 thousandths of an inch smaller than the bore. With a .38 caliber gun, the diameter of the ball is 375 thousandths of an inch.

"Then with the ramrod push the ball and patch down on the powder, and make sure you hit it down solid on the powder," Monty said. "If you leave the ball up in the bore about six to seven inches, it leaves a space between the ball and powder that creates a tremendous pressure and sometimes it will blow up the gun.

"But the mistake a lot of people made, they took these guns and loaded them with smokeless powder, and then they'd blow up. Smokeless powder is progressive burning, and black powder, well, it will burn unconfined as fast as it will burn confined. Smokeless powder, you light it unconfined it'll burn like alcohol. When you confine it, it makes a terrific pressure." In other words, flintlocks were designed to handle black powder instead of the smokeless powder that came into use in more modern times.

"By all means, don't forget to put the powder in," Monty cautioned us, "because if you do and get that ball down in there, you'll have one hell of a job. You gotta take a little pair of tweezers, or a straw and work powder in through that flash hole, and get enough behind the ball so you can shoot the thing out.

"I've done it before and I think everybody who's shot muzzle loaders has done it. They do have what they call a screw that they put on the end of a ramrod. It's nothing more than a wood screw, and if you're lucky, you can push the ramrod down there with the screw in the end of it and get it into that lead ball and pull it out. But usually a lead ball is in there tight enough so that this won't work."

When the barrel is loaded (gunpowder and ball in place), then you fill the flashpan with powder. Now put the frizzen down and cock the hammer. Set your second trigger by pulling it back, aim, and pull the first trigger. First you will hear a small bang that will be followed by a cloud of billowing white smoke. A second repercussion follows immediately, much larger, and that's when you feel the kick of the gun.

Monty told us how we could measure the speed of the bullet we had just shot. To do this, Monty said we needed to use a chronograph. "Once I put this flintlock on a chronograph that a fella made. It was a piece of rod four feet long. It had a disk of cardboard on either end of it. A belt connected the rod to a motor, and the motor caused the disks to spin at an enormous r.p.m. [revolutions per minute]." When Monty shot through the two disks, the bullet had to pass through the two disks

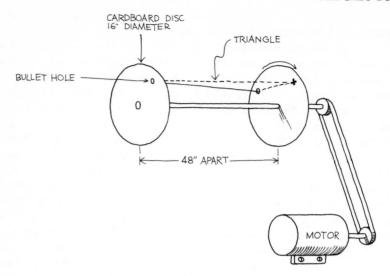

279. Chronograph.

at the same distance from the center of each disk. "While the bullet was going through the first disk, the second disk would spin so much. So then you could figure out the angle between these holes.

"The fella could figure out how fast the bullet was goin' in these four feet, which would give him the feet per second that the ball was actually going. It was just simple trigonometry how he figured this out.

"And the first shot [from a flintlock] I fired through this thing, well this was about ten feet in front of the muzzle. I blew both of his disks all to pieces. I was too close to it. Powder 'n' wad 'n' everything come out so he had to put some new disks on the thing.

"I forgot how many grains of powder I had in it, but it went thirteen hundred feet a second! That's real slow for the speed of a bullet nowadays, but it was just travelin' right along for a couple of years ago."

Monty told us that the bore on a flintlock "wore out real fast because black powder had saltpeter, sulfur, and charcoal in it. After it was fired, the gun had a residue that collected moisture and rusted real fast.

"Water will absorb that stuff a lot quicker then any kind of a gun oil or anything, and hot water will absorb it all the quicker. So I just pour hot water through it and let it come out the flash hole. I clean it off with water and then dry it and oil it."

"Flash in the pan" isn't the only expression that has come out of gunmaking, Monty told us. "A saying that got its beginning from gunmaking is 'lock, stock, and barrel.' This meant that a person made the whole gun, lock, stock, and barrel, instead of buying some of the parts and making the rest.

"The English made some of the best flintlocks in the world. Their test was to load the gun, put the powder in the pan, and then hold it bottom side up and see if she'd fire.

"If it fired bottom side up, then it was a good flintlock, because the powder was all in the air when it ignited. But most of 'em wouldn't fire bottom side up."

Monty told us a story to illustrate the value of old guns. "A lawyer down in Connecticut bought a house, and while he was pokin' around in the attic he saw a box with a gun in it. When he opened it up, there was a Parker shotgun in it. He didn't know much about guns, so he called a friend and told him he found a Parker shotgun in the attic of the house he bought.

"And this fella said, 'Well, what kind of a gun is it?' Does it have birds on the side, or dogs or quail or what's it got?' No, he said it wasn't that.

"He kept going through the grades of shotguns explaining the different grades, and finally the friend said, 'Well, there's only one left and it can't be that. Invincible.'

"'Yeah, that's what it says. It's marked right on it,' he replied. Last year the gun sold for $100,000 out in Chicago. So that was a pretty good buy the fella made on his house!"

As for making a flintlock, Monty summed it up this way: "Well, it's like knittin' an afghan or makin' a quilt. You start at one end and you keep on goin' until it's done."

Reid Chapman

*Story editing by Ernest Eaton, Regan
  McPhetres, Seth Hanson, Mark Serreze,
  Karen Eames, Kathy Giles, and Anne Pierter.*

Interviewing by all of us.

"Well I'll tell ya . . . it's just like when you do anything. Ya have a
feelin' when things is right and you go by the weather. You got a feelin'
what the weather's gonna be. I can't explain it to ya, that's the way I do
it.

"I've done it so long, all my life, so it's just naturally a feelin' come to
ya. You know how to do it some of the time, but the weather, ya can
never depend on the weather. That's why it's so interestin' to grow a
garden because it's a gamble.

"If it 'twas somethin' you manufactured, you'd know what it cost ya
and ya'd know all about it, but when ya plant a garden, the gamble in
life is so exciting when you win. Once in a while you get an awful kick,
and then if you don't win or get a good crop, there's that sad feelin', ah,
ya know ya licked . . . and ya always tryin' to lick the weather and the
bugs and everything.

"It's the gamble in life that helps make it so interestin' . . . I've made
a living, but I never made no big money. It was never money I was
after, I don't know. I liked what I was doin'. I dug in the dirt so much I
couldn't get away from it, but I've made a success in life, and enjoyed
people and got a big kick out of life."

It was an autumn day in Maine four years ago when we first heard
those words. Reid Chapman was standing in his corn field talking to

280. (*Photo by Jay York*)

four or five of us. His voice rang out across the clearing, up the rows of corn, down to the squash patch, and beyond to the potato field.

When he said he got an "awful kick" out of winning the gamble in life, it was like a shout of joy, and his blue eyes danced, the crinkles around them laughed, and his feet moved as he leaned toward us intently, almost on the point of doing a jig, it seemed. Before long he was singing. "Do you like to sing?" he asked two of the girls. "I do." And then with the warm September sun catching his blue eyes and their young blond heads, he took off his cap and sang, "I Love You Truly."

When he said, "If you don't win or get a good crop, there's that sad feelin', ah, ya know ya licked . . ." the vibrant voice dropped to a lower pitch, the blue eyes looked inward, the laugh lines mourned, he leaned on his hoe, and we could feel the full weight of blighted potatoes, unripened corn, and stunted squash.

Later he sat on the back of his old pickup truck and grew reflective, sharing with us what he had learned in almost eighty years of living. His voice softened and the blue eyes reached out to us: "Ya have to go through the sad and good part to get a kick out of life . . . take the good with the bad."

That was some day. A diamond of a day, a glowing synthesis of what life is all about, compressed into one brilliant translucent experience. You could live a lifetime and have one day like that and count yourself lucky.

Since then we have gone back again and again to see Reid. We have gone in the depths of winter when we sat around his kitchen table while he stoked the wood stove and told us hunting and fishing stories. We have gone in the spring to help him plant potatoes, and in the summer when he is busiest, always out in the field. One winter we took a large group of visiting students from northern Maine's potato land to see Reid. He loved it. He was waiting for us on his porch impishly ringing an old brass school bell. He had rigged a crude bleacher system with two long planks stretched across logs in his small kitchen. He gave us oranges, asked each one, "Who are you?" Then when he got us all straight in his mind, we talked about potatoes and people.

A newcomer to Reid might think that some lively blue-eyed elf had sprung up before him from a hidden hillock. His back is rounded with arthritis and his pants billow down his trunk and legs, jacked up by a pair of suspenders. His hands swell around the handle of a hoe like gnarled notches on a tree. On his tractor he's a cowboy, riding with his cap pushed jauntily to one side.

Reid is tough. Last year his tractor ran over him. "I was almost skwushed! You could hear me hollerin' all the way to Kennebunk [two miles]." The tractor had run over his chest, dragging him by his suspenders until it hit a tree. "I was a damn fool!" Three days later both Reid and the forty-year-old tractor were back out in the field again.

He's no saint. Many's the tale he's told us that began, "Well I was feelin' full of Old Ned one day and I . . ." He liked his liquor when he was younger, still does, but had to give it up years ago because he decided it was getting the best of him. He had an eye for "a kippy woman," and that he hasn't given up. "I love women," he says. "I love men, too." And then, "I love people.

"I ain't an all wonderful Christian, but I believe in God Almighty, and all the wonderful things. I've done a lot of things wrong, but I've enjoyed it and I've worked hard and I'd probably do the same damn thing again if I had to."

Over the years at one time or another, almost all of us have gone to see Reid. It's as if each new crop of students need to know him to reach fruition. For who can better understand the long slow maturation of humans and plants alike than a man who says about his garden, "The more you watch it, the more you'll love it, an' the better it will grow for ya."

—P.W.

Reid Chapman was 84 years old in May and he is still doing what he likes most . . . farming. He was born in Wethersfield, Connecticut, and grew up in the town of Rocky Hill with his parents and older brother. He went to school in a one-room schoolhouse with a big coal stove in the middle of the room.

"My mother and father come down here to Maine on vacation and I was sickly. I had what they call consumption. I was fifteen years old. Of course, my mother took me to a specialist. She was a woman doctor out in Farmington, and she said, 'If you don't get that boy out where there's pine trees, he'll die.' I heard it from behind this big curtain and I remember it as I grow old. Of course, there's big pine trees all around here. There is everywhere. I lived here for 69 years and I lived in Connecticut, on a beautiful farm down there."

He worked outdoors in the garden and grew up big and strong. "I grew up amongst farmers and my father was a swell gardener. I never made any money to speak of, but I made a living, and we lived beautifully. Eventually I married a good woman. She was a Scotch woman, her name was Calhoun. She was a smart woman. We disagreed once in a while, but we lived forty-six years together, and raised two kids, two girls.

"Sometimes there'll be a little argument, and in the Bible it says that the man is the boss. I never used to dictate too much. I never told my kids what they got to do. They chose their own life. I used to let my wife have plenty to say and let it go at that. I never wanted to make a slave out of her. She helped a lot and she could do almost anything. She was an awful good cook."

When he laughs and tells you he is 84, he makes it clear that his way of living must have had something to do with it. He says he has enjoyed three things in life: farming, fishing, and hunting. Farming always comes first.

Farming

"Well, I'll tell ya. You got to raise yourself a garden and you want to be doin' it all the time every day, and study it so to see if it wants something to eat. See if the bugs are eatin' it and see if the woodchucks are gettin' to it. The more you watch it, the more you'll love it and the better it will grow for ya.

"Well, I plant by the moon . . . when the moon is full. But it doesn't always work. Most generally if there's a full moon there's a frost with it . . . along May and sometimes into June. Sometimes the frost comes and kills everything whether there's a full moon or not.

"Weather is a tricky thing. A lot of people plant by the signs, and I don't know, I plant by the feelin' of it. I seem to know when to plant and when not to, but I get stuck sometimes. This year is a miserable one 'cause it rained every day for pretty near two months. Gosh, you couldn't plant 'cause you couldn't get on the ground. And then when you did plant it, it was so wet it didn't grow good. I kind of plant by the date and the weather, how it is, and guess at the rest of it.

"This is a hard place to plant up here in Maine anyway 'cause you've got such a short season. You only got . . . well you can't figure much on June. June you'll get a frost sometimes and it'll kill everything. Well, you've got July and August and ten days in September, 'bout fifteen in June. That makes it . . . well you ain't got three months to grow stuff. It makes it kinda hard.

"You plant so much, you have the weather and the bugs against ya and ya get a nice crop once in a few years—or get a nice crop once in ten years. You get an awful kick, and all the other time you have to have discouragement. You get so much discouragement, but the two go together. Ya have to go through the sad and good part to get a kick out of life . . . take the good with the bad.

"You've got to spray your vegetables. Ayuh, you've got to spray 'em. This organic farmin'—there's a lot of good stuff in it. In fact, I've been doin' it all my life.

"They claim not to use any commercial fertilizer. But you've got to have plant food and plant food is potash, super-phosphate, and nitrogen. Well if ya ain't got it in the soil you gotta put some in.

"You can't take and go out here and plant a garden on this stuff, on this ordinary stuff. Ya won't get nothing. If ya had it analyzed, they'd send it back an' tell ya you needed everything.

"But you have to build it up year after year. What builds it up is good old cow manure, or chicken manure. It is full of nitrogen, not much potash. It's full of ammonia and ammonia is nitrogen, it's a form of ni-

281. Reid and Kathy Giles of *Salt* (*Photo by Jay York*)

trogen. You put rotten stuff in and it's not good enough. I always plow in my leaves, lettuce, and corn stalks and that builds the soil year after year. It rots and makes the soil.

"Well, the organic gardeners say they won't use anything that's grown with commercial fertilizers. They claim that, but they sell grain that's raised on commercial fertilizer. Well, that's rotten stuff they put on the ground. It can't raise anything. It's raised by the mile out west, and it's all fertilizer grown. They sell it to ya at these stores and claim it's organic grown. Well, it's just a money-making scheme. You still need good soil to begin with and some good commercial fertilizer.

"They say not to use any sprays either . . . well there used to be enemy bugs that would eat bugs. There ain't enough of them now to kill all the bugs. This year was a tough year, because this year was cold and wet, and the bugs didn't hatch out until late. They hatched out late and when they hatched, we had all them damn bugs that we had never heard of before.

"So you see the idea? Then you had to spray everything. Well, now you see, vegetables are high priced. Now take this morning. The price of cabbage is five dollars a box in the wholesale market in Boston. It's because you can't spray cabbage good. It holds its poisons right in, the same with cauliflower, and a lot of other things just like lettuce. They have this chemical that works for four or five days and in seven days you can eat it. But who in heck wants to eat it? Even after seven days. So I don't dare use it on cabbage.

"But all our worms. We never used to have worms here in the north before. They've all come in from shippin' vegetables from the south up here. See the idea? Where it's hot they hatch out. Now we have everything here in the bug line to eat vegetables.

"Look at my cabbage out there. I couldn't raise cabbage all summer for the maggots et all the roots off. And you see it rained so much. You put stuff around the roots to kill the maggots an' the rain washes it away. An' you have to dope 'em all up again. An' butterflies hatched out and hung over the cabbage all summer long and laid eggs, and there's holes all through it, and ya can't spray that cabbage . . . I don't dare to. 'Cause I don't want to be eatin' it.

"There's nothin' I like better than a good cooked cabbage. I don't spray it. You can put salt and stuff like that on it. It don't kill 'em. It just hinders 'em, see. The cabbage is hard stuff to stick to. I generally put salt and lime and a little rotonone, which you can eat, but it will kill the bugs. I hate to use that even, but you have to do it sometimes. The best way to do it is to shake it out of the bag and it gets on the leaf. Well, you can stop some of 'em.

"I have to spray my corn . . . I have to spray every four or five days or I don't kill the bugs. There are three or four kinds of corn borers, ya know. It's got so you can't raise without doin' a lot of sprayin'.

"Another thing. Everybody's got so many cats. They catch a lot of birds . . . the birds catch a lot of bugs. And then came the borers. Borers first came from the south. The south is hotter. They have more bugs than we have up here. I've seen these fruit dealers, used to bring corn in when Maine wouldn't allow you to. You never heard of that did you? Well, they used to have a law in Maine you couldn't bring no corn in. On account of corn borers. Well, these big fruit dealers would pack it under their stuff when there used to be a full demand down there in Portsmouth. We didn't used to have any bugs here. All we had was potato bugs and that you could take care of pretty well."

One day we went to see Reid when he was digging potatoes. We asked him how he got them to grow so big.

"I fertilize 'em and spray 'em and get good seed. When they're blossomin', they're makin' little potatoes, and that's when they need a heck of a pile of water, thousands of gallons. Then the potatoes will grow. I sow a little 5–10–10 fertilizer to tune 'em up a little, and then you can grow the smoothest.

"Seaweed is a good fertilizer. It's got everything in it. It's got ammonia, nitrogen, super phosphate, and potash and zinc and everything else that the land is out of.

"Hey, look at these 'tatas, ain't they beautiful? I've sprayed these. Ain't they slick? I get a heck of a kick out of something like that.

"I liked to work and I still like to work. I used to have a lot of animals, you know. I used to have pigs and cows out here. I used to cut the grass over here and in the back field. I worked hard early in life. I didn't make much money, but I did something I liked. My brother used to call me a damn fool for workin' so hard."

When asked how he used to sell his vegetables, Reid replied, "Well, up here in Maine we couldn't sell much to stores 'cause there weren't many stores. Used to have to raise somethin' and go out and pick up a route. That's the way they used to do it all over the country. Sell your stuff. Pick up customers. And I sold stuff to Kennebunk Beach for, well I started up with an ol' horse and ended up with two trucks a day till the crash came.

"In sellin' and marketin' my stuff, I used to run two trucks to Kennebunk Beach there for pretty near thirty years. I had the same business in Sanford. If a fella got his peas before I did, I was tickled. He just beat me, that's all. There was one time I said to this fella, 'Let me up on that street, I can't sell nothin'. He had peas and cucumbers before I did. And he was a good sport, he swapped some of his peas for my beans or new potatoes or something. That's the way we got along. I always used to like to see everybody live.

"But I kept at it. I had a route in Sanford that I had to give up here just a few years ago. Beautiful people. Sanford was a great town, a little town back in the woods. It paid, the textile business paid. They paid better wages than any place in the country of their kind, and the people . . . you'd tap on their door and they'd holler 'Come in,' and it was certainly a great town. I sold a lot of stuff to a lot of nice people and made a livin' that way.

"Never made no big money because I couldn't have any help. But I scratched along, and here I am today.

"I've learned to talk because, I'll tell ya, I go away with a load of stuff and in them days people couldn't get enough talkin'. You didn't have to say nothin' and it's a funny thing. You start in on the end of your route to sell stuff and if somebody wanted celery or onions or potatoes pretty near every customer along the line would want them. Ain't that somethin'! And if two or three customers didn't want anythin' much, that's the way it would be all day. It's a funny thing.

"And most generally, you had to talk to come back with the money in your pocket. You had to talk hard, you had to talk a lot. Some days you had to, to get them to buy, but it would be a hot day in the summer and of course you had to sell stuff, but that's why I guess I talk so much.

"All my life I sold stuff [vegetables] to women. Rich, poor, and all kinds. To hold your business you've got to be a gentleman. Of course, when you first start doin' a business, you don't know anything about it. The customer is always right. Of course you let people come to your cart and paw all over your stuff, and they damage quite a lot. Well, I used to let them do that. I can't do that now, I'm getting too old. I can't take it. It's really a bit too much to holler at 'em to lay off it.

"I've got arthritis and it hits your weak spots. I used to go to these rubbin' doctors and they'd fix ya up. They don't rub ya anymore 'cause they're just damn lazy. They just give ya medicine and get money outa ya.

"I've seen all kinds of people and done business with them. There's some beautiful rich people and there's some stinkers. You always get ahold of a few of them, but you can't say nothin' back. There's only

282. "All my life I done business with women." (*Photo by Anne Pierter*)

three women in thirty years that I called anything. I lost my head. They was terrible. I would have a hundred and fifty dollars' worth of strawberries and raspberries, and it would be a hot day. There was one woman and she'd come out and paw around, and there would be three or four more people waitin' around to buy stuff. She'd pick them up and throw them back down. And you'd take 'em in the house, and she'd make you take them back. Tell you it was too high.

"Well, I swore at her. I won't tell you what I called her, but I guess I called her everything. I'd a thrown that woman in the ocean. My wife come along. She had one truck and I had the other. She got ahold of me and told me to stop it. She says, 'Well, you lost one customer.' I says, 'I hope to God I have.'

"There's another woman who used to come and bother me. She didn't buy nothin' and she found trouble with everything. She held me up when I was busy. I just didn't bother with her. She'd pick me up on the road, and I'd stop and tell her to get goin' or something. I don't know whether I told her she was no good or not.

"There was this very rich woman and she come from Worcester. 'Twas an awful hot day and she ordered some raspberries and currants. Currants and raspberries make the most wonderful jelly. I had 'em for her and I showed her the price. She said, 'I can get them up in Worcester two for a quarter.' 'Well then,' I said, 'why the hell don't you get 'em up in Worcester? Why don't you stay in Worcester?' She banged the window down and that was the end of her. You know, she got my goat. After she had ordered them, see. Well, she didn't come back the next year. I lost her, and I'm damn glad I did.

"I can tell you about a customer I sold to for almost forty years up in Sanford. I liked her and her husband, but I never liked to sell her anything. She picked everything all over and took the very best. I used to hide stuff sometimes, and she'd find it. She'd leave it for somebody else once in a while. This time she picked up some nice cucumbers. She used to come over at night about nine o'clock.

"The company didn't send me the right seed. They'd been sendin' me some punk seed. I was honest about it, and I told her they didn't send me the right seed. She fussed and fussed. It was dark and I was tired. I says, 'If you don't want 'em, don't keep handlin' 'em or you'll wear 'em all out.' Her husband says, 'Take 'em.' So she took them, and she didn't come back that year. And I'm glad she didn't. Now, I never lose trade, but she was hard to wait on.

"Next year, when the stuff started comin' in, they drove in. Her husband came out with his dog, he used to bring it down here and let it run. He said, 'Hi, Reid.' And I said, 'Hi.' Knowing people for forty years or more, you get to like 'em. She got out, and I had some cucumbers on the stand. Just the kind she liked. I didn't know she was comin'. She waited quite a while before she came over. She said, 'Hi, Reid. Can I have some of them cucumbers?' I says, 'Of course you can.' So she bought three or four dollars' worth and didn't pick quite so much. I can't take the gaff like I used to. I haven't got the patience.

"I had other jobs offered to me, but I stuck to farming. I couldn't get away from it. You can't get away from seein' things grow. You can never tell what you're going to get. There's always something new. You're still learning."

Fishing

"You couldn't get off the farm very well because I was tied down, but I got off a few times. I'll tell you a story about fishin'. I'm tellin' you the truth about everything as it's remembered, and I'm not makin' it up and I'm not exaggeratin' it.

"Most times you go fishin', you don't get anything. But once in a while you do. That's when you get a kick. Well, I sneaked away in the middle of May. That's when the fish really begin to bite. I didn't tell my wife. I didn't say nothin' and I slipped away. Of course we had cows and chickens and a lot of farm stuff, and my wife used to help in the work. She loved to go fishin'. I went over to Branch Brook. They didn't bite and I had a lot of work to do at the time, so I came back. When I came back my wife and daughter had slipped away. I had two trucks then, and they went fishin' 'cause they had an idea that I slipped away.

"Well, my wife got a nice bite and a nice fish. She kept backin' up. My wife backed right up into a deep hole and went down over head. My daughter was quite a good-sized girl by then, and she pulled and tugged and got her out. When she came home, I happened to come around and I saw something that looked like a muskrat runnin' into the house. See, her clothes were all wet," Reid laughed. "I didn't say nothin' and of course my daughter told me about it. She got ahold of roots and things and she got her by the hair. She probably would have drowned if my daughter wasn't there to pull her out. So that ended that fishin' day.

"I had a chum, he's dead now, by the name of Stuart Ashton. He came down one snowy day in the wintertime and he said, 'Chappy, let's go ice fishin'. Can't you make it today?' I could, and all I needed to do was catch some tommy cods or shiners to use as bait. Stuart had all the rigging in his car—an old Chevy. He had a canvas and hatchets and chisels and all the stuff we needed to build a fire.

"We went two or three miles up to a place we used to go. I guess it would be Alewive Pond. We set the traps and started a fire. We always had something to eat like hamburger or deer meat, and we had a teapot. We took turns tendin' the traps. We would cook and eat and we always had a jug of cider or a pint of gin or whiskey. We was happy. We was all cozy, and we had a canvas so the snow wasn't on us.

"Stuart was a rather long-legged guy and I was short legged. A flag would spring up [when the fish was caught] and he'd say to me, 'It's your turn, Chappy. Run, you short-legged son of a bitch, and get it!' Another flag would go up and he'd be fryin' some hamburger and I'd say to him, 'Stuart, flag's up. Run, you long-legged bastard!'

"We was havin' a good time there one day, and you could smell that hamburger. Most generally we had hamburger and onions. We were up at Long Pond. We were cookin' this hamburger and onions when all of a sudden, we looked around in back of us and there were these two damned nice women. We spoke to 'em and said, 'Where do you skirts [women] come from?' They said, 'We smelled onions cookin' and we told our husbands up the pond there, that we was comin' down to see where the onions was.' So we cooked 'em a sandwich, and I guess we gave 'em a drink. It wasn't long before their husbands came down. That's what happens when you're cookin'. Lots of times the game wardens would come down and smell the onions out half a mile, cookin'.

283. "Want to hear another free fish story?"

"Do you want to hear another free fish story? Harry Davis said to me, 'Would you like to have some fun? I have a pond over this way, a little swamp pond.' There was a punt that leaked. We let it soak. It commenced to soak up and we started to fish out of this punt. Harry started first. The thing kept leakin' and I kept bailin'. And he commenced to catch trout. Oh, they were about eight inches long. I imagine it was a stock pond and they multiply fast. The water was in there [the punt] and he'd throw 'em in, and they swam all around our feet. They were still alive. Finally he said to me, 'I'm damn sick and tired of catchin' trout!'

"He wanted me to try it so I commenced to pull 'em in, and he started bailin'. I don't know how many trout we had, but we had an awful mess. Seven to nine inches long and beautiful trout. Just as fast as we could pull 'em in. When we came home we had plenty of fish. That's a fish story, and it's true.

"Byron Gooch and I was great friends. [Byron ran the local fish market.] He always had quite a bit of liquor in his office. I was drinkin' then, and he'd always give me a drink. Well, I knew this colored chef. His name was Gilbert Hamilton. Gilbert was a nice man, a good Christian. He was a friend of Byron's and a friend of mine for years. Gilbert would like to fish down where Byron throws the old guts and things down through the hole [in the fish market into the river after fish had been cleaned to sell]. Catch those little smelts or something. And in the fall of the year when the season was over, we used to go down there. Byron would set out a couple of pints of whiskey out there, and we'd set and fish through that hole.

"We were outside fishing one day [next to the fish market]. We'd catch 'em and throw most of 'em over for the sea gulls. Byron would pass out a drink every little while out the window. Gilbert wasn't supposed to drink. He'd say, 'No, my doctor says I can't drink.' But every time Byron would pass out a drink, he'd reach up and get it. We was feelin' good and along come this man with a nice little boy. The man says, 'What are you catchin'?' I was full o' hell and I said, 'Mountain trout.' Gee those smelts were swell eatin'. Gilbert says, 'Why in hell did you want to tell them we were catchin' mountain trout?' The kid went out and he bought a line and he started catchin' mountain trout.

"That was just one little thing that happened. There was this lady, a kippy little woman, and she was goin' into the fish market. And I said, 'Hey, lady! Want a bunch of flowers?' She was a cute little thing. She stood there for a minute or two and looked me all over. And I was gettin' a heck of a kick out of it. And she said, 'You sellin' em?' I says, 'No, givin' 'em away.' That stunned her then for a minute. So she kept comin' nearer and I was all in overhauls and dirt. They were a nice

284. Reid with his forty-year-old tractor. (*Photo by Anne Gorham*)

bunch of flowers. She didn't know what to say and I happened to think, 'I gotta think of something quick to tell her.' So I says, 'They're compliments of the fish market.' So she took them and thanked me. And she went in and she said to Byron, she says, 'Thank you for these beautiful flowers.' So I went in around the back door. Byron and I was always raisin' the devil. He was wise, he'd seen me out there. And he said, 'What in hell will you think of next?'

"I was peddling vegetables over to the beach for thirty-odd years. And if I had corn, I knew Byron liked it, I'd dump some on his truck, especially if I had some left over. Or shell beans or string beans or cabbage or any damn thing. I'd see his fish truck go around and I'd throw something on. That's way back when they peddled ice. Pete Nedeau was the ice man. And Byron asked Pete, 'Who the hell was puttin' vegetables on my truck?' 'Well,' Pete said, 'I think it's Chapman.' Well the first damn thing I knew, I got fish on my truck. Big halibut, well mostly swordfish and haddock. Big rolls of fish. We never said nothin' about it. Ha! We'd talk, but we never mentioned it. We went on for years doin' the same damn thing.

"Bert Spiller, he's dead now. Nice guy. We used to swap everything the same way. If I had something he wanted, he never paid me [for the vegetables], and if he had something I wanted, I never paid him. I used to go down there and plant with him. Help him plant. He was an older man. And we raised the darndest crops down in the Intervale [road] there."

Hunting

"When we lived down in Connecticut when I was a boy, all we heard about was goin' down to Maine and goin' deer huntin'. And there were the partridges. They were thick and the rabbits were thick. You'd go out in the woods and 'twould be just like hens out there, you know. Shoot all kinds. We loved the outdoors and the pine trees.

"I'll tell you a deer story, you want to hear it?"

Reid sat down on the back of his truck and we gathered around him while he recalled the adventure.

"I met this old fella, a nice fella, and I was goin to buy some chickens. It was up by where he used to live. He says, 'Let's go and see if we can see some deer comin' back.' So, on the way back on the truck

285.   "You can't live alone. You've got to mix with people a lot, get amongst all kinds." (*Photo by Jay York*)

we went down this back road. We had two or three hundred pounds of pullets in the back, and it was always a hard job. Well, we see all kinds of deer, four or five on the way back. So that give me the fever.

"We were there about a week or two afterwards and there were deer all over the place. It was a game preserve and we didn't know it—there was no sign. And I wouldn't have been there for all the money in the world. But there was no signs and I was packin' this old .32–40 rifle that my father used to have.

"I was goin' across these plains and this other fella is about two hundred yards away. And I see this damn head stick out from this little bunch of oaks. Honest, it was a fourteen-point buck. So I thought, 'We got to be careful not to shoot each other. Especially on these plains with these little clumps of oaks.' And this is what went through my mind. 'Hell, there ain't nobody there, there ain't nobody in that direction.' And I pulled that gun up, it had a white sight on it this old .32–40, and I got my sight right on his neck. The neck's a great place to shoot a deer. I snapped off the trigger and he went around, rolled around, and laid down. Of course, I stuck him [stabbed him] and he was beautiful. He was fat. I said, 'There's probably a doe in there.' The gun was a repeater so I jammed another shot in and that doe went out of there [the clump of oaks] like a streak of lightning. I popped a shot at her and her tail went down and she went right over to where the other fella was, and he shot at her and chased her for a half a mile on those plains. He got her, but she was all shot up and she wasn't worth nothin'.

"Well, I got the buck home and I hung him in the barn on a pulley. That's the way we used to keep 'em. We used to tie the hide around them in the winter. I tried to give this buck away, 'cause generally an old buck won't eat good.

"Well, one day I was out sawin' wood and I come home to dinner and my wife had this damn nice piece of steak cooked there. I said, 'Where did you get the meat?' She says, 'Down to the store in Kennebunk.' Actually, she went out and let the pulley down and cut a steak off that buck. I didn't know it was deer meat. It tasted just like steak. And I'm going to tell you, that buck, I never had any deer meat so good. Now, generally deer meat has a taste of its own. But he had fat on him real thick. He'd been eatin' acorns. They're just like grain to a deer. But that deer et so good that I gave some away.

"I'll tell you another one. I know this fella by the name of Lester Pike. Every Saturday afternoon he'd come through here and take his hound dogs and hunt rabbit. And the rabbits was thick. They had great big long legs. In the wintertime it was a big sport, and people would hunt them in the snow.

"The rabbits would walk a regular path. You would walk along and the dogs would chase them. And he'd come up every Saturday with his gun over his back, with the rabbits all tied together, three or four of 'em. They used to eat 'em, they're nice eatin'. Sometimes he might shoot a partridge. Then he might do what I used to do.

"I had an old one-lunger shotgun that I used to carry through the woods to Sanford. I've shot deer with it. I used to shoot deer with a ball in it. Well, partridge would be on the stone walls. I'd shoot two or three goin' up and two or three comin' back. Then in my back field I might shoot a woodcock or somethin'. In three or four days, when I had enough, I'd skin 'em all out. Then we'd have what we called a game pie. There would be woodcock, rabbit, squirrel, partridge, and occasionally a pheasant in it. Everything was blended in together. When I was off sellin' stuff, my wife would say, 'Come home early, don't be too late, cause I'm gonna have game pie for supper.' She'd make it in a pan like a big baking pan. I'd be home early. If a customer wanted four or five dollars' worth of stuff, I'd say, 'The hell with you, I'm goin' off to supper.'

"I love this country. And to have had the head of it be in such a jam just makes me disgusted. It's a darn poor thing for these kids to come into.

"Everyone's after the thirty-five-cent dollar. And when they got that, they ain't got nothin', have they? I always say a little prayer for the President because he's got a big job. I'm a Republican, but I say it for the Democrats too. And I always say it for him."

Then Reid asked *us* some questions. We talked about religion. "Do you go to church on Sunday?"

"Every Sunday."

"What church?"

"Saint Monica's." (The local Catholic church.)

"Oh, ya? Well keep it up. It's all heading for the right place, whether you're Catholic or Protestant. Do you read the Bible? I don't know much about it. It's quite interestin'. I read it a little. There's two gates. There's a lot goin' through the left-hand one, and there ain't nobody goin' through the right-hand one. Ya know what I mean? God will let you do all those things, but He's got your number all the time. Don't worry about that."

Havin' a Good Time

Reid began to share some of his adventures at the fairs with us. "When I used to go to the fairs years ago, you'd meet a lot of folks that you know. I used to like to bet on the horse races. I'd go as high as fifteen or twenty dollars. You had a good time doin' it and it's pretty reasonable. I generally break about even, betting on the horse races. I remember one time I was up in Fryeburg. I was talkin' to someone there, watchin' the horses race up and down before they start. The woman I got talkin' to, she was a horse woman. Of course, we had two or three drinks amongst our friends, and we was just feelin' good, you know. She said, 'That little mare might come in first place.' I had a lucky feelin' and I said to myself, 'I'm goin' to buy ten tickets on her to place.' I rushed out and got my ten dollars in just as the bell rang, and they were off. I went back to where the horse race was and my son-in-law come, an awful nice guy. He said he was listenin' to what that woman and I was talkin' about.

" 'Did you bet on that mare, that little one?' he asked.

"I said, 'Yes, I have these two tickets for five dollars in my hand.'

" 'Well,' he said, 'she just placed.'

" 'Well, that's what I bought,' I said.

"There were two New Hampshire policemen there and I was feelin' good. He told me she just placed and I jumped into the air. I jumped right up by the police. I came down and those guys started to laugh. They knew I had had a bomb or two. My son-in-law looked at my tickets. 'Hey, they paid eight dollars and something cents for a ticket.' So I made forty some dollars, didn't I? You know, you have to have a lot of fun when you have the day off. Course you get a kick when you win something. There's a sad feelin' when you lose."

We asked Reid what he liked best at the fairs.

"Everything. There's the hoochie coochie shows. You know what them are. Stripteasers, is that it? Well, they have one place where you go and pay a dollar and these stripteasers dance around a pole. Then they charge you another dollar and you go into another room. They're stark naked and they dance around a pole. Some of these fairs don't let them do it, but I guess most of them do.

"I'll tell you where I get a kick is seein' a girl and a fella next to a box and peekin' around a corner. They don't want anybody to see them lookin' at these three or four girls [stripteasers] trying to get a crowd. I get a little pair of spy glasses, and I watch 'em. I get a heck of a kick watchin' them, and they don't want anybody to see them.

"I like cattle pullin', I like the horse racin'. I ain't so much for the faker stuff, these guys where you gamble money and take chances. I ain't so much on that. I would never play poker 'cause I never liked to take a poor man's money. If I did, I gave it back to him. Once in a while if I was out huntin' or fishin', I'd do it just to be a sport. But I never gambled much, and I was never much for stealin' stuff.

"I was pretty square cornered. I told the truth to all my customers.

Whenever anybody told me they had a bad head of lettuce or a bad peck of potatoes or a bad chicken—I've dressed thousands of chickens and sold them at the beach—I'd pull right in my pocket and give their money back. That's the way I always done business. But I had a good time at the fair. When you go anywhere, you go to have a good time.

"I remember the World's Fair in 1933. That was in Chicago. I had a heck of a time, I went with a nice man by the name of Paul Russell. We went on an excursion on a train. It was like a convention of all farmers and teachers. It was an awful long train. There were six hundred people on it. We went and looked at Niagara Falls on the way down. In the morning we went across on the train and traveled all day through the rolling plains of Canada. It got kind of boring after a while, you know just riding.

"Well, I was raisin' hell with this girl, a nice red-haired girl. She was up in front of me and I kept pullin' her hair. She had two aunts, and she was from Cape Cod. There was another girl that had two aunts and she was playin' the accordion. I grabbed her and we sat for about half

286. "The more you watch it, the more you'll love it, and the better it will grow for ya." (*Photo by Jay York*)

an hour. She used to live where I used to live in Connecticut, and so we got acquainted. She started playin' her accordion so I danced down the aisle. Then everybody started to dance. We was havin' a good time, then. How do you like the story so far?"

The train coming back from the World's Fair left the group at Detroit, where they took a ferry across Lake Erie. "I asked this woman [the one from Connecticut] comin' back on the boat if she wanted to go outside and sit in the trough where you could look around and see the different lights. It was a great big boat. She says, 'Can my aunts come, too?' 'No,' I said, 'three's a crowd.' So she went off. So I met the woman from Cape Cod. She lied to me, I know. She was full o' hell. She was married and she said she wasn't. I says, 'Hey, you want to go out on the trough?' She says, 'Can my aunts come, too?' I said, 'No. Two's company, three's a crowd.' So then the other girl come back alone—the first one. She says, 'Let's go!'

"We went out there an' it was kinda dusky. We'd been there maybe ten minutes and out come this second one, and she said, 'Oh, there you are!' She turned and switched herself around and went in."

After going across the lake on the ferry, the group picked up a train that brought them back east. "Comin' home on the train, they ganged up on me. They wanted me to play cards. This gal from Cape Cod, she had some great big fat aunts. Great big tubbas. We got to playin' cards and they grabbed me. Them big women pushed me down and tickled me. And the only way I could get up was to tickle their legs. They had me right down on the floor. It was quite a mess, you know, but they were smotherin' me. Paul is there sittin' across the way, and he's laughin' till he's cryin' with tears runnin' down his face. Well, I went to have a good time. And I had it."

We talked about other things, and then Reid glanced off into the woods. "I've still got an old work wagon in there, one that the old smithy made. It's going to pieces in the woods now. A good blacksmith could make a beautiful carriage or a nice work wagon. Oh, them nice wheels and they'd chuck and chuck, ya know. Everything was done by horse, an' farmers made a good livin' in those days, some of them.

"I feel sorry for you kids in this respect. You don't know what a good sleigh ride with a skippy little horse is like, you know what I mean? You know what an automobile ride is, which is nice. But a sleigh ride with a robe over ya and a nice skippy little horse to trot along snappy, and with the bells around you . . . jingle bells. They used to use them all winter ya know, 'cause they didn't have lights like they do now. And you could hear those bells, ya knew somebody was comin', see. That is a beautiful ride with a horse that'll snap right along. Everybody had a driving horse in those days. They'd raise their own horse, and have a colt every two or three years for power.

"Here's something I am going to tell ya. You get in a sleigh with those jingle bells an' a whole mess of bells around a horse—a nice little horse that'll step along—and get your girl and give her a ride. Oh, we used to have an ol' bear fur robe. You used to put it over ya, an' get all dressed up against the cold. It's a pretty slick ride. Now, I'm tellin' ya, I feel sorry for the young folks that ain't had it.

"What we used to do, some of us, we'd take a horse out and drive him out through the countryside with the sleigh. And we'd stop him and give him his dinner, feed him some hay or give him a bag of grain. Or perhaps we'd go fishin' there, and he'd be used to stoppin' there. It was a place he would remember.

"I'm comin' to somethin' now. Well, we'd have a girl at night, a nice crispy night probably twenty or ten or around zero, an' snappin' right along when you'd come to this place. First thing you know, this horse would zag right in an' stop, and come right over where you had fed him. Well, of course, that's what you wanted him to do. And that would give you a little chance to park awhile. That's some of the things we done in those days.

"I used to drink and I used to smoke. I didn't until I was in my twenties. I used to swear and I used to chew tobaccy. I've made a hell of a lot of mistakes, but you have to make some mistakes to learn somethin'. But if you make too big ones . . . that's when I start to worry about the young folks. They make too big ones and they're licked.

"Of course, I'm old-fashioned and it's hard for me to turn to the new. I like new ideas, but some of them I can't go along with. You get more out of life by livin' it. You can't live alone, you've got to mix with people a lot. Get amongst all kinds of people. Rich, poor, and all kinds. You'll find nice stuff amongst the whole of them. Everybody's got a fault. Everybody's tempted. You've got to stand on your own two feet when you're tempted if you want to live a half-decent life. I hate to see people dishonest and tell lies. I like the truth. I've lied, everybody's lied. I think the Bible says all men are liars. I ain't a wonderful Christian, but I believe in the God Almighty and all the wonderful things. I believe in the Savior. You've got to believe in something and have faith in order to get anywhere. Of course, I'm preachin' a sermon now, ain't I?

"I wanted to be a minister when I was young but I could never lead a life good enough. I dug in the dirt so much I couldn't get away from it. I've made a success out of life. I never made any big money, but I made a good life, and enjoyed people and got a kick out of life. I'm on the end now, down to 84 years old. Yeah, what else do you want?"

Barns and Barn Raising

Story by Lyman Page

Interviewing:
  Emily Howes
  Lyman Page
  Anne Pierter
  Nancy Beal
  Herbert Baum III

"YEARS AGO ALMOST EVERYBODY HAD A BARN"

"You ever hear tell of a barn raisin'? They get the whole neighborhood together and have a picnic. Then they make the sections right down on the ground. That's where the barn raisin' came in.

"They peg them right down on the ground. Then you bring one section up. Takes plenty of help. Then you bring up another section and peg them together with cross sections."

Lester Wildes, a long-time dweller in the Kennebunkport area, was sharing his knowledge of Maine barns with us. Since we've started our interviewing, we've come to appreciate the barns in our area even more. Many barn owners in the Kennebunks were willing to talk to us about their barns.

Bob Bartlett, who once owned and operated one of the major saw-

287.   (*Photo by Carl Young*)

mills in the area, told us, "Now years back, there was a man in town called Ren Grant. Ren would be a nickname. He built this barn here; most of your barns were built by carpenters.

"Way, way back, a man had—most every farm had—hired help that they hired for a dollar a day, or seven dollars a month and your board and something like that. You'd live at the place, so if a fellow had that much know-how, why he built barns; he built his own barn.

"I've heard them telling about leveling a barn up. They'd take a basin and fill it full of water, and to level a sill they sit this basin on top and fill it full of water; and they would lift the side of the timber up until the water in the basin was level.

"They didn't have the tools. All they had was a hammer, saw, and adz. To level anything, they'd use a basin of water. Some of these old timbers were terrific. They take 'em and a man with an adz would take and straddle that timber, and he'd cut some off, and he could make a timber pretty square. There would be little notches in it where the adz hit it. They did a lot of work; labor was nothing when you hire a man for five to ten dollars a month."

Barn Architecture

New England barns were connected to the house, mostly for convenience, Mr. Wildes told us. "You didn't have to go out if you didn't want to in the wintertime," he explained.

"Well, there's a lot of 'em like mine [barns connected with the house]," said Mr. Bartlett. "That was, a lot of the barns were years ago.

"Not too many barns being built anymore, and those that are now, are built back of the house to keep the smell away. But barns built years back here—so hell, you went out to feed your cattle and you didn't have to go out of doors to get to them.

"You'd go out through your buildings. You didn't go outdoors. If your barn and house weren't connected, you put on boots and heavy jackets to go out into the horse barn or cow barn and when they were connected together you just threw on a jacket and a pair of slippers or shoes and just went out through. You didn't have to wade in the snow."

"Well, now that is a New England feature, I'd say," Elinor Nedeau told us when we asked about attached barns. "And, out in the Middle West, well, the people from there think it's so funny because no barns were attached to the house [in the Middle West]. In fact, most of them were across the road. Course that's fire protection.

288. Earl Bibber's connected barn. (*Photo by Carl Young*)

"That's done in lots of places, actually. But around this area most of the barns are attached to the houses.

"It's a great convenience. You didn't have to go out in the cold. Years ago we didn't have heated houses. We had nothing but stoves. When we moved into this house, there was nothing but stoves. We had no furnace.

"It's cold and nasty, and you've got six or eight cows and a horse, too, that you've got to go out into the cold and you've got to walk, say a quarter of a mile, to a barn that's way out in back somewhere. It's quite something. Of course, there is a greater danger of fire. And hay is combustible, of course. It's still a great danger."

Earl Bibber, who had a tunnel connecting his house and barn, told us, "The tunnel was not an unusual feature in this area of New England where they had hard weather in the wintertime. It was very easy for them to go from one building to another through tunnels or runways between, and they didn't have to go outdoors to feed their cattle or things like that."

In Kennebunkport, Mrs. Cecil Benson said, "We had a shed between our house and our barn, but we tore it down. It was a way of getting into the barn without having to go outdoors."

Her husband added, "Some of the barns, they had a big connecting L and in the connecting L was the milk room and the wood room. Years ago they had to have quite a lot of wood. They had a wood shed, that's what they called it, and they had a place for their equipment and wagons."

If you take a look around now, you'll find a number of barns that aren't connected. Upon inquiry of the owners, we found that one of two things had happened. Either the barns had once been connected to the house years back and had been rebuilt apart from the house later (which mostly happened) or the barn and house were connected by an underground passage (which was more unusual).

Several people talked to us about the roof line of Maine barns. "I'll tell you a little bit about my own barn," said Mrs. Nedeau. "It was built around the turn of the century, so you see it's really not too old. It may seem old to you, but it's not really.

"Well, it's unique in a way because of its roof. It has a Mansard roof which matches the house. That's a French word. I don't know what it means, but you can look it up." Well, we looked it up, and it a type of roof frequently used by a sixteenth-century French architect named François Mansard. "The barn's unique in that it matches the house.

"Now if you notice, most barns have pitched roofs regardless of what the house is like. Most of them had no particular architectural features for beauty. This barn, you see, is really an addition to the property.

289. Elinor Nedeau's Mansard roof. (*Photo by Carl Young*)

290. A 45° pitch roof. (*Photo by Lyman Page*)

"And, of course, it's upheld. It's not upheld by the foundations. That sounds sort of silly, but it's upheld by the roof. Now I can't explain that to you, but it has four iron rods. They go from the roof right down through. It holds the barn up because my foundation is so bad. When the contractors were here two years ago, they went over this barn and they said, 'Well, you don't have to worry about the foundation. This barn is upheld by the roof.' "

When we asked Lester Wildes what type of roof he had, his answer was, "I really don't know. I think it's a 45 [degree angle]. I don't know. It has a steep pitch.

"I think the old people were smart building them like that. The more pitch you've got, the longer the shingles will last because the water drains off. It doesn't drain off if you've got a flat roof."

In our area, there are four major divisions of barn roofs. There is the gambrel roof, in which there is a large attic area. There is the Mansard roof (or Mansard-shaped) which, in many cases, was used as an aristocratic status symbol. There is a hip roof, which has fantastic ventilating qualities if it has a cupola on top, because in the summer, when the cupola is open, the hot air rushes right out. Then there is the common peaked roof which is probably used so much because it is easy to build.

"The roofs, years ago, most of them were put on with wooden shingles," Mr. Bartlett told us. "I can remember back when I was a boy we used to buy cedar shingles. They came from northern Maine and the

291. Gambrel roof (*Photo by Carl Young*)

292. Hip roof.

southern part of Canada. We used to sell carloads of the things. Everybody used wood. Wooden shingles are dangerous. You get a spark, if you've got a fireplace—that's how so many houses burned—you get a chimney fire and the sparks come down on the roof."

Years ago the boards in the barn roof ran from the ridge pole down to the eaves, Mr. Wildes told us. That way if you got a leak at one end of the barn the water wouldn't run along the boards and drop at the other end of the barn. Instead it would just run right off. "I could stand in my barn and see daylight in a hundred places, but it never leaked," he said.

Then he went on to tell us about the shingles. "Down East, north of Lewiston, they use cedar shingles. Cedar is your best wood. Up here we use pine, anything we can get our hands on. Bartlett's sawmill had a shingle mill."

Many barns had a cupola which was used for ventilation purposes. In the winter the farmer would somehow close off the cupola so that the hot air would stay inside the barn. If a barn didn't have a cupola, it most likely had holes drilled in the side or in the peak, or it had some ornamental design cut out.

In many of the barns we saw, there was a special set of windows over the doorway. "Those lights going all the way across the barn door," Lester Wildes said. "You can't buy them anymore." The windows are an unmistakable characteristic of some of the barns in our area.

293. "Course, the old barns years ago were boarded up and down." (*Photo by Carl Young*)

Construction

The boards on the sides of the old barns ran up and down so you wouldn't have to put shingles over them, Mr. Wildes told us. The water would just run right into the ground.

"Course the old barns years ago were boarded up and down," Mr. Bartlett said. "That was way, way back. The modern way is crossways. On the old barns they used wide boards, run 'em in the ground straight up. They'd glue them right together once they'd put on what they call a batten. It'd be an inch- to maybe three-inch-wide piece right over that crack. That kept the weather from blowing rain through.

"When they put a board on it they put it tight. The sun would shrink it an eighth of an inch or maybe a quarter of an inch over that, so when it rains against that the water will run down. It won't go through. It keeps the wind out."

We asked a number of people where the wood comes from and what type one would use when constructing a barn. Mr. Bibber said, "I would say most of it came from this area. It is spruce." Mr. Wildes told us that most people used whatever they could get. He said that there were advantages and disadvantages to different types. He said, "Hemlock and spruce, once you put a nail in them you'll never get it out."

Since Bob Bartlett had owned a sawmill, we thought he would be an excellent person to ask about wood. "Well, I guess your code calls now for spruce, hemlock, or fir," he said. "But all your old buildings back, years back, the framework was all pine. When I was in the lumber business, pine was the thing, an' I think they're making a big mistake [now that it's not being used as much] 'cause it's one of the best materials, best woods to stand weather and moisture. You can take a piece of pine, you can take a piece of spruce, hemlock, and put 'em all together where there's moisture and that piece of pine will be there, and the spruce and the hemlock will be rotted out; but spruce and hemlock have more spring.

"We don't have that much oak that grows around here. There's some along on the seacoast, you get it, but you don't find too much oak. Oak is so heavy they would never use oak unless they had to, and once a piece of oak is dried, it's a tricky job to drive a nail into it, bend them more than anything. It's a hard wood, a rugged wood. I don't know, if you boarded a roof with oak and then tried to shingle it, I don't believe you could do it. The nail would bend right over. Oak stands up pretty well, although there's nothing that will stand up like cedar; it will outstand anything. And I really think pine will withstand moisture longer than oak."

There are a number of different ways people connected their beams. Lester Wildes told us they were mortised, and Bob Bartlett explained how that was done. "In the old barns they'd use pegs. They put the beams together—bore a hole. They'd cut out a square place, and the timber would fit into that. They'd take piece of inch material and put the two together like that. They'd just drive it right through, and that was two pieces right togetherr with a pin through it so it couldn't pull out."

Ernest Savignano, an antique dealer in Kennebunkport, showed us the way his barn was constructed. He pointed out an unusual way of connecting the beams and eaves. "That's a staple," he said, "except that it's eight inches across and six inches deep. It's just a staple, that's what it is. See the way that's joined in there? That's where it takes all the stress and strain."

Cecil Benson pointed to the timbers in his barn. "They cut the stuff and make the splices and pull them [the timbers] together with a trunnel. You know what a trunnel is, don't you? It's a wooden peg about a foot long."

Most of the foundations in our area were made of big granite blocks secured from now-defunct granite quarries.

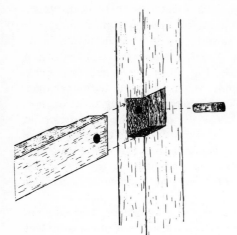

294. Mortising in. (*Sketch by Regan McPhetres*)

295. Another way of mortising in. (*Sketch by Regan McPhetres*)

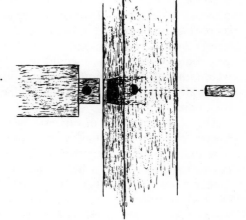

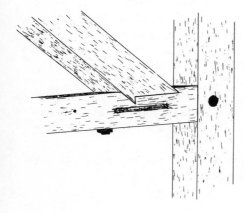

296. "That's a staple, except it's eight inches across and six inches deep." (*Sketch by Regan McPhetres*)

"The foundation of this barn," Mr. Bibber told us, "is of heavy fourteen- to eighteen-inch granite blocks. The blocks could have been brought in here from the quarries by oxen. There's a quarry right over here in Arundel. Many of the homes in the area are built with a foundation of large granite blocks."

We saw many barns that had granite foundation blocks with a length of seven or eight feet and a height of three or four feet.

Many barns had trap doors where they could shove the horse or cow dressing—better known as the manure. The dressing pile would grow pretty large during the winter and then when the spring came, the farmer had all of his fertilizer. Mr. Benson told us, "In some barns, the farmers, they used to have the skuttle, they used to call it. It would be a trap door. They put the dressing in and it would go downstairs and they hauled it out in the spring." Bob Bartlett said, "Some of 'em had the trap doors behind the horses, some had leantos, and some just went out in the open."

We were told some stories about a normally overlooked feature of many barns. Although most of the attached barns now tend to be painted the same color as the house—white, yellow, federal gold, or gray—red used to be the predominant color.

"Years and years ago," Lester Wildes told us, "red paint was the cheapest thing you could buy. Everybody used it for protection. I've heard several stories about it. In one of the stories, I heard about a salesman coming down the state of Maine selling red paint to everybody from York County on up. I guess it's a good color."

Bob Bartlett said, "It's because it was the cheapest paint. Back years ago red paint was just red lead, that's all. They mixed oil with it, and I

297. Special set of windows over barn door are characteristic of barns in our area. (*Photo by Carl Young*)

suppose that was one of the cheapest things they could use. I suppose that is why they used red. It goes right into the wood, and I don't know what it takes to get it out. But I judge that the reason everything was painted is 'cause it was the cheapest way to make paint."

We found that there were three different ways that barns were laid out. They either had three floors, two floors, or just one floor. All three had their own advantages. It just depended on how many barnable possessions you had, and whether your barn was a farming barn, a carriage barn, or a half-farming half-carriage barn.

Earl Bibber told us about the divisions of his carriage barn. The interior of the barn on the first floor is in three sections. One was known as the harness and grain room, another portion was known as the animal area, where they kept horses and a few cows; then the big area was the wagon area. This barn is a little bit different than the standard farm barn in that this was used principally by a family who had horses as a mode of transportation but not work horses.

The second story of the barn was for hay storage. It could be dropped to the first floor for feed. Also, there were shoots that go clear

298. (*Photo by Lyman Page*)

299. Many of the barns had manure doors. (*Photo by Jay York*)

to the basement of the barn. This way they could easily get food down to the cellar animals.

Mrs. Nedeau's barn was also divided into three parts. The cellar was used for the cows that were kept there. The first floor had a harness room and plenty of room for carriages. Then the loft, or third section, was used for hay storage.

Lester Wildes told us that in most of the New England barns cattle were put on the south or southeastern side, and they would stack the hay up on the north or northwestern sides in bags. This way the hay would act as insulation from the cold northerly winds during the winter.

"Over the horses there was a scaffold," Bob Bartlett said, "but the other half of the barn was just space, and then they just piled the hay up as high as it would go." When we asked him about the loft or second stories in barns, he replied, "Well, they did that 'cause they wanted to use the lower space for maybe wagons or machinery or something like that. They had what they called a loft or scaffolding up maybe seven or eight feet, and the hay was on top of that. Ordinarily, the barn had one side that was for cattle, and on the opposite side the hay was right down to the floor."

Then he told us how he used his barn. "This barn of mine, I can remember when that was a hundred feet long and solid full of horses. We used to use all horses. Course we were in the lumber business, and we had about four or five double pairs, two or three single horses, and a couple of cows. Then the barn burnt in '27 and burnt 'em all up. My grandfather bought some more. Then, when I got the place here in '32 I changed over to trucks. I kept one pair of horses until World War II.

"I never had any horses since. You'd get up in the night and hear kicking and banging. A horse has got colic or something and you have to get a syringe and give him a shot or something for the stomach-ache. That's all right for some people, but I've had my share of it.

"We used to have one box stall in case we had a sick horse. Ordinarily they were just tied up in stalls. I remember there was a partition, oh, probably six or seven feet long and I guess they were roughly four or five feet wide, and the horse went in and there was a big crib in the front end of it with a chain to hook him on and a door in front of that where you put the hay and the grain in. And when he came in at night he'd go into his stall and you'd hook him up and he'd stay there 'til morning.

"If a horse was sick, something like that, you'd put him in the box stall, but we never, hardly ever, used a box stall for the simple reason if a horse got real sick, chances are he died, and if he only had a stomach-ache, you could give him a shot of 'Humphre's FF' we used to call it, just like when you've got a stomach-ache, you take some peppermint."

When we asked Bob Bartlett about everybody having barns, he replied:

"Well, you know, if you get back of 1930, practically everybody had a horse or a couple of driving horses. Therefore, they had a barn. For a couple of horses, they had to put hay in the barn for the year, and that's the reason for all these houses having barns."

A MAINE BARN RAISIN'

by Anne Gorham, Anne Pierter, and Mark Emerson

"Does anyone have any questions on what's going to happen?"

"Ya, I know, I know. Lots of questions, lots of questions. Wrap it around the beams. Your job is to hold it. Take the rope and wrap it around."

300.   (*Photo by Anne Gorham*)

"Ya, you've got to foot it. Let's go. Altogether, one, two, three, UUGGHH! Slow now, anyone straining? O.K. we're going to walk down there slow. Easy, easy, hold it right there."

"Hold it right there, hold it right where?"

301. "Ya, you've got to foot it. Let's go." (*Photo by Anne Pierter*)

"Get the pikes in place. Keep her going up. All right, get your foot out of there."

"This is something else."

"We're doing good. We need a little on the other end."

"Put your pike right here. Pull on the ropes. Jab that pike right in there."

"Wait a minute, Stacy."

"Actually, he's gotten a little carried away. I got it right here, Stacy. We got it."

"This is going to go up just like the other one."

"Bring the bottom over this way, ya. You can push that post that way can't you? Push the main upright that way to get it in, then bring it back. I think it's about right. Can't you push that?"

"Have to go way to hell up. Push the post up."

"Let's get the pikes on there to lift it up there, whoa."

The other day we went to a barn raisin' at Stacy Wentworth's. The barn which has been in Stacy's family for five generations was dismantled and moved from its original site near Kennebunk Beach to his

302.

303.

304.

OCEAN SIDE

←ROAD   MARSH→

NOTHING   50 X   40 X   40 X   30 X   30 X   20 X   20 X   10 X
NONE   NONE   NONE   NAILED   ROTTEN

TOWN SIDE

←MARSH   ROAD→

NAILED
1TX   2TX   2TX   3TX   3TX   4TX   4TX   5TX   6TX   6T   7TX   8TX
NAILED   ROTTEN   ROTTEN

305. This sketch was made by Tommy Wentworth when the barn was dismantled. Stacy Wentworth said, "While the building set down there [Kennebunk Beach] we labeled everything east and west, and then the town side and ocean side." Because of the condition of the wood and the size of the barn, they shortened it from seventy feet to fifty feet in length.

farm in Arundel. When we arrived early that morning a few people were already at work assembling the first side.

Stacy explained that years ago "There would be a master barn builder in each area fairly close—within probably a sixty, eighty-mile radius—that had a crew go around doing barns. You'd tell him what size barn you wanted. That's why you get into different styles of barns in this area. They'd cut a tree down; they'd hew it right there and they'd make all the pieces and then lug 'em to the barn site. Then the family would get together their friends and they would put it up."

306. Lugging the plate to the center of the barn floor so the uprights and braces can be fitted. (*Photo by Anne Gorham*)

307. Fitting the corner upright into the plate. (*Photo by Anne Gorham*)

308. Close-up of a corner joint showing original peg hole. (*Photo by Mark Emerson*)

309. Tommy Wentworth redrilling a peg hole through the plate and upright. (*Photo by Anne Gorham*)

310. The oak pegs, most of which were about 1¼″ × 1¼″ × 9″, were first pointed at one end with a hatchet. (Size pictured here is 3″ × 3″ × 9″.) The pegs were then driven through a series of holes in an iron bar until they became the size needed. (*Photos by Mark Emerson*)

311. Pegging a beam with a beetle. (*Photo by Mark Emerson*)

The Barn's History

"My uncle [Ed Wentworth] got that part of the property [the original site of the barn near Kennebunk Beach] when my grandfather died. I'm not sure just how the property was split up, but my uncle got the farmland, and he's always farmed there ever since. My father got the hotel, The Wentworth.

"A couple of men at the Beach [the Coles] went in together and bought the property, some land next to the Wentworth Hotel. The barn set in the right of way to the property. In other words, the Wentworth Hotel was on one side which was sold to the Wallace Jack family, and then on the other side was what used to be the original homestead of my great-great-grandparents, who came in 1803. The only entrance to the property was right through the barn. The Coles and their partners didn't want the barn. Originally, I guess Art Hendricks was gonna take it down, and either rebuild or just use the timbers. Then he died, so they were left with the barn and nothin' to do with it. And they put an ad in the *Wall Street Journal* to sell it. My mother works for the Richard Cole family and she heard they wanted to sell the barn. I called them up and made an offer to take the barn down and bulldoze the cellar hole in and smooth it off. And they thought that over for a week or so, and finally they said yes, they'd like that. This was August, and they gave me to the following April to get it cleaned up. It would be three years last April that the barn has been down.

"There was a lot of hay and just an assortment of junk that accumulates in barns, so we kind of pecked away at it through the winter. We used to go over Sundays, and I put a little wood stove in one corner. We took the family over there, and we finally got it all cleaned out along about the end of February, I guess. And then around the middle of March we started right in, full steam ahead. Tommy Wentworth, Peter Sargent, my brother-in-law, and myself, the four of us. It took us about a month or five weeks to get it down and get it over here [to Stacy's farm in Arundel]. When I got it over here, I was originally planning to put it back up that fall, only put it up at ground level. And one thing or another, we just didn't get to it, which I'm glad because that winter I began thinking more and more about what we were doing out here and our needs for a barn. It became apparent we weren't gonna

312. Stacy Wentworth. (*Photo by Anne Gorham*)

313. The barn at original site. (*Photo by Gillet Page*)

314. The foundation of the barn. (*Photo by Mark Ruest*)

have as much space as we needed. So I began thinking about putting a foundation up like we have now.

"I just saw so many beautiful foundations and the way they did things, it just seemed to make sense to build the foundation up in the air, and build a couple of earthen ramps. Really get the use of that space. So last fall we went ahead, Peter Sargent, Tommy, and then a fellow who had been camping on the property that summer. He kind of wanted to exchange camping space for labor, and he helped us do the foundation. My back gave out about one third of the way around." Tommy Wentworth said, "It took three or four weeks, about a week each side." Stacy continued, "And those guys finished it, did a remarkable job. We got the granite from the local quarry which was nice. Many of the old barn foundations were from this quarry up here in Arundel.

"So then we got the foundation and we thinned out our pine grove out here [in back of his house] which isn't much, and we bought the rest of the timber to do the barn floor, about eleven thousand feet of lumber in the floor. We got that all done and *still* couldn't see our way clear to be able to do all the repair work and have a raisin' before winter. And of course, laying in the field for two years, the weather did take an awful toll on the timbers. But it came through, and we had enough wood so we didn't have to buy any new wood for the frame. We had enough out of the twenty extra feet that I took off the barn 'cause the barn originally was seventy feet long."

We asked Stacy what kind of roof was on the barn. "Most of your barns in this area have what they call a gambrel roof, that's the one I have to work with. Later—in the middle of the 1800s—they began putting on a Mansard roof. On the original barn roof was a cupola which Stacy plans to put on their barn. He explains, "Course the major purpose of the cupola is for ventilation, putting freshly cut hay in, you get so much heat. It's an awful expense to put on the cupola. It's just one more place it leaks, and so a lot of farmers say no.

"I really expected to find a date on the barn. I've done a lot of carpentry in the area, and frequently I find a date some place on the building. It's the habit of every carpenter to always write something. And I've carried that on. I always write under cabinet bases and any place that's going to be undisturbed for a long time. Well it's fun. We never found a date on it. The cupola had some dates. Lots of initials and we're gonna put the boards back up in this cupola. I think the oldest date we found there was 1888 or 1887, but we know it's older than that."

315.   To help guide the upright into place, a small board was nailed to the sill. Originally, the uprights had 2″×6″ tongues which fit into mortise holes in the sill. Stacy explained, "The reason I didn't take a saw or a chisel and chisel the holes in the floor was that I decided I was getting cramped for time. I had all this wood [parts of the side] over the deck and to mark precisely where those mortise holes were would have been a two- or three-day job. So now I'll just put on a three-quarter-inch railing around."

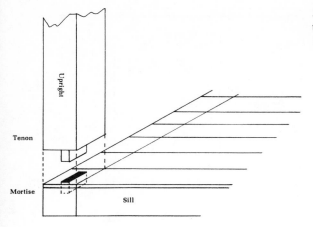

316. Stacy would have preferred taking the time to mortise in the sill. (*Diagram by Anne Gorham*)

317. Tommy knocks the upright in place with the commander, a large beetle. (*Photo by Mark Emerson*)

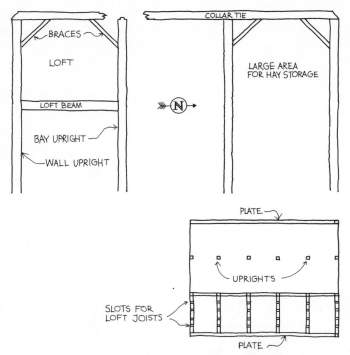

BRACES

LOFT

LOFT BEAM

BAY UPRIGHT

WALL UPRIGHT

N

COLLAR TIE

LARGE AREA
FOR HAY STORAGE

PLATE

UPRIGHTS

SLOTS FOR
LOFT JOISTS

PLATE

318. Diagram of bays (front and top view).

319. The bays are lifted upright into place and then pegged. This photo shows the erected bays. (*Photo by Jeff Bonney*)

320. The sides are then pulled together so the collar tie will fit on the corner upright. The first collar tie is being fitted on upright and brace. (*Photo by Mark Emerson*)

321. Using a block and tackle and pike poles, the men hoisted the second collar tie in place. After that was done, everyone broke for lunch. (*Photo by Mark Emerson*)

322.   "The people who have a barn raising generally provide most of the food, which we did. We had a turkey and five watermelons and tons of potato salad. All the usual things. And everybody who comes brings something to add to it."

323.   . . . and the kids went swimming.

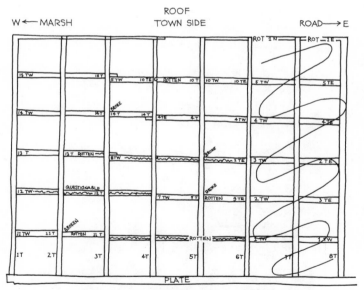

324.   Diagram of roof by Tommy Wentworth.

325. The roof was laid out on the barn floor a few weeks before the barn raising and remarked. "It might have been the ink faded over the years or something, anyways we lost probably eighty per cent of the markings. There were a couple of us working at least three weeks prior to the barn raisin' to remark it. And we used a different system, you know, anything that seemed to make sense. I painted 'em on and they stayed this time." (*Photo by Anne Gorham*)

326. Hoisting the first ridge beam. (*Photo by Mark Emerson*)

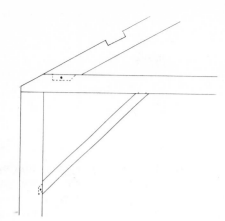

327. Diagram of rafter and collar tie. (*Diagram by Anne Gorham*)

328. Fitting the rafter into the collar tie. (*Photo by Anne Gorham*)

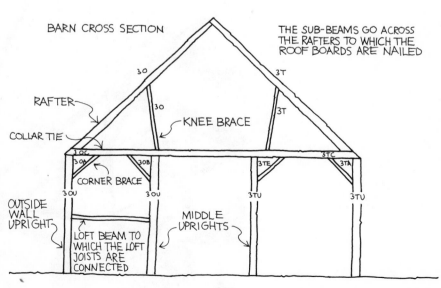

BARN CROSS SECTION

THE SUB-BEAMS GO ACROSS THE RAFTERS TO WHICH THE ROOF BOARDS ARE NAILED

RAFTER

COLLAR TIE

30

30

3T

3T

KNEE BRACE

3 OC

3 OB

30B

3TC

3TE

3TA

CORNER BRACE

3 OU

3 OU

3TU

3TU

OUTSIDE WALL UPRIGHT

MIDDLE UPRIGHTS

LOFT BEAM TO WHICH THE LOFT JOISTS ARE CONNECTED

329.

330. The first two rafters showing the slots where the subbeams will go. (*Photo by Anne Gorham*)

331. Connecting the two end rafters. (*Photo by Mark Emerson*)

332. Ed Loija using a pike pole to help guide the rafter. (*Photo by Anne Gorham*)

333. An honest to gosh OshKosh. Close-up of a pike pole made by OshKosh Tools. A pike pole is twelve to twenty feet long with a sharp iron attached to one end. It was used to help position the beams. (*Photo by Anne Gorham*)

334. After placing the subbeams, the rafters were pegged. Finally the ridge poles were placed. (*Photo by Jeff Bonney*)

335. Placing the ridge poles. (*Photo by Anne Gorham*)

336. Stacy thought the tradition of nailing the tree on the barn came from Norway. "I think it's just to signify the new growth of the barn." Stacy's son, Jason, added, "If that tree's for good luck, maybe some day we'll wake up and it will be shingled and boarded." (*Photo by Anne Gorham*)

337.

Self-sufficiency

A few days after the barn raisin', we asked Stacy what his plans were for the barn. Smiling, Stacy leaned back and said, "What we're doing is we're headed for self-sufficiency. This farm isn't going into the agribusiness. Baled hay is typical of a big farm, and we're headed the other way. We want to eventually have work horses, and that means we're gonna have to have hay for the animals. We'll probably cut the hay with the horses and haul the hay wagon and something that doesn't cost us a lot of money."

The barn is situated to take advantage of the sun during the long, cold, winter months. The sides face the points of a compass and the corners face northeast, southwest, etc. Lester Wildes told us that the cows were on the south or southwestern side and hay was stacked on the north or northeastern sides. This way the hay acted as insulation from the northerly winter winds.

"On the north wall I'm gonna have traditional board and batten [a thin, narrow strip of lumber used to seal or reinforce a joint]. I guess that will be the side that we'll store the grain and hay. And then on the ends, I think on the front end which would be the northeast or east side, I'll probably clapboard that and oil them, I guess, leave them natural. We have the original barn door, and we're going to paint a big mural on it. The west wall will be shingled, and the south wall will have animal stalls in it. My workshop will be on the third floor from the ground level. The basement area will be animals on the south side and animals on the first floor, and we may have my wife's pottery shop there." Stacy's wife, Marilyn added, "The south side since it has nourishing sun is going to be for animals and people all the way up, and the north side can store stuff."

Stacy continued, "And the second floor will be for my sons, and Tommy and myself—our workshop. We'll probably have some sort of insulation. I'm gonna put some solar panels on the roof and try to heat the workshops using the sun. There'll probably be some solvent antifreeze solution circulating through the panels that will go to probably stone or water. Heat that in the floor of the barn, the basement, keep the water warm, and I'll circulate in the areas to heat.

"In the northeast corner we're gonna have a big root cellar. In the northwest corner will be equipment storage. In the middle, where I have the door opening, will be the manure spreader. We'll just park that right down there and then fill it up, and either take the stuff directly to the fields or to a compost area."

"Pretty Damn Sound"

The beams in the barn are pine wood. "Ya, they're all pine. Probably cut right there [at the original barnsite]. What timbers in the barn that are sawn are from an up-and-down saw. From what I've read, you can usually tell the age by the regularity of the marks. If they're very regular, it means it probably was powered by something. If they're irregular, then it was maybe a pit saw where men sawed the timbers by hand. I have the feeling that most any wood if you take it and keep it dry and well ventilated, that you'll never have a problem with it in building. It's pretty damn sound you know, the timber is."

The floor of the barn was built with new pine. "I think we had dropped a beam from quite high at one point. Well it broke a couple holes in the floor without us noticing. With all the people jumping around up there some of the others [pine floor boards] let go, and it's a problem with pine. It doesn't have any elasticity really, it doesn't take shock, like a spruce will bend. A pine reaches a certain load limit and bang, it especially can't take a shock. So I've got to repair the new floor already.

"A building deteriorates much more rapidly when it's nailed together than when it's pegged. If you just keep a tight roof on these so that they don't let the moisture in, they'll go on forever. The timbers are big, but

338. "A building deteriorates much more rapidly when it's nailed together than when it's pegged. I think it's a beautiful way to build. It just allows for so much flexibility." (*Photo by Jeff Bonney*)

yet it's not holding up that much weight. The roof is steep-pitched so it won't get the snow load that a shallower pitch ranch-type house will get. The snow won't stay very long. And the way that it's structured, each stress point has got a brace there and the rafter mid-point has got that knee brace which is letting that load go down through the knee brace, down through the post, to the post underneath the barn. So the weight is just transferred perfectly right to the ground.

"I think it's a beautiful way to build. It just allows for so much flexibility. You can have so much more open space. After we took the barn down, I really got so interested in mortise and tenon that we built a house that way, Tommy and I. I'll never build anything different. You don't need a whole pile of two by fours to hold up the wall, your beam and post do it. I hope that more barns will begin to get built this way again. Not with hand-hewn timbers, but with sawn timbers and put together in that fashion.

"You know, two hundred years says something for pine."

Town Meetin'

by Valerie Gould
  and Anne Pierter

Photography by
  Seth M. Hanson II

"Any further questions? If not, all those in favor of this motion please manifest by raisin' your right hand, and those contrary minded? And by your vote you have so voted it, and I so declare it, and it will be so recorded."

And so ends another article of the annual Arundel town meeting. That snowy March evening, approximately 130 were present out of the 325 voters. Arundel is one of the smaller communities in southern Maine. We went there hoping to hear "old-time democracy" at work. When we left, we were far from disappointed.

"Town meetings, the way we have it, is one of the oldest and most democratic ways of living, because you have the final say. You vote, this is the way. You get up and the moderator will let you go on as long as you are keeping within the article that you are doing. But you're not supposed to be able to go on forever, like some of them do, because everybody there should be able to have their say."

Colonel George C. Martin, moderator of the Arundel town meeting summed up his feelings about town meetings just before he rapped the meeting to order. Because Colonel George earns his livelihood as a country auctioneer, he brings to town meeting the same brand of showmanship that he uses at an auction. However, beneath his jovial manner we found a strong belief in the importance of what happens at town meetings.

He seemed to be a good reflection of the attitudes of the crowd he

339.

moderated. They joked and exchanged light banter, but most of them carried well-thumbed copies of the proposed articles with pencils or pens ready to figure or make notes. It was clear they had come primed to say their piece.

"Mr. Moderator."

"Yes?"

"Henry Tilton."

"Yes, sir, Henry Tilton."

"I make a motion that the request and appropriation [for schools] be accepted as indicated—[the whole] $188,000."

"Motion has been made."

A lady from the back: "I'll second it."

"And it's been seconded. Been moved and seconded, $188,790.58. Now . . ."

"Mr. Moderator "

"Now, yes."

"Charles C."

"Now wait a minute, Mr. C., I mean Mr. Credit was ahead of you."

"Was he? O.K."

"Thank you."

"My name is Credit as you well know, and you think I'm a nuisance, but I got confused there a little bit. The appropriation [requested] is for $188,790.58 for the public schools, but the Budget Committee recommends $163,798.53. Now what does that mean? That they can run the schools for that amount? Why do they need $188,000?"

"Fine now, Mr. Credit, let us do this. Let us first ask the School Committee why they need $188,000; then we'll come back to the Budget Committee and why they cut it. So now, I'm gonna call on the school department to give their figures. As you go along, you may ask questions, but do it through the chair."

"Mr. Moderator."

"Yes, Mr. Tilton."

"I think that the motion has been made and seconded."

"That's right."

". . . for $188,000 to be accepted. I think that in view of the fact that I represent the school board, this is our approval, this is what we need. I think that I can testify this is the minimum for the school budget."

"Mr. Moderator."

"Wait a minute. Have you finished, Mr. Tilton?"

"Yes, I have."

Mr. C.: "Mr. Moderator, if you remember on the school budget last year, it went for about $132,000. Now that was what we were supposed

340.

to spend. Now it seems to me that we don't have anybody representing
the schools that has a check on it. Every year they're gaining on us. I
read that they overspent $29,000. Now who's responsible? Who's going
to pay for that, you and me?

"I'd like for them to have a business and run it the way they're running this town. There's none of them that gives a damn! [Sharp banging
of the gavel follows.] Pardon my English. They don't care about the
money, and they want you to listen to them, and they're telling you anything. If you're gullible to go for it, then you're wetting your voters in
and out. And you're voting them in, and boy you got a mess."

Moderator: "Now just a minute. Did he answer your question?"

Mr. C.: "What a mess, what a mess."

Mr. W.: "In the beginning of this article, ah, when you read this article . . ."

"What a mess."

Mr. W.: "You said we were gonna hear from the school board. How
come you slipped in a motion?"

Moderator: "What was that?"

"When you read this article, you said you were gonna call on the
school board."

"Right."

"How come you snuck in a motion there?"

"They have the right. You're supposed to have a motion, actually,
before you take any action."

"Why did you say you'd call on the school board?"

" 'Cause I thought we were gonna call on them."

"Well, he gets up and makes a motion."

Moderator: "Well, that's perfectly all right, perfectly all right because . . ."

Mr. W.: "Hit the gavel." (Gavel is struck.)

A man to the side asks, "Will you tell me the duties of these teachers'
aides, and tell me why do we need them? I think if we pay good money
for a teacher, we should have a teacher who can handle the children."

Moderator: "Question has been asked about why you need teachers'
aides."

Mr. C.: "We never had them in our schools. They'll put sixty children on a school bus, and they expect the driver to have complete control. And they'll take a course with thirty children in the classroom, and
they expect to have an aide to help them. Now it just doesn't make
sense."

Moderator: "Can anybody answer that question? Why they need
aides? Who wants to make the—Mr. Bernard?" (Mr. Bernard is the
superintendent of schools in Arundel.)

341.

Mr. Bernard: "In this particular school now, we have overcrowded classrooms, and we have more than thirty youngsters in a good per cent of the classrooms, approaching forty in some classrooms, and I guess there are forty in one or two. This is a way of compensating for the overcrowded conditions. If, at the point we have ample square footage or classroom space for a reasonable class size, probably we'd reach the point where we wouldn't need the teacher's aide. This is just another compensation if you will, of a way to give individual attention for what they need."

Mr. W.: "Don't you think that if the teachers had better control, we wouldn't have to have all this extra help? We could have more money to pay for new desks. We wouldn't have to have all those things. Why can't they take better care of the school? The desks—it's a shame that they can have children sitting in a place like that."

Mr. C.: "I agree with ya."

Mr. W.: "Why can't we get the government to give us better discipline, better aid?"

Mr. Bernard: "Well, I've just been with you a couple of months, sir, and we're working on it, believe me."

Mr. C.: "Well, you better do something."

Then the moderator recognizes Mr. Tilton. "Yeah, I'd like to make a couple of points here, and I think they might be pretty apropos. I hear Mr. C. and Mr. W. say a few things about the school and how it's run. They ask why we have teachers' aides, the conditions of the desks, and so on. We're asking for $188,000, and believe me, this is only *just* enough!"

Mr. C.: "Buster you!"

Mr. Tilton: "Let me say something else to that."

The moderator interrupts, saying, "Mr. W., sit down, please, 'cause Mr. Tilton has the floor."

Mr. C.: "Well, he's talking to him . . . he was talking to me, too."

Mr. Tilton: "How many times have you attended our school board meetings? We have them every month."

Mr. C.: "No, ah . . ."

Mr. Tilton: "They're open to the public."

Moderator: "Mr. C., sit down." (Banging of gavel.)

Mr. C.: "He's talking to me, yes, he is, ask him."

Moderator: "Sit down, Mr. C., or I'll move you out. Now, sit down."

Mr. Tilton: "If Mr. C. has suggestions, I don't think the town meeting on March 11th that comes once a year is the time to come and be critical of the school board. I think that we need—we open these to the public; we ask people to come. We have meetings after meetings and no one shows up—just a few. Not the people that are here complaining, but other people. Their suggestions would be more than welcome.

"And as I said, we are asking for $188,000 because we have given this hours and hours and hours of thought. And this is *just* enough. It

342.

isn't gonna give us any frills or improve a lot of things that need to be improved.

"We're very conscientious people. We've worked hard on this, and the one thing we've tried to do is to come up with a budget that is workable. We realize it costs money. We know a large percentage of the tax dollar goes for the schools, but we are placing our faith in the kids today. And these are the kids who are going to be our leaders of tomorrow.

"The town does not have a broad tax base. We realize how you people feel. I feel the same way and, believe it or not, I'm one of the largest tax payers in the town. Look it up in the book. I don't even have any children in school, and we have worked hard on this, and we're asking that it be accepted because we know that this is the bare minimum that we need to operate the schools for the coming year."

Applause follows accompanied with the banging of the gavel to restore order.

The debate continues for over an hour more. A man in the back asks for some figures to explain the debated proposal. A member of the budget committee goes through all the figures and explains which ones they propose to cut. A young woman in the back stands up and says, "Please speak up; we're having another meeting going on back here and we can't hear a thing." With a few sharp raps of the gavel, the moderator replies, "There'll only be one meeting in here, just *one!*" And the meeting continues.

A heated debate develops over two proposed cuts in the budget. After several minutes of discussion, the moderator brings order by saying, "Now, ladies and gentlemen, there is a motion. Motion has been made and seconded that the requested appropriation by the School Committee of $188,790.58 be accepted.

"There has, however, been an amendment of $164,910.87. Now, the amendment is to reduce it. You must vote on this amendment first, and if you down it, then, we'll have to go back and vote on the main motion. Any further questions? If not, all those in favor of the budget of $164,910.87, please raise your hand. And all those who are against it, please raise your hand, all those against it.

"Now, if we're gonna do it, we gotta do it, we're gettin' paid by the hour. There seems to be a little question of doubt. Neither one of us seems to agree, so I'm gonna do this. We must do it over again because I want it right, and I know you do. A motion has been made and seconded, and I lost the paper."

After things were straightened out, they voted again by standing to show their approval. After the votes were counted, those who disapproved stood up.

343.

344. The ballot clerks.

"Ladies and gentlemen, the return is, seventy-four for and forty-five against. You have voted for the amendment, and it automatically throws out the other thing."

They then continued to vote on the motion with the amended figure. It passed with a majority of ninety votes.

"Ladies and gentlemen, the ballot clerks with the town clerk find it hard to count and tally, which is an important thing. If there's no objection, I would like to declare that room across the way here as part of the town meeting. Is there any objections? All right, if not, all those in favor of letting me use the room across the way to count the ballots with the four ballot clerks and the town clerk, all in favor, please manifest by raising your right hand. Contrary minded? By your votes you have voted to let them. So, you go ahead, Ah, constable?"

A man in the front row asks, "Is this going to be under supervision?"

The moderator replies, "Yea, we have four lovely ballot clerks and we have the town clerk and we have a constable."

Mr. Credit replies, "The constable is also married to someone who's running on the ballot."

"That's true, Mr. Credit."

"You don't have to call me Mister, you know my name."

"I'll still call you Mr. Credit. Now. Mr. Credit, she is running unopposed, so I'm sure she is not gonna cheat herself."

"Why don't we declare fifteen minutes recess and let them count right here where we can see them."

Mr. C.: "I second the motion."

"Now wait a minute. We've already voted. Now, ladies and gentlemen, you have voted to do it there. Now, I know they're not going to make everyone happy, but this assembly has voted to let them go in there, and we're going to let them go because it was your vote to do it."

"We will now move on to Article Eighteen, we're half way through. To see what sum of money the town will vote to raise or appropriate for the town dump. The Budget Committee recommends—if you people that want to talk, why don't you go outside so the people can hear the warrant."

Mr. C.: "It's too cold."

"Why don't you keep your mouth shut? All right, the Budget Committee recommends $4,200. Now, what do you wish to do with this article? The chair waits your pleasure, and speak your mind."

Mr. B.: "Mr. Moderator."

"Yea, Mr. B."

"I'm curious now. I'm starting to wake up now, I slept all afternoon.

How much is going for the dump and how much is going for the Road Commissioner to clear that road?"

"Well, it says the town dump."

"What is the contract? Let's break it down, now."

Mr. Harris, a Selectman: "I move that we appropriate $4,200 to the town dump."

"Motion has been made to appropriate $4,200 for the town dump."

"Second it."

"And, I have it seconded. Now, it is open for questions, and can you answer Mr. B.'s question, please?"

"Mr. Moderator."

"No, I'm talking. Mr. B. has asked a question and we're going to try to answer it."

Mr. Harris explains the financial situation. He explains that the town needs money for the lease of the land and an additional sum to upgrade the road to the dump site. They then argue over the cost of the gravel for the road and the amount to be used. Mr. Harris goes on to explain the problems and needs of the dump such as vermin and rat control, resurfacing of the dump entrance and its accessibility to the townspeople.

"Any further questions?"

Mr. Credit asks why the town isn't willing to pay him $300 a year for the lease of his land, and they would pay $300 a month to someone else. He is reminded that the town voted down his proposal.

"Motion has been made and seconded for $4,200 for the town dump. All in favor, please manifest by raising your right hand. And those contrary minded? And by your votes, you have so voted to accept it. And I so declare it."

The time was fast approaching 11:30. We had been there since 7:30 and had experienced four hours of "Democracy in Action."

A few days after the Arundel Town Meeting, George Martin met with us to share his experiences moderating town meetings over the years. "You have to be a diplomat, lawyer, and somewhat of a ham," George said. "You have to keep them happy. They get mad, you know, and you have to smooth things over.

"Town Meetings can become very interesting. You always have the occasional groups or individuals who have been out and had a little tonic and been in the 'sausperilla'—sometimes they can become very disorderly, like this fella gets up in the Town Meeting and says, 'Mr. Moderator,' he says, 'we know we ought to build a new school,' but he says, 'I put a motion before you that we build the school out of the bricks of the old school, but under no consideration should you tear

345.

down the old school house until the new school is built.' That's how well off he was that day.

"So one day we're going to build a bridge across this stream. One man got up and said, 'Mr. Moderator, we don't need a bridge across this brook.'

" 'Why?' says the moderator.

" 'I've looked,' says the man.

" 'You're out of order,' says the moderator.

" 'I know I'm out of order. If I was in order, I couldn't hold this much rum.' So these are the way things are."

George told us how he began his long and colorful career as town meeting moderator. "So when I got back to what was then North Kennebunkport, which is now Arundel, I became their moderator, and at that time I was the youngest moderator in the state of Maine. I am now probably one of the ones who has done it the longest of anybody in York County. I've had over thirty years of experience and some very interesting stories.

"Now, years ago, we used to make it an all-day affair. When it come noon time, we would have a recess. The Grange or the Woman's Guild would sit down and they would have a big spread. DINNER! Of course, that was something for the Grange or Ladies Society. Then, they would pick up after dinner; they would get back into session again.

"All right now, for a meeting what do you have to do? You have to post a warrant, got to be posted on five different places, but be sure it's posted on the place where you are going to have the meeting. Just recently in York you read in the paper, they got up there and they called the meeting together. After the moderator was elected, he said, 'I'm sorry ladies and gentlemen, but we got to adjourn to another time,' because the meeting had only been advertised for six days. It has to be advertised seven days in advance.

"I guess you know that they were mad. They had an editorial in the paper about it. Kind of upset the dear old lady for a day. You know, she didn't know what she was going to do. She's been planning going to the town meeting, got there, and she only stayed about as long as they elected a moderator by secret ballot. Then, the moderator tells them that they have to go home. It just happened recently, so it wasn't a mistake that they made years ago because they do. That's why they have erasers on pencils. People make mistakes.

"How do these articles get into the warrant? Articles don't have to go into every problem. You may decide that you're going to fix the Smith property. You go out and you get ten names on the petition. Years ago, they didn't do this; years ago the selectman done it. Selectmen say what we need, the court sends them. Now, times have changed. You have today, project committees. If you're going to get things to go into the warrant, you've got to go out and get a petition.

"All right, so now we begin with the meeting. You've elected a moderator; then you go into article two. That's the one to open the polls of the day, to choose your municipal officers. The polls are open; it's up to you to choose a town clerk, selectman, assessors, and overseer of poor for three years' term.

"Now I say, 'What do you wish to do with this article? The chair waits your pleasure and please speak your mind.' Somebody gets up and moves that we proceed to ballot. 'Do I hear it seconded?' Then seconded. 'Any questions?'

"Then I open the ballot box and show it to everybody there, so that there's no doubt that it's already stuffed. See, that's what they call it. Years ago, they used to go up to the cemetery and pick out names. Of course, they didn't know that they voted, but they used to do this years ago. That's the old way of doing it, but times have changed, laws have changed, this is it. Now they count the ballots. They usually put them in a pile. Now you hope that they have as many ballots as they have checked off on the checklist. You don't have 460 ballots when you've only got 455 checked off. But as it's happened, we've always had it that way.

"So after they get done voting, you close the polls, and I always say this three times about two minutes of 7:00. I say [banging gavel] 'Anyone else wish to vote, anyone else wish to vote [bang], anyone else wish to vote?' [Bang.] You've called it three times. 'By your votes you have voted that your polls are closed at 7:00,' and poor John Brown is still on the floor coming through. It's too late, next time he'll get there on time."

Colonel Martin then went on to explain the voting procedure. "In a larger town there are two checklists, one for the women and one for the men. Giving your last name first and your first name last, you're checked off and handed a ballot. Then you go into a booth which has a specimen ballot to tell you who your candidates are. You go in and mark your ballot. You are checked off, and you drop it into the contribution box which is the ballot box, and walk out. You don't go back and socialize, you go out.

"Times have changed. Years ago, we used to wander around. I remember 'cause I used to do it. 'Hi, what are you going to do tomorrow?' Well, today they would have a sheriff on you now, escorting you out. Well, anyway, this is how it's done. The polls are closed and we go and say to the clerk, 'You count how many have voted.' You write the tally down, 455. We take the two checklists together and I come over here and I take the key to the ballot box.

"The moderator has the most power over anybody there that day. He has more power than selectmen, but he has great responsibility because he has the laws that govern him, too, and he can be fined. The fine is much more than the pay you get out of moderating, so you have to be careful.

"You go over, dump the ballots out of the box, turn to the town clerk and say, 'How do you find the ballot box?' 'I find it,' she says, 'I find it fair.' I turn it to the ballot clerk. I says, 'How do you find it?' Then I turn it to the people in the crowd, let them see, 'And I, too, find [bang] the ballot box fair.'

"While they're counting the ballots, you still go on with the regular order of business. Now for instance, Article Sixteen, to see if the town will vote or appropriate the sum of $2,100 for street electric lights for the town. 'What do you wish to do with the article? The chair waits your pleasure and speak your mind. Do I hear a motion? [Bang, bang.] Motion has been made. Do I hear it seconded? Seconded. All in favor please manifest by raising your right hand. Those contrary minded? By your vote you have so voted it. Sorry, you're a little late, sir. We're going to have street lights for the ensuing year.'

"This gives you an idea. All right now, we come to an article where there is going to be a little fire in their eyes. There's going to be a little controversy. So this is where you let the opposers of the article stand up and exhaust it out of their veins. Now we have here an article, it's a controversial one. Article Fifty-one, to see if the town will vote or appropriate to raise the sum of fifty thousand dollars for two fire trucks. One to be used at Blaisdell Corner, one to be used in East Lebanon.

We didn't want to get involved because the thing of it was we didn't want to get our houses burned. We wanted to leave it to the people. If the budget committee recommends they don't want to do it, well now, maybe we're not going to be doing our civic duty, but if we had a fire, they might forget to report it in, you know.

"So we kept quiet on it. This is a touchy thing. I say, 'Now ladies and gentlemen, we're going to hear from the proposers of this article.' After all, you've called the people here to hear it, the people who are interested. You don't want somebody to get up and move and postpone it and somebody second it. Then, maybe two weeks later, they have another town meeting. 'Let's hash it out here,' that's what I tell 'em. I said, 'I wish there's one thing that I want you to do. I want you to vote, each and every one of you. I don't care how you vote, that's your right and privilege but,' I said, 'I want to tell you one thing. When you're voting, I want you to know where that's coming from.' I said, 'You see that pocketbook? That's coming out of your pocketbook and don't you forget it.'

"He [proponent of the firetrucks] gets up and talks about why they

346. "You have to be a diplomat, lawyer, and somewhat of a ham. You have to keep them happy. They get mad, you know, an' you have to smooth things over."

need the firetrucks. He's told you why you need it, he's selling the town a bill of goods. That's what he's there for. Now I say, 'The chair waits your pleasure, speak your mind.' Naturally, one of the fellows who's interested says, 'I move a motion, Mr. Moderator.' He must address the chair, that's important. He can not speak, not until I've recognized him. 'Mr. Moderator.' 'Yes, Mr. Brown.' 'Well, I move that we accept this article.'

"Now, a couple of fellas get up, start in, don't even address the chair. Well, with a rap of the gavel [bang, bang], I say, 'Now you keep quiet!' If he carries on, the man can be removed from the auditorium, right out, and stays there until after the meeting, because he's disrupting it.

"The only thing that you can do is what you have told them in the warrant. All right, they've got in the warrant that they want to build a new school, but you and I have decided that we don't need a new school, we need a new town hall. They want a school, so they get up there and the moderator reads the article.

"You and I might get up there and say, 'Mr. Moderator, we don't need a school, we need a town hall!' I make a motion that we build a town hall. She seconds it, and right off the bat it's illegal anyway, because you haven't warned the town that you're going to build a town hall. You've told them that you want to build a school.

"The last thing legally now that comes before the meeting is the last article to adjourn which I don't let them do until Article Two, which is election of officers. I never let them close—if you can close the meeting while you're still having elections. You recess until a certain time.

"Then when they get done counting, you give the returns of the elections, which is Article Two. The moderator gives the returns. After each and every one of these are elected, they are sworn in. They have to take an oath which the moderator or town clerk does.

"I usually do it. I line 'em all right up. They hold up their hands and they repeat after me, 'I [the name and the office going into] do swear that I will uphold the Constitution of the United States.' After Article Two is taken care of, you now go through the last article.

"Now, you're ready to adjourn the meeting, but you may have a complaint. Someone says, 'Mr. Moderator, I would like to have the selectmen print the town reports in darker ink so I can read it better.' Well, O.K., that's a suggestion. He can take it or leave it because it isn't in the warrant saying that they could do it or that they have to do it. But, if it's in the warrant then, that they're going to have the town reports next year in red covers, then the town so voted, it better be in red covers!

"This is the way it is now. The last article is just a polite article to adjourn your meeting."

Stone Walls

Story by Mark Serreze

Interviewing by Mark Serreze,
  Jay York,
  Tim Good,
  and Karen Eames
Photography by Jay York,
  Mark Serreze,
  and James Jannetti

Robert Frost had a poem. The old fellow said that stone walls ought to keep something in. Frost said there ought to be some purpose to them. He said, "I can't see any purpose to this. A stone wall is here to keep the pine trees from eating my neighbors' apples."   —Harvey Bixby

> My apple trees will never get across
> And eat the cones under his pines, I tell him.
> He only says, "Good fences make good neighbors."
>   —Robert Frost

One autumn day we went to see Harvey Bixby, our school's recently retired librarian and long-time friend, to learn how to build stone walls. Harvey is a man of many skills. He has built his own house atop several acres of ledge in Cape Porpoise and filled it with furniture which he has either built or refinished himself. On the walls hang Harvey's paintings. Outside, his stone retaining walls outline terraced gardens he has created.

347.   (*Photo by James Jannetti*)

Many of the stones Harvey uses in building his walls come from the ledge beneath his house. He has taken more than a thousand wheelbarrows of stone out of his cellar, breaking them out by hand. Harvey told us that he learned masonry from his father, who in turn learned from Harvey's grandfather. Both men built stone walls on the farm in Massachusetts where Harvey grew up. Before he showed us how to build a stone wall, Harvey wanted to make sure we understood his interest in the subject. We gathered around his fireplace while he told us some history.

"It seems that stone walls have been with us for a long time. It isn't just a matter of piling one rock atop the other. Stones serve a great purpose for civilization. They have walled people out, and they have been used to build homes. Some of the most magnificent walls you've ever dreamed about are in South America. How could they ever cut them so close that you couldn't even get a piece of paper between the stones? That's a dry wall—without any mortar—that you can hardly pull the stones out of. Goodness knows how many years stone walls have been around, but they've been with us for a long time.

"Here in New England they used stone walls not so much to keep the Indians out or anything like that, but to keep cattle in or to keep cattle out. In the old days they walled in the gardens and let the cattle roam.

"In New England, which is largely rocky and hilly, they had all these stones. So, naturally, they wanted to clear the land. They simply moved the stones to the edge of the field. They used the stones for boundaries, they used them for enclosures, they used them for foundations under their houses, they used them for barn cellar walls, and they used them for sea walls.

"My grandfather, and men before him, spent time building those stone walls. Every family had someone in the family that was good at building stone walls. And they built them with a purpose."

Harvey explained that there are two types of stone walls, dry walls and masonry walls. A masonry wall is laid up with cement or mortar cement. A dry wall uses no adhesives to hold the stones, relying on the skill of the artisan in wedging the rocks together.

"Most of the old-timers used dry walls, and those walls have stood up for generations," Harvey told us. "All the walls at my home were dry walls, and they stood up for a hundred years or so. They were still up when the barn was torn down!"

We went outside to the back of Harvey's house, where we met Johnny Thompson, his friend and neighbor. Johnny helps Harvey whenever he needs to hoist a stone into place that is too big for one man to move.

The type of wall we learned about was the dry wall, which is most typical of New England. Harvey and Johnny began to tell us how it's done.

"You know, originally they just laid the stone walls over the ground as is. When you are simply moving the stones, such as clearing a field and finding a place to put the stones, that's one thing. This is probably why a lot of them you had to go over every year, replace loose or fallen stones. There are all kinds of things, as Robert Frost says, that don't like a wall. Something is always tearing it down, whether it's hunters, animals, or even frost.

"However, if you are laying up a dry wall and you want it to stay up, you might be a little cautious about what was underneath, whether you were over clay soil, ledge, or sandy soil.

"If you were over sandy soil, it wouldn't make too much difference. If you were over heavy clay soil, you might want to use loose rocks, called grout. You put these on the bottom. It might give a little drainage. I suppose if you really wanted to do a good job, you would probably dig down about a foot and put in a layer of loose rock. This will prevent heaving with the frost.

348. Harvey Bixby on the left, talking to his friend, Johnny Thompson. (*Photo by Jay York*)

"It all depended on the purpose of a wall. If you had a wall in a pasture, you wouldn't bother about putting anything under the rocks, you'd go up over ledges and everything else, you wouldn't bother too much about it liftin' a little bit, nor would you bother to try to face the rocks or get them even.

"If you are building over a ledge and over a fill [a soft space], a dry wall will have a little give to it, whereas if you build a masonry wall over a ledge and over a fill, you will probably have to put some kind of reinforcement underneath. That wall, if it settles over a fill area will probably crack, but with a loose wall you've got more give."

Harvey had his tools laid out in his wheelbarrow, and we asked if he would show us what they were used for.

"We do have some tools to work with, but not many. This is my stone hammer. It has square jaws and weighs four pounds. It was used primarily in granite quarries for trimming granite blocks. It can be used for trimming the edges of stones. It's sometimes called a 'triffle.'"

Harvey showed us another tool, a crowbar about five feet long, used for moving heavy stones into place. "You'd use a crowbar for moving rocks that are too heavy to move otherwise. Crowbars come in all different weights. A lot depends on your preference and the use.

"If you are doing real heavy work, you might prefer a bigger bar. With a longer bar you can get a bigger pry. You might have some that are slightly bent. I've got one that's about six or eight feet long. It has a curve in it. Well, with that curved bar, you can get a bigger pry. I've used it, but you have to be careful about the curve in it. If you don't get it absolutely right angles to your work, it will pull you right over.

"This is a sixteen-pound sledge hammer. It's got a fancy handle on it. It [the hammer] was made here in Kennebunkport. I couldn't get a handle to fit it, so I made one. A four-pound stone hammer will break

349. Tools Harvey uses are a pick, pry bar, sledge hammer, and shovel.

some stones, depending on how hard they are. A sledge hammer is for a rock that requires more severe blows.

"Here's the shovel. I use that if I want to loosen up the soil at the base of a wall, when I start to build it."

Choosing the right stone for the right spot in the stone wall is where the real artistry lies in building a stone wall. As Harvey began to work, he explained that he uses two kinds of stones—trap rock and granite.

"Trap rock is a fine-grained, dark-colored rock commonly found in New England. Granite is more coarse grained and has many colors. You've got different weights for different stones.

"When I take rocks out of the cellar, breaking them out, I'm really quarrying that rock. When you lay up a wall with quarried rocks that have been broken out of a ledge in a very informal way, as compared to cutting them in a quarry, it leaves a sharp edge on the rocks. Now, with

350. "Granite is coarse grained and has many colors." (*Photo by Jay York*)

351. Harvey picking out pieces of grout from his grout pile. (*Photo by Jay York*)

these edges you can lock rocks together. You'd be surprised. Even the top layers, if you sort of weave them in together, you'll think you can pick that rock up, but you can't. It's sort of locked in there.

"When you are building a wall, you always want to put your flat rocks aside, to use them as topping. You have a tendency to use them up. Then when you get to the top, you can't get a good level wall."

Harvey pointed to a pile of small stones. "See there? These are grout which I use for chinking up spaces or to keep a rock from rolling. Now if you have a stone that wobbles, then you put grout underneath and in back of the stones. That will begin to pick up the weight of the stone, and make that rock good and solid."

Harvey took some stones and started laying up a section of wall. We noticed he started with the corner, choosing stones with two flat sides. We asked why he started with the corner.

"You've got to have something on the end. If you had a pile of wood and you didn't have stakes or something, you wouldn't have anything to hold up the pile, see," he replied, explaining that it was the same with stones. "So you've got to sort of bind your corner in there, lock it in."

352. Harvey starts the wall by laying the corner stone. (*Photo by Jay York*)

353. The corner stone is now lev-
eled off by inserting a flat stone
under it.

After Harvey laid the first stone (the corner stone), he continued laying several stones on the bottom layer in a line even with one of the flat
surfaces of the corner stones. Then, using a second layer of stones and
grout when needed, he worked back toward the corner stone.

"If possible, you build away from the corners a little bit. Then you
can build into it and your rocks won't fall away from you.

"Now we're making around a corner. This one here is a square
corner. Now, I'm having trouble with these bottom rocks, but I'll take
this one here, set that on top, and it holds the corner in place.

"We've got a little wobble there. Jack that up and put a rock in back
like that. You see how that's sitting now? That's fine. You've got that
level, so we can put another stone in there, in this fashion, see. I break
that joint there."

We asked what he meant by breaking the joint. "Well, cross the joint
between two rocks," he said. "In other words, if I had put a rock in like
that [parallel with the face of the wall] this joint will be open. I really
close the joint, that's what I do."

354. Laying the bottom layer.

355. Grout is inserted underneath the stones to keep them from wobbling.

356. The completed corner.

"You don't lay 'em seam to seam," Johnny added. "You break up the joints." (See photo 356.)

By now Harvey was laying stones in two directions from the corner stones, picking up a stone, then walking the length of the bottom layers to see where it would fit best. We asked if he always worked the whole length of the wall simultaneously.

"That's right. So if a rock doesn't fit over there, it will fit here. In building walls, you've got a help if you're building a long wall against a short wall. When you're putting up a wall like that with a long run on it, you take and you look the whole length of it. If it won't fit here, try it over there.

"If you're building a short wall, you've got corners. If you are building a chimney, you pick all corner rocks if you can."

When laying a dry wall, you don't have to worry as much about the face of the wall as with a masonry wall, Harvey told us. "You just take them as they come. When you are doing a masonry wall, you will probably pick and choose rocks with the best faces.

"Usually, people laying a dry wall aren't too particular about having a square or flat face. They don't care if it sticks out a little bit. As a matter of fact, a lot of people prefer to have that wall very rough. When you're laying up this type of wall, you are not too particular to have joints even, you know, the same distance. You leave irregular holes or spaces in between your rocks," and these are chinked with grout.

"Regardless of how well you lay up a dry wall, you have to go over it every few years because people and frost and water put pressure on it. Especially kiddos. They love to walk on a wall and they loosen it up. So you have to go over it. I spoke to you about using grout to chink the rocks up. Well, that grout will sometimes slip out a little bit, so you have to force it back in.

"A lot depends on whether you have a free-standing wall, that's a wall with a double face, or a single-faced retaining wall that's built into a bank. You have to lock a free-standing wall in from both sides. If you have those walls too narrow, they'd just fall down. In other words about sixteen inches would be right. In some cases the rocks might be too large, or you might have to have it wider. If it's a dry stone wall without any mortar, you've got to make it wide enough so that it won't tip over on you."

To build a stone retaining wall, "the more irregular the wall is in the rear, the better that wall will stay in there. Against a bank you might slope your wall inward a little bit. That will keep it from heaving out.

"You fill in the back of the wall with loose rocks, grout, and earth. That would give pretty good drainage. If you use soil in back of a stone wall, and you should take that wall down after a number of years, you'd find that the stones had almost consolidated with the earth. That earth would sort of stick to them. It would hold."

Harvey had a big stone he wanted to lift into place about midway up one section of the retaining wall. For this he needed Johnny's help. "That rock there probably weighs four or five hundred pounds. We're going to roll that stone up here on these planks, and then we jack the rock up. Johnny and I have done this many times. Roll it along, and then we take crowbars and we slide it into place with a crowbar. Now if we didn't get that stone up there, where we wanted it, then we'd tilt it and put a piece of stone under the crowbar. Then we get a little pry and lift it up higher and put another stone on top of that—in other words, sort of jack it up."

Sliding the big stone into place, Harvey said, "You got to play every rock differently because of the balance of the rock, the shape of it, and what you're trying to do." The large stone seemed unstable to Harvey

357. "We're going to roll that stone up here on these planks and then jack it up."

and he wedged a medium-sized stone beneath it on one side and a smaller stone toward the center, "The frost action will move those small rocks, won't it, Johnny? But it won't move the larger one sitting on top of it."

We began to realize that our ideas about stone walls were all wrong. We had thought that a well built stone wall was a wall that didn't move, something solid, unchanging. Now we understood that a wall must move, and that a good craftsman like Harvey builds his wall so that it will move the way he wants it to.

"Now when you get a rock like that in place," Harvey continued, "you do something to make a top on here, depending on how high you want this." He laid some flat stones on top, using grout between the topping and the big stone.

"This is all done by eye. This wall, see I didn't use a string or anything. I just laid it up by eye, and sometimes by curses," Harvey laughed.

358. Jacking up the rock and putting grout underneath.

359. The large stones are topped with flat rock with grout in between to keep them from rocking.

"That goes with it," Johnny agreed.

If Harvey had a stone that wouldn't fit in a wall, he might have to trim it. We asked him if he could show us how it's done.

"When you do stonework, you try to avoid scarring. Some of these stone walls on these big estates are all trimmed and fitted. They did a lot of trimming. More than we would bother with. We want it natural. I knew some people, if you ever laid a chimney for them and you showed a scratch in the face of a rock, they'd shoot ya."

Harvey took his stone hammer and started hitting a nearby stone lightly.

"You set up a stress with light strokes. After you do that several times, you just give it a tap and it will break. The fracture will be on the stress point you set up. You can throw a stone in a fire and it will crack, because it sets up a stress. It's like breaking a cake of ice. What you do is you take an ice pick and sort of marking and tapping, you set up a stress. You just go back and forth a couple of times and then give it a tap and it will break.

"A good stonemason tries to avoid breaking rocks. See, when you fracture rocks, you get a fresh surface. You want to try to keep the weathered look to your wall. When you are laying up a dry wall, even a masonry wall, you bang those rocks around and you leave white scars. So the best thing to do is to avoid trimming." And the way to avoid trimming, Harvey explained, is to keep looking until you find a stone that fits. "That's what an old-timer would do."

But stones aren't as plentiful as when the old-timers were around, according to Harvey, making it necessary to trim stones sometimes.

"An expert will pick up a rock and look at it. He will see by turning it three or four ways how it will fit. I've seen people pick up a stone and throw it back down when all they needed to do was turn the face of it and it would fit in."

Some of the stones that Harvey uses are field stones, shaped by time and the elements. But most of the stones come from the ledge in his cellar, shaped by his chisel. He invited us down and showed us how he would break them out.

"I start with a half-inch cold chisel to get into a seam. A seam is just a crack. It's where the two pieces come together. I can see a seam here. You take a cold chisel and you have to be careful, because it's hardened steel. You'll hit it and it will bounce. I've got some humps on my hands where it bounced.

"Now I get a larger and larger cold chisel until I get to the size of big wedges. Iron wedges are a lot better. A wedge will have the tendency to spread the seam open. I'm going to get sections of this ledge. I'll take out large pieces of rock and crack them up into smaller pieces to get

360. The corner of a retaining wall.

361. Harvey trims a stone.

362. A retaining wall at a cemetery.

363. A double-faced or free-standing wall.

them out.

"I've estimated that I pushed maybe five hundred tons of rocks out of here by hand. That's quite a job.

"Granite goes with the grain and across the grain. You know about that in wood, but would you think of it in stone? Stones have what they call the riff and the run of the grain. Now, if you fracture rocks with the run of the grain—that's with the grain—it's a lot easier. Trying to fracture with the riff doesn't break as easy."

Harvey says it takes an experienced person to tell the riff and run in a rock. "Especially on a rock that has a fine grain to it. You can get some stones that are very, very fine grained. You can get coarse-grained particles that are as big around as your little finger.

"You've got different weights for different stones. Granite will weigh about two hundred pounds per cubic foot. With some of these big ones, I don't know how they moved 'em. Those old fellas [who built long ago], I think they must have had a lot of hernias.

"I grew up on a farm, and I saw the barn cellar that my grandfather built out of stones seven or eight feet high and possibly three or four feet deep. As a little boy I remember wondering, how did they get them there?

"But you see, these old-timers, they did this. They had what they called a drag or a stone boot." Harvey explained that the stone drags were made of six or eight planks. "If you were fortunate enough to have had an uncle who owned a sawmill, perhaps he could cut those with a little bit of curl in the front, see. It would be almost like a toboggan. Then the horses were hitched to the stone drag so as to lift the front end of it up and keep that drag from digging into the earth.

"And so the old-timers, what they would do is build the wall up so big, fill behind it, and then they would get those rocks on the stone

364.

drag, and drag the rocks in with horses, up to the edge of the wall and then, with crowbars, they would put them into place in the wall. It's amazing how some of these old-timers could move a big rock with a small crowbar."

We told Harvey that we thought there must be a lot of patience needed to put up a stone wall.

"Oh my, yes," he replied. "You might say there is a lot of love for stones. I love stones. I love the different textured stones. The slopes you get in them. Like that weathered look that you get in each stone. And getting your own stones and estimating the number of stones you need for a job.

"And that is why I say that agility isn't all the stuff you learn from being a good stonemason. I think some of it is what the Lord has given you in the way of skill, in that respect."

Fiddleheads

by Jay York and Stephanie Wood

Photography by Jay York

Monty Washburn, a long-time friend of *Salt,* invited us on a fiddlehead picking, cooking, and eating expedition one May weekend, and we wasted no time accepting. We went to his hunting camp in Upton, a small town nestled among the mountains of western Maine, near the New Hampshire border.

The road to Monty's camp seemed to take us nowhere but deeper into the woods. Finally the trees gave way and we looked over a sea of spring, rising to cover the nearby mountains with its green tide. At the edge of the clearing sat Monty's small, cozy-looking camp.

We'd go out picking fiddleheads later, but first Monty greeted us with a pot full of beef stew and a head full of stories.

"I wish you'd known my father. I'm telling you, he was a character. I guess he never went to much more than the fifth grade, but he had a wit that was just unmatchable.

"He dearly loved to play jokes on people. One day there was a new minister come into town, and he liked to go hunting, so he shot a deer that year. And my father met him downstream one day and he said, 'Well, Everett, I hear you got a deer.'

"'Yes, I did,' he says. 'I got an eight-point buck, a real nice one. The Lord was with me that day.'

"My father says, 'Oh, how'd He make out. He get one, too?'

"One my mother told me one time, she said she was out in the dooryard when she was a little kid. This little boy came up the road, hiking right along, and he says, 'Dad's lost a heiffer.' He says, 'We think she's gone to hell. If you see anything otherwise, let us know.'"

Then Monty told a story about fiddleheads. "One year my wife and I went up to Vermont to trap shoot. It was over Memorial Day. I'll tell you, they had the trap-shooting range right up side of the Capitol, right up side of the river. And I looked out and you wouldn't believe the fiddleheads near it. Almost all gone by. There was just loads, just acres and acres of 'em.

"So another fellow come from Maine and I said, 'Hey, Jesus, I wonder if there's any out there to pick.' So we took a target box and we went out and started picking 'em. Four or five come up and said, 'What the hell are you picking?'

" 'We're picking fiddleheads.'

" 'Fiddleheads, yarrk! Them damn things. Just as soon rake up the back yard and eat it.'

"So he [the other Maine fellow] had a camper trailer up there and we took 'em over and cooked 'em. We gave three or four people a taste of fiddleheads. Before long we saw another guy with a target box going over with another guy. Pretty soon the whole side of the river was full [of trap shooters] picking fiddleheads.

"Better stop the story telling for a few minutes. We gotta go and get some fiddleheads," Monty said, handing each of us brown paper bags to collect them in.

Soon he was scrambling down a steep river bank to point out the clumps of newly sprouted fiddleheads. They looked like the scroll on the head of a fiddle, from which they get their name. As they grow, fiddleheads uncoil into large, leafy ferns. There is a dry, brown skin which is wound inside the head. "There's a thing like an onion skin here. That's the way you can tell a real fiddlehead, by that little onion skin."

What kind of areas are you most likely to find fiddleheads? "Places

366. Fiddleheads.

367. Overripe fiddleheads.

along the river usually, where the water goes up and then recedes in the early spring. You'd find it's best there. You find them sometimes on high ground, too. I know one place up on the back street of Upton that there are some. It's a little, kind of reserve spot."

Commenting on how fast fiddleheads grow, Monty said, "Now I was in here yesterday and I picked over this place and you can see how many there is today." While we were picking, Monty declared that he'd seen fiddleheads grow "about two inches a day."

How long is the growing season for fiddleheads? "Oh about two weeks and they're gone." The best time to pick fiddleheads is in early May. "Usually you can depend on it [the season] beginning within a week, one way or another, of Mother's Day. That's the easy way to remember it."

After picking enough fiddleheads for a hearty meal, we headed back to the camp to clean them. Monty slowly shook out the fiddleheads from the bag into the wind. "It's better to get all the stuff out of them first before you wash them. All that onion stuff." Another way to clean them that Monty had heard about was to "take a vacuum cleaner and turn it backside to and wind 'em in front of there." Using this method is convenient when there is no wind available.

The cooking of fiddleheads is up to the individual's taste. Monty

368. "Wow, look at this big bunch here! I think those have come up since we've been here."

369. Monty cleans the fiddleheads.

boiled them like most greens, in a pot with just enough water to cover them. He added no salt or spices.

As the fiddleheads cooked, the water around them turned dark. "Now this dark water is caused by a little bit of extra onion skin," Monty said. We tried to decide what they smelled like cooking. "I would describe it as a definite fiddlehead smell," Jay laughed at last. The closest we could come to it was "kinda like artichokes."

"Mmm . . . look at them. They're looking pretty good." To go with the fiddleheads, Monty had been baking beans since early that morning, and now he had Johnny cake in the oven. Except for fiddleheads and dandelion greens, "I'm more of a meat and potatoes man myself," Monty said. "I find something I like and I like to stick with it. I don't like experimenting with all these different dishes."

After the fiddleheads had boiled about ten minutes, Monty took the taste test and popped one in his mouth. "Mmm . . . I think they're done."

"Okay, everybody start some fiddleheads here. Slobber 'em up with a good lot of butter. Put a lot of it on. This is Jud's butter [homemade by Fred Judkins in Upton]."

Monty leaned back and his smile broadened as he watched us gobble down the fiddleheads. "How do you fellers like those?"

"Delicious."

"Mmmm . . . good."

"This is my third serving."

"Ha, ha. I'm kind of reluctant to get too many people eating these things because I won't find any to pick!"

We tried to give a name to the flavor. Someone said, "They're a little bit crunchy."

"That's how I think of them," Monty agreed. "Something like nuts, nutty flavor."

After supper, we were able to appreciate the view from the cabin window, looking out over the vast forest and mountains of Maine. As Monty told more stories, his snug camp became too warm and he had to open the door.

"I remember the year I built this camp. My buddy and I snowshoed in just before hunting season. It was twenty-two below zero and I'd never been up here in the winter. We thought we were going to build a big fire to keep warm. My stove got all stoked up to the top of it. In about fifteen minutes I got quite comfortable and in about another ten minutes it got damn uncomfortable.

"We opened the door and a great big rolling ball of vapor come under the door and right in the bedroom. Well, finally it got cooled down so it was bearable. So we closed the door and in ten minutes it was so damn hot we could pop corn on the floor. It was about two o'clock in the morning before we got this place cooled off enough so we could sleep.

"And my buddy says, 'Damn it, next time you build a camp, don't build it so tight.'"

It wasn't much later before Monty was reciting *The Cremation of Sam McGee*—verse after verse of it. Maybe the hot stove made him think of the old tale about two woodsmen caught in the depths of a cold north woods winter. Monty's voice rang out in hearty fashion as he recited. We were spellbound.

Then he told us about some neighbors of his. "There's an old couple lived over the road from me down in Kittery Point. And he was a Harvard graduate and his wife was a Radcliffe graduate. He worked on the *Wall Street Journal* when he got out of college for quite a while. Finally he decided that wasn't the life for him, and he built a farm. And he started raising chickens and cows and that's the way he lived till the day he died. And to go into the house, you traveled right backwards in time for a hundred years. And boy, I'm telling you, after TV got going full blast I used to enjoy going over there. He didn't have a TV or telephone or anything, and you could go over and talk with those people, and they're the nicest people. Sometimes I think there's too damn many conveniences in the world.

"People don't have time to talk anymore. They have washing machines where they used to have little wash tubs and a rub-a-dub scrubboard. Many's the time I've stood there and thought it was real fun to turn that ol' ringer when my mother was doing the washing. She had two tubs there, one on each side of that ol' clothes horse, a boiler on the wood stove. Boil those clothes and reach in there with a crotched stick and twist 'em up and put 'em in the tub, ha, ha, boy."

Soon the talk turned once again to the mountains rising around us with their fresh green foliage and the contrasting dark pines.

"Come up here, whether it's summer, winter, fall, or spring, and I think, 'Boy, this is the best time of the year. I come up here in the winter time and the snow is blowin' and howlin' and it's nice and warm in here. Gee. Boy, what a nice place. In the spring, all the leaves come up and the flowers come up. Oh, I think, spring is the best. In the summer I go fishin' and that's the best time. In the fall all the leaves around you all red and gold and pretty. Gee, how could I ever think that summer was nicest!' "

Thinking about the snow blowing and the wind howling reminded Monty of one more story. "There was a fella that lived right on the line between New Hampshire and Maine. And one day he looked down at his back pasture and he saw a bunch of surveyors down there. So he walks down and he says, 'Hey, what ya doin'?'

"And they say, 'Years ago when we surveyed the line between Maine and New Hampshire, we made a mistake. It should be up in back of your farm instead of in front. In fact, you've been living in New Hampshire for all these years, and you never knew it.'

" 'Thank God,' the old man says. 'I couldn't have stood another one of those Maine winters!' "

Wild Honeybee Hunt

by Mark Emerson,
  Ann Bernier,
  and Sean Riley

Photography by Mark Emerson

"After you've hunted bees long enough, you can tell by the sound of their buzz whether it's a honeybee or whether it's a bumble bee, and you can learn to recognize them quite a little ways off.

"Now a honeybee, I always thought sounded more like a housefly. Their hum is high pitched. A bumblebee bumbles along. He isn't supposed to fly, according to aeronautics experts, but he doesn't know it."

Monty Washburn was bending over his cucumber plants trying to catch a wild honeybee. He learned to catch and hive bees from his father over forty years ago when he was a boy. Today he was passing his knowledge of bees down to us.

"This is my old box. I guess you'd call it a bee box. My uncle made it for me when I was just a little kid, probably ten, twelve years old."

The bee box has two sections. The top section has a screen cover over it and a sliding door at the base. It's about 4″ by 6″ and fits into a bottom section which contains a piece of honeycomb.

"They don't have to be like this box," Monty explained. "You can make them out of anything. You can take a plain box and if you can get a bee into it, you can put a piece of bread in the bottom and put sugar and water syrup into it."

Monty held up an old Cain's Mayonnaise jar full of liquid. "It's just a plain sugar and water syrup. There's about six spoonfuls of sugar in this.

370.

"We'll put a little sugar and water in the comb."

Monty rustled his cucumber plants in search of a bee. "Last week this place was alive with 'em. But we still won't have any trouble gettin' 'em goin'.

"Here's one in here. There's two of 'em. Now we'll take these two up and see if we can get 'em goin'."

371.   Top section of the bee box.

372.   Bottom section.

Monty put his hat over the top of the bee box. "I'm gonna put this over it because if we don't they'll stay right up on the screen.

"If it's dark in there, they'll start crawlin' around to find a place to get out. They'll get on the sugar and water and they'll stay there and work.

373. Monty adds the sugar-water mixture to the comb.

374. Monty traps two bees in the box with his hat.

"Got one down . . . there goes the other one. They'll be goin' great guns in a few minutes here."

He put the box on a four-foot pole in a clearing. Then he removed the top section. We watched the bees loading the syrup, and then they flew off.

"Now they're spreading the message. Yep, see 'em. When they come out of the box, they'll circle and circle and circle and circle, and you'll lose sight of them nine-tenths of the time.

"It'll take sometimes four or five trips before they'll settle down. And finally they'll come out of the box and take right off in the direction where their hive is and they won't circle at all.

"And when they bring the other bees back with 'em, the other bees don't follow them. When they get into their tree or hive or wherever they are, they do this little bee dance. And they tell the other bees in the hive where the source of the honey is by the direction of the sun."

"Quite a Society"

While we waited for the bees to return, Monty told us more about bees.

"When I was just a little boy, my father used to go bee hunting. One day my father found some bees and he said, 'Why don't we take 'em up. We'll get a hive and we'll cut down the tree and save the bees.'

"So we did. And he says, 'All right, they're yours. You take care of them now.' He told me how to go about hiving them and so forth when they come out. And I worked 'em up into twelve swarms.

"There was a big rock out across from the house where we kept the bees. I used to lay out there on my belly by the hour, and just watch those bees work, and different things they'd do. It was quite an education.

"But the fella that made that box, my uncle, he used to take two weeks off every year just to go bee hunting. Like some people take a vacation to go fishing or hunting, he'd take his vacation to go bee hunting. He loved it.

"He had his own hives that he sold honey from. But I never bother with bees now. I find a swarm of bees and leave 'em alone.

"Because there's so few of 'em that it's a crime ta kill 'em. And they do an awful lot of good in gardens and orchards and so forth. They cross pollinate the flowers.

"The poor flowers, male and female flowers, they can't seem to get together. They haven't any legs and the bees perform that service for them.

"They're interesting little creatures. They have quite a society.

"They air condition their hive on hot days by taking a whole bunch of worker bees and they'll line right up in front of the hive and almost stand on their head and just fan their wings to blow air through the hive so the honeycomb won't droop.

"And the drones being the males, they don't do any work. They don't lay any eggs. Their only purpose in the hive is to mate with the female.

"They have it pretty easy during the summer, these drones. They don't do anything. They just sit around, eat honey.

"But in the fall, they don't have it so easy because the worker bees drag 'em out and kill 'em. They don't want them eating honey all winter 'cause they haven't helped gather it in the summer.

"Oft times, two swarms of bees will get fighting, and the only way you can cure them—and sometimes this don't even work—is to narrow up the entrance of the hive.

"See the entrance of a hive is the whole width of it, probably a foot and a half. So you take a piece of wood and you narrow down the entrance of the hive to about three inches. They'll put guards up in front of this entrance.

"And every bee that comes in the hive, these guards'll feel 'em all over. And if he belongs in there he can go through. But if he don't, all hell breaks loose!

"They'll take him out. They have a grand fight outside."

We asked Monty if he had seen that happen. "Oh yeah, yeah. I watched 'em drag the drones out and kill them. And ventilate the hive.

"A worker honeybee has no sex. They're undeveloped females. And there are thousands and thousands of them in a swarm. There's maybe fifteen or twenty of what they call drones, and these are the male bees. And there's one female bee, which is the queen.

"Now these worker bees work so hard that their lifespan is only about twelve weeks, so the queen has to continually lay eggs to keep the swarm healthy and large.

"The queen will lay maybe fifty thousand eggs during a season, probably more.

"You can tell brood comb from honeycomb by the way they cap it over. The honeycomb'll be flat or slightly indented, each cell . . . and the brood comb will be concave.

"In the spring she'll lay eggs that are quite different from those that hatch out worker bees. These queen eggs are deposited in what they call queen cells, and they look like unshelled peanuts, and they hang down on the bottom of the honeycomb. The queen lays the same egg in this queen cell that she lays for a worker bee, but they feed it a different substance called royal jelly. It hatches into a queen.

"When this new queen hatches out, a great percentage of the bees, maybe one half of them, will follow her out and make a new swarm. This is how they propagate.

"When a queen comes out in the spring, she flies in the air and there's probably fifteen or twenty of these drones that fly after her, and she keeps going up and up and up. One by one the drones will drop off, and the last one that is following her will mate with her.

"When they're ready to swarm you can go out in the evening and there will be a little bunch of bees hanging down the outside of the hive. Each day this'll go on, bigger and bigger and bigger and you can tell that they're going to swarm very shortly.

"And one morning you'll come out and there'll be bees all through the air and you can hardly see the sun for bees.

"And they'll what they call 'pitch.' Now this means that a queen will light on a bush or a branch or something and as soon as she lights, all the rest of the bees will light on her and pretty soon there'll be a big bunch of bees hangin' off this branch.

"So then you take a new clean hive and there's two different methods you can use for gettin' the bees into the hive.

"One is to spread a sheet down in front of the entrance, cut this branch off and shake this bunch of bees onto the sheet. If you watch 'em, maybe it'll be five minutes and pretty soon you'll see every bee turned to head for the hive, and they'll go in it, just like a waterfall. This is when the queen's gone in.

"And the other method is to take the top off a hive and take this bunch of bees and cut the branch right off and just shake 'em off in the top of the hive and put the cover on. And in 90 per cent of the cases, they'll stay in the hive and start workin'."

"They're Friendly Little Devils"

By this time the bees had made several trips back and forth and were making a direct beeline to the woods. There must have been forty or fifty honeybees flying around the bee box at this time.

"Don't be afraid of 'em. Don't slap at them. They won't sting you. Honeybees can only sting once, and they know it. So they're very careful of how they use their stinger.

"They're friendly little devils. Sometimes they come up to the screen when I'm sitting there [inside] and wonder where their sugar and water is.

"If you chop the tree down or, you know, agitate them enough, they will sting ya, but they can only sting once.

"You can get up close to them. They won't hurt ya. They're attracted by bright objects, like your glasses, wrist watch, rings, earrings, even your eyes sometimes.

"Apparently a bee can sense that you're afraid of him. One thing, if you're working with bees, they don't like the smell of sweat. So if you want to have a swarm of bees, it's a good idea to take a bath first and get all the sweat smell off of you. And they don't like horses 'cause horse sweat smells a lot.

"But these little fellas are real friendly."

Monty brought some colored chalk and explained that he was going to mark one of the bees. "Now this stuff in here is something I bought quite a number of years ago just for bee hunting."

The reason for marking the bee is so that he can be timed as he makes his trips back and forth between the bee box and his hive.

"Quite a number of times you'll get three or four swarms of bees going at once and if you paint different bees different colors, you'll finally get a red one maybe that's going this way and a yellow one that's going that way. But we'll just use blue chalk. Cause we only got one swarm of bees going here.

"Hold still, you little devil. There. I got him painted. He's right down there.

"Well, I think our bee left. Four minutes and 15 seconds past ten according to my watch. Keep watching the box and see how soon he comes back.

"You keep watching these, and tell me just where they're going. Because we're going over and see if we can find 'em by and by. Right up against the dark background down there. I can see one goin' way down there.

375. Marking the bee.

"When they really get goin' they'll come out and take right off, and you can see them right against that dark tree background. There goes one.

"These bees are a young swarm because they're awful anxious to work. If they've got plenty of honey, it's awful hard to get 'em to work. They've got enough, so they kind of quiet down like a man that's retired. Like myself, you know.

"They claim that honeybees fly seven minutes to the mile, so if they're half a mile away, they'll be gone seven minutes. A round trip being a mile takes them about seven minutes.

"It isn't a hard-and-fast rule, because a lot of times they'll have a tree where they have to go in and crawl way up in the tree. This takes 'em some time. It also takes time for 'em to unload.

"When they take on the sugar and water they have to unload it like a tank truck would.

"They're taking on fuel. They're pumping it in I guess. They have a little tongue and a tube that they suck it [syrup] in, and sometimes they'll get overloaded.

376. Chalk for marking bees.

"They'll be a little greedy and they can't fly. They'll have to let some of it out before they can go home.

"There's a little story I'll tell ya. It isn't a bad story. My mother told me this quite a long, long time ago. When she was a little girl, which was back in the late 1800s, the people used to go out in the fall and they'd find bees. Course they only hunted 'em in the fall 'cause they was after the honey, and this is when you find most of the honey in the hive.

"So after they took the bees up and got the honey, it was customary to invite all the neighbors in the next Sunday for a feed of hot biscuits and honey. So this particular family, we'll call Benjamin Smith, went out and he found a swarm of bees, and, uh, he got the honey and there was quite a lot of it.

"So they invited all the neighbors in the next Sunday for this feed of hot biscuits and honey.

"Well, the neighbors started arriving, and there was quite a few of 'em. So Mrs. Smith decided that the dish that she had the honey in wasn't big enough and she couldn't think of what she could use.

"So she went upstairs and she brought back this old earthen ware chamber vessel complete with the cover and the whole works . . . that people plant plants in now. She brought it down, she put the honey in it, and set it on the table.

"The women commenced to eye it and look at it. And finally one of them said, 'Mrs. Smith, isn't that kind of an odd dish to put honey in?'

"Well, the old lady bristled just like a porcupine you'd poked with a stick. And she said, 'Why, that's just as clean as any dish in this house. It was never used but once or twice when we had company!'

"He should be back most any time. Seems like. You can tell, by the way these work and how many come back, approximately how far away you are.

"If the swarm is quite a ways off, your original bees will work quite a long time before any follow them back. But if you're fairly close to 'em, they'll come back real quick and it'll be a lot of bees very quickly.

"There he is! See him? The blue paint on his back? Now he's been gone just about six minutes.

"They're goin' just about south. Six minutes, they're a little under a half a mile away."

Monty considered setting up the bee box in another clearing to get another line on it, but decided he didn't need to. "Where it's only gone six minutes, I think we can find 'em.

"That field should be just about in line with where they're going. Right over on that little ridge over there somewhere, or down this side of it, or over on the other side, but they're over in there somewhere.

"That would be just about the right distance, and according to the compass, it would be just before that ridge starts down."

We started walking in a southerly direction through the woods.

"South right now is off this way. We figured the bees were somewhere right over in here. So we'll go over here a little ways and start looking in trees.

"Don't look exactly at the tree. Look out in the sky, or against the tree and see if you can see insects going every which way. This is the easy way to find 'em."

As we walked along, Monty told us what the bees liked to make honey from.

"They'll make honey on most anything. They'll make honey from pine trees, certain times of the year. And sumac blossoms when they're green before they start to turn red, corn cobs, cucumber blossoms, squash blossoms, Indian tobacco, milkweed, the big milkweed that has the big pods now, they love that.

"They go crazy. In fact, when they're workin' milkweed it's almost impossible to get one to work the box. They like that so well. Buckwheat. Any kind of blossom."

We wanted to know how long a swarm usually lives in one tree.

"Oh, for years and years. Or it might rain all season and they might die during that winter because they couldn't store enough honey. But if it's a big tree, and a good swarm, usually they'll be in it maybe for twenty-five or thirty years."

Monty explained, "They'll have to have a lot of honey stored up to get them through the winter. Probably forty or fifty pounds at least.

"I've found 'em in two hours and I've hunted for 'em for two weeks sometimes. You can't tell. Well, this is gonna be a fairly good-sized tree that we find these bees in, if we find 'em, and it'll probably be somewhere near water, within two or three hundred feet, because they have to have water in order to make their honey.

"They know that in here there isn't any trees big enough, those little small things. Often you'll find them in hemlock trees. I don't know whether it's because they prefer hemlock or because there's more hollow hemlocks, because they have to have a hollow tree.

"I have found them in old houses, in under the eaves or going between the walls, and once in a while you'll find them right out in the open. They can't find a tree anywhere, but there's a swarm and they have to start gathering honey. That's their nature. So they build their comb right on a limb right out in the open and they invariably die there during the winter.

"Sometimes you'll find a tree that'll have twenty-five to thirty pounds of honey in it. A lot of times you'll find one that doesn't have but five pounds, depending on the size of the swarm and how long they've been in the tree.

"A new swarm that comes out in May, usually by the end of the year will have enough honey to last them through the winter and some besides.

"There's an old saying that 'A swarm of bees in May is worth a load of hay. A swarm of bees in June is worth a silver spoon. And a swarm of bees in July isn't worth a fly!'

"The entrance to their hive might be anywhere from a foot up from the base of it, up to thirty feet high . . . trees that are big enough.

"So we'll have to look 'em over very thoroughly. If the bees were in any of those trees, you'd see 'em flyin' out from between the branches and lookin' up against the sky you'd see 'em, too.

"So they aren't here. The wind is blowin' and the leaves are all movin' and you can't catch the movement of the bees so quick."

We walked on in search of the tree. Several other large trees seemed possibilities, but we found no signs of bees. Then we came up to an old tree in a thick grove.

377. Monty carving *Salt*'s initial in the bee tree.

Monty circled the tree. Then he spotted some bees. "Look. Right this side of the second branch. See the little imperfections in the tree there?"

It had only taken us about two hours to find the honeybees. Monty said this had been an easy hunt. "I've only found about three more swarms any quicker than that." As he had explained, sometimes it took as long as two weeks.

"If you was going to get the honey out of that, you'd have to cut down the tree, then take the saw and saw into it below and above that hole about half way through it, and take an ax and split the pieces out and tip 'em up and get the bees out that way.

"When the people used to find a swarm of bees in the old days, it was an unwritten law that if you left your initials on the tree nobody else would touch it. They might find it, too, but if there's someone's initials on it, why they'd leave it alone.

"Why don't we put the old-time law into effect and we'll carve the initial in the tree?

"I'll tell ya. We'll put an S on it for *Salt,* how's that?"

Cottage Cheese

by Fran Ober

Photography by Anne Gorham

I got my idea for this story when my mother was telling me how expensive cottage cheese was getting at the supermarket. She said she could remember when her mother used to make cottage cheese at home.

Mom would be coming home from school and she could see the cottage cheese hanging on the line. Mom knew that every time she saw that cheese hanging on the line, she would be having it with her supper.

I decided it would make an interesting story, and my grandmother, Elinor Nedeau, agreed to make it for us. I bought a gallon of whole milk from a farmer and took it to her on Wednesday so she could start the process of making cottage cheese.

"To make cottage cheese at home, you must have whole milk right from the cow, not pasteurized. Usually you use whole milk with the cream in it. I let it set. It's been setting since Wednesday—Thursday, Friday, and today, Saturday.

"Well, it started to clabber last night. That's how long it took. If you use rennit tablets, that makes milk clabber faster. I can't tell you any more than that. See what the milk is like? This has the cream on it."

I asked Gram if it is possible to buy rennit tablets. "I tried to get some downtown, but I couldn't get any. You probably could get them somewhere. I don't know.

"Years ago when I was keeping house as a young woman, I used to make cottage cheese. I don't anymore. We used to use a bag to drain it in, because then, most everything came in a bag, a little cloth bag. Sugar

379. "I just want first to take off this cream."

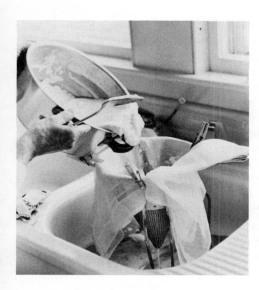

380. "Now you pour it into the strainer, thusly."

381. "This would be what you'd call the first washing."

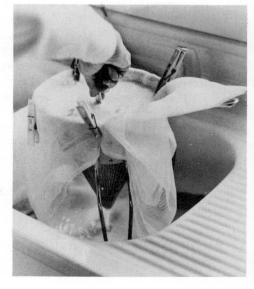

378.

came in a bag. Salt came in a bag. Housewives used those little bags for just about everything. Sometimes they were little, sometimes big, depending on how much sugar you bought at a time.

"Now, I want first to take off this cream. I'll tell you why I did it this way, and let that cream sour on there. Sour cream makes wonderful cookies. We'll save the sour cream to make cookies. You'd be surprised the cookies that cream will make.

"Looks pretty awful doesn't it! If you smelled it, it smells even worse than it looks. The cream is just this yellow. The cream always comes to the top when you set milk. This is what they call setting milk, when you put it in a big pan.

"We won't try to get all of that [sour cream] off, just enough so you girls can see what happens. Looks like a dreadful mess, doesn't it?

"Now, you pour this into your strainer thusly.

"You know I shouldn't be doing this in a pair of pants. In my young days, women did not wear pants, I'll have you know!

"This has to be what they called washed, with lukewarm water. That's to take out the bitterness, some of the sourness. Yes that's washing it. I could have done it faster if I hadn't put so much [water] in there.

"You use the same amount of warm water for each washing as you had milk when you started. I had four quarts of milk so I'll use approximately four quarts of lukewarm water, and pour it down over there.

"This would be what you'd call the first washing. After I get all the water poured into there, you have to let it drip till that's practically all dripped out and your curd is almost dry. Then, you do it all over again. You do it three times—you wash it in lukewarm water.

"It takes all day, because it drips slow. After your last or third washing, you just wrap this up and take it out on the clothesline and just let it drip till it's dry as you'd like to have it. You can tell by squeezing the bottom of it. You know, just how thick you'd like to have it.

"That's the end of it as far as making the cheese is concerned. That's all there is to it. If you want it to be real tasty, you add a little bit of sweet cream and some salt and pepper. You've got a real delicious bite. Add salt and pepper, a little cream butter, melted butter, it really is some delicious.

"Look, now you can see what it looks like. It looks just like what you can buy in the store. It's still got a bit of cream in it, but that won't bother anybody. It's got to be washed two or three times. That's what I say. It takes all day to get the thing made. You wouldn't want to stay here all day waiting for it to drip and dribble. If it comes out the way it used to when I made it years ago, it will be just lovely. A lot of things we used to make at home. Everybody made them if they liked them."

Maple Syrup

Story by Louie Burns

Interviewing, transcribing:
  Louie Burns,
  Kathy Burns, and
  Beth Mann
Photography by James Jannetti

After the long gray winter, the light warmth of April seemed to bring a feeling of expectancy from the snow-filled woods. It unlocked the streams and filled them with rushing snow water. The south-facing shoulders of the worn, rolling, time-softened hills looked like harsh, vicious brown scars on the pureness of white.

It is a time of subtle, secret awakenings and stirrings in the muddy earth beneath the snow and in the hardwood and pine forests that surrounded the valley to which we had come. Behind the saphouse a stream could be heard splashing down from the woods, from the maple woods above to the fields below. The dirt of the barnyard was moist and smelled of the earth and wholesomeness, sweetened by the mellow aroma of sap steam that billowed out of the saphouse in a whirling cloud up into the bluish white sky. And all the time you could see diamond flashes in the woods as a crystal drop of sap caught the sun and glistened for an instant like a sequin.

The sap was running.

James Jannetti

Going up the hill-surrounded road lined with maple trees, we could tell right off that someone was tapping trees. There were sap buckets hang-

382. Sap buckets hanging from the maples.

ing on almost every maple tree in sight.

We figured we had to be nearing Donald Wood's house, which is at the end of a mile-long dirt road. "There it is," I yelled. And sure enough, waiting at the end of the driveway was Woody.

It had been a cold week in February of 1975 when I came to meet Woody. Little did I know that I was going to interview him for a story about maple-syrup making a year later. But here we were, in South Tamworth, New Hampshire, where maple syrup is always on the breakfast table, and we were beginning to learn how it got there.

"Well, actually I guess we should start from the beginning. We wash the buckets. Putting them away we don't wash them because the sap coating helps keep them from rusting during storage.

"Then in the springtime we take them out and wash them and we wash the spiles." Spiles are cone-shaped funnels measuring about three and a half to four inches with a lip at one end. They have a hook attached to hold a bucket and are inserted into the tree to funnel sap into the buckets.

"Go out to a tree and, using a brace and bit, drill a hole about one and a half inches, just long enough to stick the spile in, drive the spile just right up to here [two inches], tap 'em in with a hammer, and then hang the buckets on.

"Eventually, you go along and look at some of these big maples here and pretty soon it gets hard to find a place to tap them. Because when

383. Entering Woody's camp.

you tap a tree, it kills all the wood about an inch or two around it, so the next year you have to tap where there is good wood."

The kind of maples Woody taps are rock maple "or what people call sugar maple. And we tap white maples up here. Tapping and hanging takes a lot of time. That's the hardest part."

384. Spile.

We asked Woody when is the best time of year to start tapping the trees.

"It varies from year to year. It's when the weather starts to get warmer, or when you think it's gonna be really nice in the day, and freezing at night, cause the sap runs best when it's freezing nights and warm days.

"It won't run good if it doesn't freeze the night before.

"This year we tapped the end of February. Some years they didn't tap until the end of March. Other years they tapped in February and were done in February.

"You can't plan. You can't say, 'Well, I guess I'll start sappin' about the fifteenth of March.' We'll go into April this year before we take our buckets down. You're all done when the trees start to bud."

How long you leave the buckets in brought another "iffy" answer just like the previous question.

"Well, this year we should have them on there for about a month, although they didn't run for a month. We started off and it ran for a couple of days and then we got cold weather.

385. Woody standing beside the Imp.

"It will vary from a week to a month. You know it goes according. It'll probably run for about two weeks. And then the trees'll start to bud out, and there you go."

For collecting on the road, Woody uses a truck, but out in the hills and across fields he uses an Imp. An Imp is an odd-looking piece of transportation that looks like a bulldozer only without a plow. The main feature about it is that it has a big tank on the back used for holding sap, and it can go almost anywhere.

When we asked how much he had collected so far this year, Woody wanted to know if we were talking about sap or syrup. That's when we found out how much sap it takes to make a gallon of syrup.

"On the average it takes forty to one. Your average collection is probably about 2.5 per cent maple sugar content, and you'll boil out about forty gallons to one." Sometimes the ratio will be more like thirty to one, if you happen to get sap with a high-sugar content.

He estimated that he had made about fifteen gallons of syrup, which we figured amounted to about six hundred gallons of sap.

"It takes a whole day or two days to collect the sap if we don't have

386. Draining sap to the outside holding tank from the Imp.

any help," Woody said. That's two men, Woody and his uncle working together. "Like, we'd collect all down the fields one day, and then the next we'd do the roads.

"If it freezes up the night before, you have to wait for the sun to come out to thaw at least some of the ice. Water just freezes out of the sap and makes a higher-sugar content. You can throw the ice out."

Boiling It Down

After your sap is all collected, you should boil it down as soon as you can if you want light syrup. If you let it set for a while in the tank, the syrup will be darker.

"Well, first we dump the sap into this holding tank. We use a screen to strain out the bugs and whatever else might be in there, sometimes mice.

"After that we pump it into this big holding tank which holds about thirty-five gallons. When it goes in there, it gets filtered again to get the finer debris out."

The first holding tank sits out in the open and the second tank is under the roof of the saphouse. The saphouse itself is a long narrow building about twelve feet by twenty-five feet. Running down the center is a wood-fed stove, maybe ten to twelve feet long, called an "arch." On top of the stove, on a gradual incline from back to front, sit five boiling tanks. The saphouse is vented to let out the clouds of smoke from the stove. On each side are benches.

"The setup we have here is made up of several separate compartments," Woody explained. "The sap comes in from the back, the holding tank. Then it starts to boil in the back tank.

"As it boils down and gets heavier, it moves to the front and gets drained through a series of four tanks, the front being the thickest syrup. Then just before the very front pan is ready, we block it off so as not to let any less dense syrup mix with it.

"Then we just keep boiling it until it reaches the right density. You could boil it down more and make candy.

"If you keep boiling it, eventually it will get as hard as rock. That happened. I don't know if it was here or somewhere else. One day someone left the pans unattended and they had about an inch and a half of rock sugar stuck to their pan. Now that was some mess. I bet that took a good day of cleaning."

As soon as the front pan is boiled down, it is drained out into cans and the plug that blocks the pans off from each other is taken out to let more sap into that pan.

387. Outside the saphouse, a long narrow log cabin about twelve by twenty-five feet with a wood-fed stove.

388. The boiling pans or arches.

"Right from the start [when the pans are empty and the boiling just started], it'll take about five hours till you get a syrup.

"After it's boiled down a little and you take off one batch, it doesn't take too long to get the next one."

We wondered if there was any difference between the way they used to collect sap and boil it and the way they do it now.

"Well, they used to collect it using oxen. The only difference between the way they used to boil it and the way they boil it now is that some of the places use oil to keep theirs lit instead of using wood. We still use wood for ours, but a lot of places are getting into oil because it's a lot easier.

"A long time ago they used to do it right out in the field. You know, instead of having an arch like we have here, they might just have one huge pan, a big caldron where they'd boil down the sap.

"Some of the big operations today, they use tubing instead of buckets. Like they might have a tube running from say twenty trees that all collects into one big pan, instead of walking around and collecting twenty buckets. This way you only have to collect one big bucket.

389. Woody checking the density of the syrup.

"The only operations that can do that are the ones that put out four to five thousand buckets. It takes a lot of money to buy all that tubing and all your other equipment. I imagine it would take a few years before anyone would make a good profit at it.

"An inspector comes in every year and checks it out. He comes and checks your saphouse. He'll take a can of syrup and check its density and color. The inspector also grades your stuff. Ya, a lot of people say it's because of white maples. It doesn't change the taste of anything, just the coloration. Some people prefer light stuff, and I prefer the dark stuff.

"You can make syrup lighter by adding marshmallow, however the inspector would know it right away. They'd make you empty every one of your cans and boil it all over again. If you get caught with it, they're awful sticky."

The inspector hadn't been around yet to check this year's syrup. "When he came last year, Perk and I were making some homemade brew. This whole place smelled like a brewery. He didn't like that."

According to Woody, there's no big profit in making maple syrup. The boiling pans (arches) cost about five thousand dollars twelve years ago. Buckets cost about three dollars apiece, spiles sixty-five cents apiece, and gallon cans about a dollar apiece.

"I know this guy up in Vermont with all his labor and everything— he says he probably makes fifty cents an hour."

Right then Woody's uncle Doug came along and took us into the sugarhouse. "I have to open some hatches here to let some of the steam out. We built this big hatch here to direct the steam up so it will go out that big opening on the roof.

390. The vent on the roof of the saphouse lets the steam out.

"Sometimes the steam gets so bad in here that you can't even see your hand in front of your face!"

He offered us each a little syrup. "Here's some that's all ready," he said. Each of us took a little sip. It was some good. "Ya, this is all ready for the market," Doug told us.

"Syrup's high," Woody said. "It's twelve dollars a gallon here now. In Massachusetts, it's about fifteen dollars. I like it, but I can't see paying twelve dollars a gallon. I can always tap three trees and get enough for what I'd want it for!"

Mary Turner

Story by James Jannetti

*Interviewing and photography
    by Jeff Bonney and James Jannetti*

Riding up to Mary's, the road gets narrower and narrower. Modern trailers give way to practical farmhouses, their barns lacking paint and looking used. The road follows a stream, and when you cross the bridge over the stream, it is just as if you were entering Mary's kingdom.

I really didn't know what to expect. This was my first interview. I felt worried about whether I had the right to investigate Mary Turner's life, but the way she greeted us changed those feelings.

"Well, what the hell you doin' down there? Get on up here where I can talk to you if that's what you come for. Come on now, come along," Mary yelled, waving imperiously with her cane and ordering us into her house as she might guide her geese into a pen.

Her house in West Peru, Maine, was formed to fit the side of the mountain; the mountain hadn't been changed to fit the house. Sheltered by the surrounding hills, it overlooked the valley.

We entered the house through a sagging woodshed attached to the side of the house. It had axes, pitchforks, cats, sacks of meal, cans of rusty nails, piles of logs, harnesses, an old butter churn and press, barrels, and fishhooks. Light coming from a dusty window was dimmed to a murky yellow.

As Mary opened the inner door we were engulfed by a warm blast of air mingling the smell of molasses cookies and woodsmoke. It seemed like a good refuge, warm and cozy, a good place to come in from the cold. Socks were drying from strings on the ceiling. Coats and hats were

391. "Come along now, come along . . ."

392. Mary's woodshed. (*Photo by James Jannetti*)

hung on deer antlers on the walls. Chipmunks were chirping and scurrying around their cage.

Mary kept up a good-natured patter of curses as she rushed around seeing we were comfortable. The worn floorboards creaked under the unaccustomed weight of so many people.

The sink was a slate sink with a lawn hose nozzle that came in through the wall. Bare wires of recently installed electricity ran across the ceiling, and the white, conspicuously new refrigerator stood in a corner. A chain saw buzzed outside as Mary's fallen chicken shed was raised again by one of her friends.

Gus sat contentedly next to the stove. It was some time before we discovered who Gus was. Gus is an old-age pensioner who has been living there so long that nobody is quite sure when Mary took him in.

We had come to West Peru to meet Mary at the suggestion of Monty Washburn, a childhood friend of Mary's. This wasn't the first story Monty had led us to, so we could depend on him. It was like a reunion between Monty and Mary, a reunion of old friends.

393. Gus.

394. "There's not too many people come here and not go away feeded." (*Photo by James Jannetti*)

"Mary's been a landmark here for quite some time," Monty said.

"I guess I have," Mary agreed, adding, "I've taken care of this place ever since I've been here."

That's been since she was seventeen years old, when she and her mother bought the house with thirty-five acres of land for a thousand dollars, two cows, and a horse. Things are different now from when she and her mother bought the land. Now Mary says she is pestered by real estate agents wanting to buy up the land.

"Them real estate agents, they kept comin', botherin' and botherin'. I told them I wouldn't sell. One of 'em said I might break my leg and *have* to sell. I said, 'Don't worry. I got crutches upstairs. So you ain't got to worry about buying it 'tall.'

"Well, I swore I'd shoot the next one to come. 'So you better be movin',' I said. And I ain't had no trouble since!"

Mary's life is tied to her land. She raises veal cattle and chickens, grows all the feed for her animals, and plants a big vegetable garden. It is easy to see why real estate people are not welcome around her place.

Not only is Mary's house a refuge for outcast animals, but it is a haven for people, one of whom was her brother Charley. "I took care of him, you know that. God, he'd a-starved to death if I hadn't fed him. He'd work just enough to get a feed of salt pork and beans, and then he'd put the rest in rum and beer."

Monty asked, "Can you remember the epitaph he wanted on his gravestone?" And Mary replied, "Oh hell yes, I can remember that."

Charley's Epitaph

Who lies here, who do you think,
Old Charley Porter, give 'im a drink,
For rum and beer have cost him dear,
Now he's dead and his bones lie here.
Many a barrel he's turned in,
Just between his nose and chin.
Strangers step lightly upon the side,
If he gaps, you're gone, by God!

"I've never got that on his grave yet. [Charley's been dead twelve years.] If I don't die too soon, I'm going to get someone to write that up and take it over."

Charley's attitude toward death was about as cavalier as Mary's attitude about religion. "I remember when I went to church to get baptized," Mary laughed. "Jesus, I thought they were going to drown me. I turned around and looked up and I said this was going to be it. Oh, I don't know. I went to the hospital and not one damn person from the church came to see me."

And then Mary exclaimed, "I remember when the minister had a service right down there by the brook. He was baptizing and one of the kids got loose and floated right down the river!"

Mary's memory seems to be exceptionally sharp, which adds to her story-telling ability on topics such as fish poaching, bee hunting and, most of all, the often-told stories about the pursuit of moose and the evasion of wardens.

"I Shot a Moose"

"I shot a moose. That mornin' I had on my red pajamas eatin' breakfast. It started raining. The old man [Gus] was down at the barn milking the cows. He milked 'em in the barn. That was ten, twelve years ago.

"It was a moose. I come downstairs, I grabbed the gun and the shells, my .30-30, and back up there I went. Well, he come down the hill a

395. "I shot a moose!"

bit, so I got a standin' broadside shot.

"Well, I didn't have the least idea I'd got him. I leaned up against the side of the building, so I could let him run. He started to run, then he slowed up, and went across to the field. I'd paunched him. I knowed I'd hit him.

"So he slowed up. I thought I'd get him again, so I shot him in the rear end. Well, he ran over and he run around the tree. Well, I was still here at half past six in the morning.

"The old cow kicked Gus off the stool. He said, 'That's nobody but that goddamn warden that would do a trick like that in the morning!" So I went in these old red trousers, you know, always red, wobbling up the road with a gun.

"I heard a car coming. I figgered it was the friggin' game warden. I'd bet you a dollar I shot twice. Well, I came running down the road just as fast as I could. And some fellas [friends of Mary's] drove up in the yard.

" 'What in hell are you running for?' one of them yelled.

" 'I just shot a moose!' I said.

" 'Well, don't you know that's pretty serious?'

" 'Well, yes, I guess it is, kinda,' I said. 'I sure don't need my name in the newspaper.'

" 'Well, just you shut your mouth or you will.'

"Well, they was over and he was down, had died. They carried two guns—one went one way—I told them where I'd seen him last, and I started to run. They put another bullet in his head, to make sure.

"I went over to see what I'd done. Well, it was a big one. They said, 'Take these two guns and head for home with them.'

"I got my feet all wound up. I was hurrying in them old red pants. I got right down on the old ground and dug both barrels right into the ground! And I hurt my thumb. It swelled all up and it was sore. I wouldn't tell anyone what I'd done.

"Well, we started in working. I went back over after I'd got the guns home, got some clothes on, so I could run if I had to. And then I went back there and they was a-skinnin' him out, and I says, 'You know, I never had a moose tongue before. Why don't we have that one?'

"So they cut him open and they got the bullet out. I was glad I'd got it, because when they was searching here, they said they'd like to have the gun that shot that moose. Well, it was right over there [Mary's own gun] and we buried it right up there in trees and everything else.

"We cut that thing up and carried it down the hill in the wheelbarrow. We put it on the floor with sheets and everything else and cut it up [at Mary's house]. And we worked like beavers all day long. And this was on a Wednesday.

"And on Friday I saw two more moose. I said, 'Jesus, I wish I'd brought my gun!'

"But somebody blowed the whistle. We got rid of that meat, and on Saturday in came the game wardens. There was six of 'em. I got two sons that live in the village. Two of 'em hit Bob's place, and two of 'em hit Johnny's. Told 'em to come here all at the same time. They timed it just right.

"Well, when they come into the dooryard, I see 'em comin' and they had a warrant, they told George. I had some meat all cooked on the table and threw it into the stove. He [a warden] said, 'She's already lighted the stove!'

"He came right on over and sticks his hand down in that fire. And he dug out some of our meat. 'Why'd you throw the meat in there?' he asked. I said, 'It stunk.' And it did, when it came out. And so he hunted around and he took that meat.

"I had some in a pan cooking on the stove, and a lid on it. They never touched it, but they looked all over everything. They hunted all over, but they couldn't find nothing else, only that. But it was all cooked.

396. "Somebody blowed the whistle."

397. Mary herds her geese into their pen.

"They was hoping that they'd find something on me, the knives or somethin'. They learned me a lot, I'm tellin' you. Ever after that, if I did anything illegal, I kept after them things.

"Keep them things clean and they can't get anything. They was lookin' fer blood and they was lookin' fer meat.

"Well, they went all over the house, down in the cellar, in the pork barrel, in the walls and all that. They come down 'cross the field and they had a leg of that moose, and George was here and he said, 'What's that? A leg of Black Angus?' Of course it was a leg of that moose.

"They looked in the well and there was a tin can. And one of 'em said, 'What is that?'

"'Well, you know, that's a game warden's hat,' George said. 'There'll be another one down there!'

"So they all got ready to leave. I heard one say, 'We'd like that gun that shot that moose.' They went out that way. I just closed that door. Gus went in this way and put the gun on my bed and laid on it, under the blanket. Well, that was the end of that.

"Then they came back. I had forgotten about the roast I had cooking, and they said, 'Is that moose meat?' I said, 'That's what you think it is.' Well, he got mad and went out. George was just cutting it in half. They took it with them.

"They asked me what was cooking in the oven. I said, 'I ain't got a thing to tell ya. Now if you looked around here all you want to see, well, get the hell out of here!'

"So if you ever catch a moose, make sure you cook the meat. They can't tell what kind it is. For all they know, it could be horse meat. So I cooked the damn thing right up.

"I took all them sheets and all that stuff, put 'em in a laundry bag and took them down to the brook, and tied it with a nail so I could wash it in the brook. I was praying they wouldn't see it, and I didn't dare go near it that day.

"I went down there Monday morning. I got that old laundry bag and come with it right up here to this swamp, and I throwed it right down to the bottom. I poked it. Them goddamn sheets and pillow cases never growed after I put them inside there. I expected they might, but they didn't. I expected they might sprout.

"They never come back. I thought they would. I went picking—that's the year I retired. I retired about '63. Poor old Gus, he had to stay here and stick it out. Every time he heard a car, he kept the door locked. Well, I figgered they'd come back, you know, but they didn't. So that was that episode. We lost every bit of it [the moose].

"Well, I don't believe I'll have another one," Mary laughed. "I just did that one for kicks, and I got a heck of a kick out of it."

Mary's Farm

It couldn't have been a stronger kick than the one we got out of Mary. As the dusty yellow light faded in the mountain dusk, the atmosphere of our group began to glow like Mary's old wood stove, surrounded by napping cats.

After a while, Mary took us out to see her farm animals, throwing affectionate oaths at each one as she introduced them. "Come on out, you rascals," she roared at the racoons hiding at the back of their cage. Cows, dogs, cats, rabbits, raccoons, and flying squirrels were described in terms of personality and character. She showed us how her flock of geese could understand her when she talked and pointed her cane.

Mary's cane was more a tool of emphasis than locomotion as we followed her up to the little clearing where, every spring, after the sap starts running, she hauls barrels of sap through the snow filled woods to be boiled into maple syrup.

"It was spring I guess and there was some snow on the ground and I was coming down the side of the hill with two big buckets of sap. I was coming down the side of the hill and I slipped right on my ass. But I didn't spill any of the syrup. I slid down the hill and I cultivated half of the hill!

"I made eight gallons of it last year," Mary said. Monty said he wished he had bought some syrup from her. "I give it away," Mary replied. "I like giving things away. It's no fun if you can't give things away when you want to."

We asked Mary about the process of making maple syrup. "Well, you have to get the sap from the trees. First you have to bore a hole in the tree kinda slantylike. You can use anything for sap buckets. I use two-gallon oil drums. They make good sap buckets.

"What you do is put a nail in the side of the tree to hold your bucket. When you tap the tree, the sap starts coming, and then, of course, you have to start gathering it. Well, then you have to start your fire. You have to watch it all the time or you'll burn your sap. I've been up all night watching it many times.

"Boy, some trees'll run like hell, and others, Jesus, they'll run so damn slow. I've got a good way of bringing them down the hill. I put them on the toboggan and they slide along real easy."

Mary pointed toward a clump of wind-twisted apple trees across on the lower edge of the field, and began telling us of something that happened there once.

"I was out here and there was a doe wading across over there by the apple tree, and then I looked, and there was a great big buck. I never seed such a fat one. That wasn't so long after I shot that friggin' moose, you know.

"And he had an apple in his mouth, and then he picked his head up.

399.

What a rack of horns! I said, 'Jesus, maybe that's another moose, and I don't want to shoot it. And all I could say was, 'Well, I wish George Turner was here.'

"Well, I musta said it out loud, because his old tail fled into the air, and off into the woods he went. Well, I went into the house and sat down, and George lost him. He could see where he had laid down and bled. But he had to come home and get a little sleep and go back. He come home on Saturday and said he took to his tracks again. He hadn't moved too awful far. He got him in the basin, then lost him again in with them other deer. He never did get him."

As we slowly ambled back into the house, Mary stopped to show us the wooden churn that she uses to make butter from the milk of her cow.

Mary seems to be a very self-sufficient person. Besides making her own butter, she grows and preserves all the vegetables she needs, cares for her animals and, until only recently, she still cut hay on her mountainside fields to use as winter fodder. She appears to be happy living with what she can make for herself, and wants nothing more.

She told us about her homemade flydope. "I usta take a pound of lard, get a can of pine tar. I'd melt the lard on the stove and warm up the pine tar so's it'll run out easier. Some of the time it does anyways.

"Then I throw that in a two quart jar and fill the rest up with kerosene. You shake it and use it and it's good. You're black, and you stink, but it's good.

"Jesum, there used to be people working in the woods, or there'd be someone going fishin'. They used to come here. I used to make up 'bouta gallon. You didn't need much of the stuff. Yep, it was pretty good stuff."

Mary must have a good knowledge of the techniques of repelling insects after years of hunting wild honeybees.

"I took a swarm of bees one time. I got a line started and I took them clean over the brook. It was three weeks [before she found the bees]. Leroy's girl, Sally, helped me. We worked and George cut wood up here, bringing it out to the top of my field. Well, we worked and worked and we found it [the hive].

"Three weeks we kept after them. They went right straight. Course if we'd beelined it, it wouldn't of taken so long. But we had to go up this road and down into a hole. George said he could hear them bees. I had the box out here.

"We could hear them going back and forth. I went up there one day and I put the box right behind that old trunk, and I started to drive up there and down into the hole. Set up my box and it weren't no time before I had that thing fulla bees. Well, then I moved it further down, and I got bees there, and I kept on goin' up and putting in syrup, you know [in the bee box to attract the bees—see "Wild Honeybee Hunt"].

"And the damn things made a swing around. They went over to Tall Brook, to a great big tree right inside of the brook. Well, George Turner helped me, and he went over there with me one day. He said he could hear the bees, and we got around and there was a great big tree there, and they was coming in and out.

"We cut the damn thing down. You couldn't keep him from cutting that tree. He had to cut it. I said, 'No, wait until we get a hive and get everything ready. You can't do a thing without that.' He cut that tree. He never let nothing stop him. They were in there all that winter, but they left before the next fall.

"Gus said, 'I'm glad you found it. I ain't had nothing to eat since you started in.' Really, I had more fun takin' them bees!

"George found one tree down the road, down towards Shag Pond. It was an ash. They went up there, and by gee whizz he took some screens and plugged them goddamn holes and they sawed her off and put screens on the bottom. She had a hole in the bottom, you know.

"He brought it home, log 'n' all, and it [the hive] laid up here for two years in that log. Then they finally left it. I don't know whether something got in there or not.

"The last honey I had come from that tree Paul and Mark had. I told 'em, 'Take the washtub with you, or a couple of pails, and for God's sake don't be foolish.'

"Wouldn't I of liked to of gone down there with them that day! I said, 'Take that washtub' and they came back with a washtub fulla honey."

"I've Got Everything"

Mary rose out of her chair to take us down a flight of cracked and wobbling steps that went into her cellar. She seemed to know the few spots on the rickety structure where it was safe to step, since she quickly disappeared into the darkness below. As we picked our way down, Mary was already describing and categorizing hundreds of jars of vegetables that were stacked on a shelf along the full length of one wall in her cellar. In one corner there was a pen overflowing with potatoes.

It seemed amazing to me that a seventy-two-year-old lady could produce from scratch enough food to fill a small grocery store. On top of that, it was all exhibited in a casual manner, as if Mary considered the practice of self-sufficiency natural—something that would surprise only naïve and ignorant people.

An attitude like that is explained by Mary's life. She worked in a sawmill for thirty-five years, maintained a mountainside farm, and raised a family, in addition to caring for all the injured or outcast individuals that came her way. We can understand why at seventy-two her back is a little bent.

We could see from meeting Mary that one of the rewards that comes from hard, honest, daily work is the ability to appreciate humor in many simple things that occur from day to day.

"I remember when Edmond was out in the woods cuttin' birch," Mary said. "He chopped down one and got it lodged in between two trees. His father come along and said, 'How you doin', Edmond?' Edmond said, 'Soon's I get this one down and two more, I'll have three.'

"One time we were out hiking and we came upon the biggest rooster you ever seen. And we couldn't leave it till we got it. We run that thing down. I guess we cornered him right up against a wall. Come to find out it was Roy's rooster. After that everybody used to say that I tried to

400.

steal Roy's cock! We couldn't leave that rooster alone. We had to have it.

"One time Uncle Al was riding on a horse and he got bucked off. Everybody come runnin' out and said, 'Where did it hurt you, Uncle Al?' He said, 'Where in hell do you think it will hurt if you fall on your head?'

"He used to say, 'If I worked for a dollar a day, by the next day I'd have three dollars.' "

When we had first entered Mary's house, we had noticed how new the electrical fittings were. Now we asked Mary about that.

"Yah, it'll be three years next week since I got electricity. I used to have a couple of Aladdin lamps, but mostly just gasoline lamps. I don't use them now unless the lights go off. We used to have a gas stove and a gas freezer.

"First I decided on gas because if I'd a-wanted to have electricity down here, they would've had to set up them poles, and it would've cost a bundle. But pretty soon other people wanted it, so then the price would be cheaper because more people would be doing it. Each one of us had to pay a hundred and fifty dollars to get electricity. And then I wanted color TV, so I got one of those. I always said to myself, 'I'm going to die pretty soon, so I'm going to live it up!' "

As for running water, she said, "Yah, I've had running water for quite some time. When my boys was small, I had to lug it from that well, and when I didn't have that well, I used to lug it from the brook.

"Hell, I've got running water now, and a washing machine. Hell, I've got everything!"

Even though time has brought to Mary a few conveniences, it seems that she'd quickly give them up for the pleasure of the old days.

"I remember when I was just a little kid my mother would say, 'What are we having for supper?' and I'd say, 'I don't know.' And we would walk down through the field, catch hoppers, and go fishin'. We would catch twenty to thirty trout, bring them home, and cook them.

"Old Gus says there's one good thing in them days. You could walk down the street without gettin' killed. Oh, I wouldn't mind livin' it all over again!

"I remember when we used to go out for a sleigh ride. We used to heat up some bricks and wrap them in newspaper and go out for a nice ride. We would ride with our feet nice and warm and have a hell of a good time. You wouldn't have cold feet for days.

"We used to go clear over to Peru [from West Peru, Maine, to Peru, Maine]. Oh, it was a damn good horse. He was so strong. Old lazy Staples. His horse could tow. They buried that horse somewheres, but I don't know where.

401.

"Yah, you could go out and shoot a deer any time you wanted then . . ."

At this point in our visit with Mary, I became acutely aware of the bleakness of modern life. What consolation are cold conveniences? I think they rob us of the nobility of self-accomplishment. When you sit watching a colored TV, is it better than feeling the warmth of a wood stove burning full of wood that you cut with your own hands from your own land?

Seeing Mary awakens me to a different reality, actually a more realistic reality, where a person's fate depends directly upon his desire and motivational force.

I ask myself what is better, what life is more fulfilling: an existence where everything is obtained indirectly, and so its value is forgotten in terms of physical exertion? Or a life in which one can see the immediate and concrete results of a day's labor, eat the next day the fruits of the previous?

I think that it would be much easier to remember and appreciate the value of what you are eating if you had just worked for it all day the day before. The simpler is much more easily recognized as beautiful, and pride is as much being able to deal directly with life and succeed as anything else.

Whether it is deer hunting or fishing or farming, Mary's life is always a direct challenge of determination against obstacles. I find it easy to respect a person who has dealt all her life in these terms.